Adequate

Adequate

Rewriting the Logics of Success in Rhetoric and Composition

EDITED BY
Timothy Oleksiak and Joshua Barsczewski

UTAH STATE UNIVERSITY PRESS
Logan

© 2026 by University Press of Colorado

Published by Utah State University Press
An imprint of University Press of Colorado
1580 North Logan Street, Suite 660
PMB 39883
Denver, Colorado 80203-1942

All rights reserved

 The University Press of Colorado is a proud member of Association of University Presses.

The University Press of Colorado is a cooperative publishing enterprise supported, in part, by Adams State University, Colorado School of Mines, Colorado State University, Fort Lewis College, Metropolitan State University of Denver, University of Alaska Fairbanks, University of Colorado, University of Denver, University of Northern Colorado, University of Wyoming, Utah State University, and Western Colorado University.

ISBN: 978-1-64642-803-8 (hardcover)
ISBN: 978-1-64642-804-5 (paperback)
ISBN: 978-1-64642-805-2 (ebook)
https://doi.org/10.7330/9781646428052

Cataloging-in-Publication data for this title is available online at the Library of Congress.

Cover art: Nafis M. White, *Oculus (Black, Brown, Navy, Teal)*, 2021, detail. Hair, Embodied Knowledge, Ancestral Recall, Audacity of Survival, Bobby Pins. In the permanent collection of the Mattatuck Museum, Waterbury, CT.

Contents

Acknowledgments vii

Introduction: A Call for Adequate Work in Rhetoric and Composition
  Joshua Barsczewski and Timothy Oleksiak 3

Part I: Sustaining Support Under Impossible Conditions

1. Solidarity as "Living": A Theory of Relationality for Community Building as Women of Color in Academia
   Eunjeong Lee, Amy J. Wan, and Sara P. Lopez Amezquita 33

2. Imagining a Critical, Coalitional Kindness: Moving Beyond Niceness to Envision a Discipline of Care and Cooperative Disagreement
   Mara Lee Grayson 47

3. Rhetorical Theory and the Fight for a Living Wage
   Olivia Wood 66

Interlude 1: An Honest Job Application
  Katie Manthey 81

Part II: Responding to Structural Inadequacy

4. A Dialogue on Un/Learning Institutional Knowledge in Bits and Doing *the Work* as Pre-Tenure Administrators
   Kelin Loe, Ashanka Kumari, and Gavin P. Johnson 91

5. Embodying (In)Adequacy: "Good Enough" as a Blow Against the Meritocratic Regime
   Christina V. Cedillo, Vyshali Manivannan, Ada Hubrig, and Bernice Olivas 107

6. Temporarily Adequate: Learning to Be Enough at the Writing Center
   Lauren Silber, Malaika Fernandes, Tenzin Jamdol, Audrey Auerbach Nelson, Xiran Tan, and Shaoxuan Tian 122

7. A Labor of Love: A Generational Conversation About Success, Living Well, and All That
   Jen Wingard and Rachelle A. C. Joplin 138

Interlude 2: Overachieving to Leave: Reflections on an Early Career in Transition
   Sara Doan 155

Part III: Adequacy as a Path Toward Change

8. Confrontations with Adequacy in Pandemic Teacher Training
   Crystal Broch Colombini, Stephanie L. Kerschbaum, and Sara Webb-Sunderhaus 159

9. Laboring Through the Lifecycle: Toward a Disciplinary Approach to Faculty Evaluation
   Laurie A. Pinkert and Lauren Marshall Bowen 181

10. This Is Fine: Reflecting on (Missed) Opportunities and Adequate Moments of Departmental Collaboration, Labor, and Care
    Brigitte Mussack 199

Interlude 3: We Will Never Be Enough (Because Academia Will Always Demand More): A Letter from a Fledgling "Crip Doula"
   Ada Hubrig 215

Afterword: Maturing and Organizing Toward/with/for Adequacy
   Seth Kahn and Tony Scott 221

Index 235
About the Contributors 239

Acknowledgments

No work is written in isolation. We would like to thank the following people for their insights and support during the development of *Adequate*: Jessica Restaino, Travis Webster, Kendall Gerdes, Jill McDonough, friends and colleagues who have shared their excitement about this project. We are grateful for Rachael Levay for her guidance early on with this process, especially her insight into the initial call for proposals. Thanks go to Sonya Manes and Robin Garabedian for copyediting and indexing work. We are grateful for Skylar Cooper, Darrin Pratt, and Michael Spooner of the Utah State University Press for bringing *Adequate* through the final steps. We thank our contributors who shared with us their work and took the aims of the collection seriously. Last, we have gathered these voices and dedicated our time and effort to putting together this collection, and we are thankful to those of you who spend time with it. So very much of the stuff that gets written remains unread, and even less is taken up playfully-seriously in classrooms and our academic writing. We do not take engagements with *Adequate* for granted.

ADEQUATE

Introduction

A Call for Adequate Work in Rhetoric and Composition

JOSHUA BARSCZEWSKI AND TIMOTHY OLEKSIAK

The work has to get done. But there is so damned much of it coming from so many sectors of our *working* lives.[1]
 So.
 Damned.
 Much.
 It needs to stop.
 Rhetoric and Composition's history is wedded in many ways to a history of us saying "yes" where others have said "no," filling voids left by those who don't understand what we do.[2] "No" is what we want to say, but without a deep reflection on how, when, or why we're saying "no," doing so can feel like or even be a violation of our ethical responsibilities. In the scramble to find someone else to do the work, we miss out on conversations about whether the work actually, really, truly needs to be done in the first place. From a different angle, in some

---

1. On the matter of increasing workloads, see Deborah Brandt's (2015) *The Rise of Writing*; Fred Moten and Stefano Harney's (1999) "The Academic Speed-Up"; and James Rushing Daniel's (2022) *Toward an Anti-Capitalist Composition*.
2. Many histories of Rhetoric and Composition are full of sad and depressing tropes about who we are and who does this labor: redheaded stepchildren, sad women in the basement, or the wives of the real professors (cf. Connors 1997; Crowley 1998; Miller 1991).

https://doi.org/10.7330/9781646428052.c000b

cases (honestly, in many cases), it is easier to just do the work ourselves rather than to allow an incompetent or destructive colleague to join in.

The discipline has developed robust research programs, paradigms, and schools of thought about how to do our work and do it well. Our disciplinary investments thus perpetuate a dual dilemma. On the one hand, folks in Rhetoric and Composition are hired and trained to take on unequal amounts of administrative labor in a higher education environment that's only getting more complex; and, since few others want to do this work, our discipline has developed a set of internalized dispositions that makes us feel obligated to do so. The combination of these pressures—external and internal—is a profound sense that we're never doing enough. That is, if we truly believe our work matters, then someone needs to do it. Developing theories, teaching writing, running writing programs, training writing tutors, and conducting faculty development are all necessary parts of our job. In our more optimistic moments, we might even think that they're valuable to our institutions and students. To say "no" to doing this work can feel like a dereliction of duty.

We want to highlight, specifically, the frequency with which folks in Rhetoric and Composition are hired to take on administrative and teaching obligations, even if these obligations are not within our primary scholarly areas of expertise. This is personal for us: At his institution, Timothy was hired to direct the Professional and New Media Writing Program, an academic minor. For most academic minors in his department, there is an expectation for cycling in and out of directorships. However, there are too few Rhetoric and Composition faculty to take over should he want or need to cycle out of the directorship. At the small liberal arts college where Joshua was hired, where teaching is by far the single most important aspect of tenure review, he is the only faculty member whose contract permanently calls for administrative work. This has meant, among other things, that a new system used to evaluate him for tenure and promotion has needed to be developed. As the director and really the only permanent member of the so-called Writing "Program," Joshua is a one-stop shop for managing first-year seminars, running the Writing Center, and conducting faculty development through a hybrid writing across the curriculum (WAC) and writing in the disciplines (WID) program. We mention these personal examples not because they are exceptional but because in Rhetoric and Composition, they are normal. Often, departments must frame new Rhetoric and Composition hires as administrators to get lines approved, as even a cursory glance at job listings might suggest, putting pressure on job seekers to apply for and accept administrative jobs even if they have not been trained in administrative research or praxis.

Rhetoric and Composition workers can internalize this structural reality in ways that can be harmful to our flourishing, becoming martyrs who overwork to make sure things get done (even if we aren't well trained or excited to do so), to make sure things get done well, and to make sure things are in alignment with the best practices of the discipline while being sensitive to local contexts. Susan Miller-Cochran's (2018) concern for souls, or that "administrative work can potentially put you at risk of losing yours," is especially on point (112). If the concept of soul is too abstract, we might add: Doing all of this work—and doing it successfully—puts you at risk of anything approaching a healthy work-life balance, likely requiring you to volunteer time to an employer who would easily replace you. Thus, we must ask: How can Rhetoric and Composition workers think about labor, work, and a cessation (temporary or totalizing) of unending and increasingly more production? Even if such a question sounds familiar, it is still worth asking given that it hasn't permeated at the level of disciplinary habitus.

Adequate: Rewriting the Logics of Success in Rhetoric and Composition arose from a desire to see further engagement with this question, and to think through how to answer it in our daily lives as professionals. We are inspired by work like Crystal Broch Colombini's "Composing Crisis: Hardship Letters and the Political Economy of Genre" (2018), which asks how neoliberalism, austerity, and economic crises affect composing practices, and Holly Hassel and Cassandra Phillips's book *Materiality and Writing Studies* (2022), which aims to ensure scholarship about writing in the United States and is more broadly reflective of the life, labor, and learning conditions of the era. Indeed, we are hardly the first—and make no claims to be—to ask about how to thrive in a profession at a moment when "success" itself seems impossible.

Two relatively recent collections do grapple with pragmatic realities of labor in the discipline by examining how such circumstances relate to epistemology and ethics. *Rewriting Success in Rhetoric and Composition Careers*, edited by Amy Goodburn, Donna LeCourt, and Carrie Leverenz (2012), engages the discipline's knowledge imperative, pointing out that professional definitions of success are often grounded in publishing and advancing the discipline's scholarly agenda at the expense of devaluing "what we spend most of our time doing—teaching, administering, mentoring" (viii). Their solution is to expand what counts as knowledge in our field (xvi). Contributors to *Our Body of Work:*

Embodied Administration and Teaching, edited by Melissa Nichols and Anna Sicari (2022), examine "institutional embodiment," or what the editors describe as "a kind of a posteriori knowledge gained through individual's experience of and within the institution" (6). The edited collection provides multiple narratives of labor highlighting experiences too often ignored in disciplinary discourse—harassment, grieving, sickness, pain—drawing attention to the layers of complexity involved in being or having a body and doing labor. They challenge their readers "to do better" and pressure the field to "rethink and rework our practices if we wish to create a more ethical discipline" (22–23). Both collections are vital contributions, showcasing aspects of academic labor typically left to the liminal spaces. Yet both continue to imagine success in the discipline, holding out that there's a way we could do our jobs (however defined) better. Alternatively, our collection asks: What if we take success off the table? What if we aim to be adequate at the work we choose to do?

In building this collection, we imagined *adequate* as a deliberate choice to value our needs and desires as workers against the material and structural realities of our present. On the one hand, we know that there's always more to do, and we value what we need to do; on the other hand, we are equipped with decreasing resources (financial, temporal, emotional, physical) to do them. Adequacy in this context, then, emerges as a form of agency—a goal for thriving by empowering ourselves to focus on the work we choose to do and to let other things go. In this way, adequacy is a possibility that lies outside of the continuum of success and failure. Many of our contributors provide their own definition of "adequacy," and as quite a few of them point out, adequacy is sometimes, often, horizontal—never to be reached.

In this way, adequacy has the timber of utopic envisioning. What might it look like to imagine labor beyond as it is typically understood within the contexts of higher education? What does our work look like if we define our sense of ourselves and our professional agency without centering publishing, awards, enduring an oppressive system, getting tenure, moving from the professoriate to administration, or teaching and mentoring beyond working hours? *Adequate* is our attempt at some answers to questions such as these.

It's Too Much: The Unethical Work Burdens in Rhetoric and Composition

As news articles about cuts to the humanities proliferate, and journalists in the *New York Times* and other blue chip legacy rags declare the liberal arts to have "lost," as Florida colleges are remade in the governor's image (Hodgson and

Kumar 2023), and as entire political campaigns (Smith 2021) are waged against the propagandized image of Critical Race Theory by people who've never read a word of it (or read it selectively), it's easy to wonder what being a Rhetoric and Composition professional is really about these days. The dismantling of tenured positions at West Virginia University (Corrigan 2023) and the reshaping of tenure in Wisconsin (Flaherty 2016) and the ongoing fight in Texas (McGee 2023) to dismantle tenure completely remind us that employment protections are not guaranteed in a political climate of manufactured financial crisis. The COVID-19 pandemic exacerbated the working conditions of millions. Entire industries did not just suffer, but came to a full stop during the early years of the pandemic.

We take as a given that we are currently working within a neoliberal, corporate university system of labor exploitation and extraction. Marc Bousquet (2008) compellingly argues that the corporate university system is not just dominated by profit-seeking behavior and managerial bloat, but a transformation of the culture of higher education. Bousquet describes how many public institutions of higher education are gripped by market consciousness; shared governance has been replaced with administrative demands grounded in austerity and driven by perpetual budget crises. All of these concerns frame and reduce the most important decisions in higher education to matters of economic solvency. Ever self-aware, Rhetoric and Composition is not immune from the cultural shifts resulting from domain corporate university structures. Donna Strickland (2004) described the effects of this on Rhetoric and Composition studies: We are often part of the maintenance of rather than resistance to these corporate cultural logics. Our colleagues have been warning us of these dangers at least as far back as Bruce Horner (2000, 2016) but also from Catherine Chaput (2008), Nancy Welch and Tony Scott (2016), and many others.

Louis Menand (2023) provides a useful working definition of neoliberalism that serves our purposes. He writes,

> Neoliberalism, in the American context, can be understood as a reaction against mid-century liberalism. Neoliberals think that the state should play a smaller role in managing the economy and meeting public needs, and they oppose obstacles to the free exchange of goods and labor. . . . The label "neoliberal" has been attached to a range of political species, from libertarians, who tend to be programmatically anti-government, to New Democrats like Bill Clinton, who embrace the policy goals of the New Deal and the Great Society but think that there are better means of achieving them. But most types of neoliberalism reduce to the term "markets." Get the planners and the policymakers out of the way and let the markets find solutions.

Leaders of higher education have internalized the logics of neoliberalism to transform the operations of college and universities into corporate machines. Administration—in the form of provosts, deans, directors of institutions and centers affiliated with colleges, and department chairs—exploits academic workers' precarity and vulnerability, and consistently asks for more. Part of what we mean by the corporate neoliberal model of the university and its specific effects on Rhetoric and Composition is articulated via Linda Adler-Kassner's (2017) idea of the Educational Intelligence Complex (EIC), which grounds proficiency and efficiency as its guiding metrics for success. That is, the terms of labor are not defined by workers but by those obsessed with branding, framing students as consumers, and moving those consumers quickly through the institution with only enough attention given to them to solicit alumni donations or to include in branding efforts.

In all of this accounting and marketing, financial projecting and contract exploiting, does anyone even notice if we're actually good at our jobs? Does a dean know the difference between a cutting-edge writing center and one that's stuck in a 1960s Current Traditional Rhetoric fix-it shop model? Does a provost know the difference between a decent composition class and an excellent one? Between an ethical and equitable grading policy and one that merely keeps problems off their desk?

Perhaps (probably) not, but still the administrative burdens increase and we need to find ways to alleviate them.[3] This is not, we admit, an easy task—nor even a possible task for all people. Tenure-track lines in Rhetoric and Composition are often connected to administrative positions, despite advice about not taking a writing program administrator (WPA) position pre-tenure being repeated so frequently that it's a rhetorical commonplace (Horning 2007; Ratcliffe and Rickly 2010). While this commonplace is almost certainly outdated (see Stolley 2015) and impractical considering that folks need salaries, the existence and perpetuation of the commonplace should give us pause. WPA positions are complex and thorny—arguably, more complex and thornier than other types of academic labor given the advice that one should have the

---

3. We use the phrase "administrative burden" to highlight the seemingly never-ending supply of work that comes down institutional pikes onto often underresourced and already overworked professionals. Writing Program Administration (WPA) can be tremendously rewarding, and the pages of *WPA*, *CCCC*, and other top journals are replete with necessary scholarship that theorizes administrative work as an agentive space to create real change on our campuses. But we are also keenly aware that many folks in the field—including contributors to this volume—turn toward WPA scholarship as a matter of necessity and not as a matter of preference. As enriching as that work can be, we cannot, in the end, scholarship our ways out of the morass of labor.

protection of tenure before taking them on. The burdens, such as they are, likely aren't going to go away. Perhaps our response to those burdens can change, though. Doug Hesse's provocative suggestion that we focus on "teaching and writing" as our core professional identities and avoid "selling our birthright for a mess of managerial pottage" is one way (2015, 131). At a certain point, not everything will get done or not everything will get done as well as it can. What's the amount of administrative burden we can do to keep ourselves whole while keeping our jobs?

At a very fundamental level, we understand academic work to encompass all those things we do in the process of knowledge production (of theory, teaching, administration, etc.) and dissemination and the surrounding conditions that make that work possible. We acknowledge that for some folks, the distinctions between work and labor are important. Labor activist Seth Kahn (Kahn and Payson 2021) describes the difference thusly:

> "I understand academic labor as referring both to concrete work behaviors we engage in (teaching, research, administration, shared governance) and the worker/manager relations (compensation, hiring/firing, evaluation, discipline) that determine working conditions. In other words, if we are not talking about how work is managed, we're not talking about labor issues" (114).

In that same structured dialogue, Amy Pason extends Kahn's ideas of academic labor, saying, "When I think of academic labor analysis we should expand out to identify the full system that we have to address to change our individual working conditions" (116). We agree. The intertwining of work and academic labor would offer a fuller analysis. With the exception of Laurie A. Pinkert and Lauren Marshall Bowen, Brigitte Mussack, and Jen Wingard and Rachelle A. C. Joplin (who offer revisions to how administration or mentorship might be reimagined), most of the ideas within *Adequate* focus on work and less on labor. We affirm the necessity of looking to focus on work for two reasons. First, work occupies the space of the moment; it is something that we can do while building an imagined future that is equitable and fair to those working in academia. Second, while the terms of work are often handed to us, we believe that in the doing of the work, gestures to alternative futures remain possible. That is, there is a relationship between what we do now and what we can imagine for the future, even as what we do now falls short of what we imagine. What we have is the unfolding of work so that we might understand something powerful about academic labor.

Central to doing the work is considering how we matter and for whom we matter insofar as we maintain. Hesse and Kahn and Pason sensitize us to the very real fact that all around Rhetoric and Composition, workers are administrators, students, and an antagonistic public that increase our emotional demands and commit us to doing things we don't want or need to do. These people who demand more of our work in order to get *their* needs met do so, frequently, without regard to the individuals they are inviting to work. And in those cases where administration *does* care about individuals as people, they often act as agents loyal to the institution. When we say "no," are we always leaving that work for someone else to do? Is a "no" an invitation to consider whether *this* work needs doing *at this time*? How can we begin to consider the ripple effects of "no" in a workplace environment that always, by capitalist design, asks for more?

As workers within the profession of Rhetoric and Composition struggle to thread many answers of "whom" the work is for, we also must contend with what our work is. One answer is clearly offered by Carmen Kynard (2021): Disrupt in a focused and just way. In "All I Need Is One Mic: A Black Feminist Community Meditation on the Work, the Job, and the Hustle (& Why So Many of Yall Confuse This Stuff)," Kynard creates a three-part heuristic that extends productively to questions of academic work. The work is whatever it is we need to do to disrupt the "white, neoliberalist, racial-affect-sanitized ethos of the western academy and its epistemological violence" (12). Importantly, Kynard understands her students, and her Black students particularly, as already doing the work of disruption. When student activists form unions for collective bargaining rights, when they make demands of colleges and universities to create courses of study, or generally agitate for better working and learning conditions, they are doing the work. We can frame and amplify their rhetorical dispositions and link the knowledge production we have been a part of to illustrate for them the coalition between our field and their work.

Kynard's notion of "the work" is useful for us to ground what we do in some meaningful vision of whom we are doing this work for. To counter the tendency of what Hesse is suggesting (i.e., that we're doing too much), we need to create a way of saying "no" without giving up or breaking down. The way to ground our choices is to ask whom we're serving—who is the beneficiary of the knowledge production and dissemination we enact? Before Rhetoric and Compositionists take up Kynard's ideas for their own use, it is important to sit with the complexity of them. Kynard grounds her notion of work in the lives of Black students and how her work is supported by their intellectual and activist actions while at the same time supporting them in these endeavors. We do not, nor do the contributors promise, the same work that Kynard does. What makes Kynard challenging for us is that she gets us to consider deeply whom our work is for. Ultimately, whom the work is for might be the most important argument in which our profession should engage.

Responding to Untenable Working Conditions

The harms of the corporate university system on Rhetoric and Composition workers are pervasive, established, and complicated. In Rhetoric and Composition we note four broad responses to these harms: leaving the profession, staying but refusing to work, echoing negative feelings, and integrating ourselves into the current structure. Certainly there are others, and in any given context one or more of them may be more acceptable or understandable; they do all cause harm, and, in the end, none of them are completely persuasive. Their very inability to persuade us necessitates a deeper consideration of adequate as a potential for a different kind of working life as Rhetoric and Composition professionals. While simplified for our purposes, we do not believe them to be straw people nor do we believe them to be caricatures of the position. For every response that follows, adequacy is often a better course of action.

RESPONSE ONE: LEAVE THE UNIVERSITY OR THE PROFESSION

One radical but realistic response to the harms of the corporate university is to leave the university or the profession. If the university is so broken and violent, so inequitable and so complicit with colonialist, racist, ableist projects that it cannot be transformed, what's the use of remaining (see Ahmed 2017, 2021)? Many professionals with strong reputations have simply left university life altogether to pursue different professions. They might still occasionally publish in the field or manage journals, but they are no longer a part of the system of the university or seek to serve the profession. We know their stories because they are spoken of in the halls of our institutions and at conferences. *He left because . . . She isn't doing that because . . .* Sometimes, we envy their reasons and admire our colleagues who move on to what they think will be more rewarding careers. Still, many others leave not because they desire to, but because they cannot live off the wages of academic work or endure emotional abuse from administrators or colleagues. We don't hear their stories as much.

Often, the stories of leaving that circulate in the halls of our professional organizations and workplaces are those who have already established themselves well enough to make such moves. Their publications records, professional advances, and cultural capital appear like a standard narrative of success *before* they left. It is easier to leave when the leaving is accompanied by financial stability, cultural capital, and professional respect via continued citation. Though the leaving may have and likely did cause emotional stress and worry over the future, stories of leaving often end with the protagonist landing on their feet. The stories of the folks who don't—often, the ones who left because they had to, because they couldn't afford academic life anymore—don't get told as much.

On the other hand, *leaving* can't be the only response. Some of us simply cannot. In countries like the United States where healthcare is linked to employment, leaving can be a matter of life and death. At many institutions, the flexibility offered by academic institutions is simply the best for those with care responsibilities. And so, while we acknowledge the symbolic power of leaving and hope that folks listen and act on these symbolic actions, walking away isn't desired or appropriate for all of us.

Finally, some of us just don't want to leave: Despite critiques of academic systems, many of us still like being Rhetoric and Composition professors. As someone who grew up in severe poverty, Joshua is reluctant to leave a job that provides him with a better financial future than experienced by many of his family or friends from home. He actually likes his job despite feeling overwhelmed at times by its demands. Wishing a job could be more manageable does not necessitate leaving said job. The thought of moving into the 9–5 corporate grind or moving from salaried position to contract work is deeply unappealing to Timothy. For these reasons and more and despite all the problems with working in academia, Timothy would rather stay put. And staying put is animated by both a sense of comfort and safety and by a deep commitment to the work of Rhetoric and Composition.

RESPONSE TWO: STAY BUT DON'T DO THE WORK

Not doing the work can look like two very different things depending on who is not working and what the consequences of this not working are. The first is simply being incompetent at your job by not being able to do the work or being so unwilling to work after a particular point in professional advancement that you stop showing up. We know the colleagues who get tenure and then refuse to serve on committees or collaborate with colleagues on real needs of the department or institution. This is the kind of unethical worker who drains resources from institutions while putting pressure on others to say "yes" when it might not be feasible or any part of a worker's career plan.

Most academic institutions have documents (handbooks, memos of understanding, union-negotiated contracts, board of trustee dictates, etc.) setting minimum expectations for work to which all faculty must adhere. While faculty might not like doing this work, rejecting it outright (for whatever reasons we might have) is not an appropriate suggestion if only because refusing minimum work expectations outright will likely result in being let go from the position. The pragmatism of minimum faculty expectations should not lead one to the conclusion that these expectations are always just. Work policies we agree to can be ableist. Rather, they must be changed through committee work and advocacy so that they are more just; an individual faculty member cannot simply refuse and expect to retain their position in the institution.

"Stay but don't do the work" may also look like quiet quitting. Since major stay-at-home and industry shutdowns encouraged a shift to increases in work-from-home situations, the term "quiet quitting" has circulated in newspapers, magazines, and social media situations. Rather than quiet quitting, we prefer the union-supported phrasing of "work to contract" or "work to rule" (Hiltzik 2022). Work to contract is a union effort to put pressure on management without calling for an official strike. It is doing precisely what your contract requires and nothing more. In college and university settings, this means the service efforts faculty are asked to do in order for upper administration to complete their projects come to a grinding halt. While work to contract is the epitome of adequacy, blanket calls for it without direct union action are likely to be as successful as boycotts of chocolate or bottled water: They would work *if only* everyone did it. The United States is currently facing an uptick in unionizing efforts, and we should take great care to not reduce these efforts by co-opting union work in nonunionized contexts.

RESPONSE THREE: DOUBLE DOWN ON NEGATIVE AFFECT

The most damaging response to tough work conditions is the emotional mindset that keeps us complicit in our own exploitation. Simply quitting or refusing to work fails to address the deeper issue: the emotional ties that bind workers to their labor. Leaving might mean students get taught by teachers less attuned to better practices (Cicchino and Hicks 2024) in writing pedagogy. We want to stay and do our jobs; what we want is for our jobs to be manageable and for us to have agency over what our jobs entails. Nevertheless, this hunt for more perfect work can function as a form of cruel optimism. We borrow "cruel optimism" from Lauren Berlant (2010), who coined the term to explain how individuals become attached to those objects that promise, but never deliver, on a good life. In the case of Rhetoric and Composition, the moralistic tendency to situate our writing knowledge through the language of harm and alarm, whether supported by research or not,[4] has the effect of creating anxiety about how to be good in the field. This anxiety can be felt most perniciously by discipline members who don't enjoy the comforts of stable employment or who do not have mentors who might guide them through the many (often contradictory) moral imperatives of the field.

Rhetoric and Composition scholarship is committed to the idea that we could be doing our jobs better. Rarely are we invited to consider what is enough. Saying that we could be teaching writing worse would hardly be a way to build a discipline, of course, but sometimes the sum total of the discipline's knowledge can be a seemingly permanent sense of *inadequacy*. There's simply so much to keep up with; we need to decide what we care about and what we're willing to let go. This is the essence of *adequate*.

Take, for example, a 2023 issue of *College Composition and Communication*, arguably the discipline's most important journal. It includes an article about how to create conditions that allow "community-engaged scholars greater institutional freedom to create and sustain strong community partnership projects" (Hartline 2023) and another article about being attuned to the knowledges students from evangelical backgrounds bring to their writing (Mannon and Privott 2023); another article talks about how syllabi can play a role in disabled students' agency to disclose or not disclose their accommodations (Simpkins 2023); still another article describes how neuroscience can help us to provide resources for students to "persist in writing-related tasks and to better realize their rhetorical and social goals" (Comstock 2023). These aren't even all of the articles in that issue. While some of those are issues we (Joshua and Timothy) know a bit about, others are completely new to us, and even the ones we knew a bit about we aren't experts in. Now that we've read the articles, we can commit ourselves to trying to think of all of this going forward—and we're going to be better professionals for it. But at a certain point, we have to wonder if the add-ons to our knowledge base can make our teaching unsustainable: If we did everything we know to be true—if we did everything we *know* can be helpful for students—would we have time to do anything else? Is there ever a point where our classes are just good enough? Can we embrace adequacy? If

---

4. One illustration of what we are talking about is that the field's rush to embrace contract grading, for example, as a response to the violence of grading was widely celebrated. This collective embrace was challenged recently by Sherri Craig's (2021) excellent piece "Your Contract Grading Ain't It."

there is a central question guiding this collection it is this: If you are invited to engage the idea of adequate, what would you find?

The felt need to commit oneself to relentless teaching is not always or ever a demand of higher education and its army of administrators. It is predicated, rather, on where our disciplinary knowledge has led us. The disciplinary work that has been done has unwittingly *increased* our emotional labor. That is, when viewed from outside our discipline, we don't actually need to be doing the things that we insist on doing and yet can never fully realize. We need to reconsider trying to cram everything we possibly can into the first-year writing class. This "cram it all" attitude has seeped into disciplinary demands that imitate administrative demands for excellence.

RESPONSE FOUR: SEEK INTEGRATION WITHIN THE UNIVERSITY INFRASTRUCTURE

Finally, another response—one we see the attractiveness of and could even be said to have participated in at times—is for Rhetoric and Composition to seek better working conditions through a more fulfilling, legible, and recognized integration into the intellectual life of the institution. Unlike the more radical response of leaving entirely, this is the option to stay and be the best. This response is both emotional and intuitional, psychological and social. Simply put, Rhetoric and Composition is less valued than other disciplines—this has been true historically, as Miller described so long ago. Her invocation of the "sad women in the basement" imagery both reflects historical codings of composition work as symbolically lower than other courses and disciplines, and describes how composition was ideologically interpellated not as a discipline in its own right but as one concerned with initiations to a higher discourse (1991, 136–142). But it's larger than just our own need for recognition from colleagues: The lack of respect has material consequences on our ability to do our jobs, as Rita Malenczyk et al.'s 2018 collection *Composition, Rhetoric, and Disciplinarity* explores in great depth. As these writers point out, one benefit of being seen as a discipline (or field) is a recognition that we have "scholarly rigor," which would allow "us to work with all students more effectively, precisely because as a disciplinary unit, we would control curriculum and budgets in ways we often now do not" (7). That is to say, recognition by others as a discipline could allow us to increase our agency within our institutions and—we might assume—fight for better working conditions, for ourselves and for others who are intellectually committed to this same cause.

Whether chasing after disciplinarity is a good thing is perhaps outside of the purview of this collection, although Bruce Horner's work (2016) on value describes the pernicious effects of commodifying the work of composition in terms of how it occludes "the labor involved in the realization of the value of that work, distorting and undercutting its demands and its potential as work both within and on the social" (122). Horner particularly points to disciplinary statements such as the Council of Writing Program Administrators' "Evaluating the Intellectual Work of Writing Administration" and its delineation of specific types of work as intellectual and therefore tenurable, as an example of how chasing after prestige and status can come at the detriment to workers by privileging some aspects of their work over others. Likewise, Donna Strickland's *The Managerial Unconscious in the History of Composition Studies* (2011) provides a compelling account of how expertise in Rhetoric and Composition prepares graduates not to be specialists in a discourse valued for its intellectual merits but for its administrative and managerial capabilities. As Strickland points out, the "Evaluating" statement gets at the heart of the problem: "Scholarly expertise in composition studies is expertise in pedagogy, rhetoric, or writing theory. That expertise is then applied in administrative settings, thus making writing program administration into intellectual work . . . but as the 'Intellectual Work' document makes clear, even the very people involved in administration understand management to be separate from (and implicitly inferior to) the scholarly, disciplinary expertise of writing specialists" (9–10).

So, we might have a frying-pan-and-fire situation: To gain respect within the institution as a Rhetoric and Composition specialist might, ultimately, lead to finding oneself "promoted" through course releases, some nominal amount of money, or appreciation, as the manager of others, someone implicated in but only possibly able (and possibly not) to improve the very working conditions that led to the drive for institutional respect in the first place.

This effect isn't, as we've stressed before, universally true. Plenty of folks have published in top journals, won teaching awards, and built stellar programs that have allowed them to advocate for better working conditions. We don't deny that. But we would suggest, perhaps, that the desire for integration in the university's system of valuation is often an individualistic response to a collective problem, and one that could very well result in professionals perpetuating the very harms they sought to alleviate. A different response, grounded in collectivity, is needed.

The Utopian Potential of Adequate Work

We champion adequacy now, years into a pandemic that has upended the borders between work and life, at a moment when self-care and resilience have been promoted as strategies for survival in the face of state failure and late capitalist chaos. At a time when institutions call on us to see one another as families, to take care of one another, to listen and be present, they also call for us to do more, to be ambitious, to be entrepreneurial. The work is getting harder, the work is unrelenting, and the emotional and material benefits of doing it all have gotten less clear. Yet, for many workers, striving for excellence is perceived as the only option. Given Bill Readings's (1996) incisive takedown of the term "excellence," we know excellence is an empty platitude that can be used to buttress nearly any initiative or ideology administrators want. But as workers with bodies that need to be taken care of, dogs and spouses and families who need our attention, as workers who sometimes just want a drunken night out with the girls or to play board games with our chosen family, and as workers with lives beyond academic production, we need something in the now that helps us imagine a better future. *Adequate* as a collection aims to engage in temporal longing, viewing a utopia where "adequacy" would be an agentive norm pushing us into spaces that may never be fully reached for all of us but that can still in the now provide a sense of clarity about our temporal and material realities. We do not refuse to address structural realities but engage with them: What does agency look like in a structural condition of inequity? In a world seemingly hell bent on destroying our bodies, what work should we do now that will allow us to flourish as academics and maybe do some good for the world?

Adequate, ultimately, says, "We will not repeat the cycles of trauma that this profession and this culture together do to us." The hope in *Adequate* is that you decline to take on burdens you do not want but that in the saying of "no," you do no harm to those for whom good work you've distanced yourself from can still take place. Early in the process of building this collection, a colleague looked at our draft call for proposals (CFP) and encouraged us to be mindful that we didn't come off too strongly as white tenure-track men complaining. There's something to that critique. We are perhaps not the best poster children for "adequate." Timothy is a highly motivated researcher with a deep commitment to service to the discipline via participation in professional organizations and who has been published in some of the top journals in the field. Joshua is an emerging scholar who has started to make his own mark on the discipline too. Both enjoy comfortable, relatively stable employment at a public research university and a small liberal arts college, respectively. Both of us want to and actually do live in metropolitan regions, have stable housing, and are in loving marriages. Part of what drew us to "adequate" as a concept is grounded precisely in our lived experiences. What we want is a way to exist within the discipline without suffering under the burdens that we feel are threatening to our work-life balances. We want, for all of us, to understand the material actions necessary for maintaining our physical and emotional well-being. We want no one to struggle with whether or not to go dancing at the club with your best Judys or filing the assessment report on a Saturday evening. If you enjoy assessment reports, file them. But if you, like us, would prefer to go dancing, then go dancing and leave the rest of it until Monday morning.

So, yes, perhaps there is an extent to which "white tenure-track men complaining" is at play. We'll own that. That's not something we can deny as editors. But what we can push for, what we hope this collection can help make space for, is a collective sense that complaining is not simply cathartic but world building (Ahmed 2021). We need to keep complaining until we have created the right conditions for a loving reception of our complaints. To our mind, some of the best resources for developing this kind of agency are located in coalitional, utopian politics.

The scholar most important to our thinking with utopian coalition politics is Jennifer C. Nash. We are listening to Nash rhetorically as a way to consider what it might be to hear how Black feminist thinking can inform what we see happening in this collection. Listening to Nash positions us as stewards of her ideas as academics whose job it is to think with the ideas of others and make a case for why these particular sets of ideas are appropriate in this context. It is, to be honest, easier for us to engage the utopian coalitional work emerging from queer theorists and queer Rhetoric and Composition studies. In citing Black feminist politics, we want to take care to suggest two important things that, helpfully enough, Nash (2020) articulates in a different context. First, this isn't a co-optation of Black feminist thought. Rather, it is an articulation of how Black feminist thought helps us, Timothy and Joshua, make sense of what is happening in *Adequate* and the affective theorizing and working found throughout. Second, it is not to suggest that Black feminist thinkers and activists have been right all along but unable to find their voice. Black feminist theorists and activists have been speaking for a long, long time (Combahee River Collective 1977; Logan 1999; Royster 2023; Spillers 1987; etc.) and finding critical uptake by scholars and activists in every space where activist and intellectual work is being done. At the risk of imperfectly taking up Black feminist thought, we offer here the ways Nash has been supportive of our thinking about the work we can imagine doing in Rhetoric and Composition.

Nash (2011) credits queer theorists like José Esteban Muñoz, Anne Cvetkovich, and Lauren Berlant with a popularization of academic affective politics. Without denying the contributions of these scholars, Nash constructs a genealogy of Black feminist love-politics that predates and surrounds queer theorizing but is situated within and around queer affect. Building upon the intellectual contributions of June Jordan (2003), Audre Lorde (1984), and Alice Walker (1983) specifically, Nash expands their notion of love-politics to create a non-identarian theory of political action. When Nash describes love, she resists the kind of surface empowerment movements that suggest positive attitudes or prioritizing the self as a process of checking out of the world or our responsibility for working in it. It is possible to love yourself so much that you no longer see yourself as responsible for doing the work. Rather, Nash argues that love is "a significant call for ordering the self *and* transcending the self, a strategy for remaking the self *and* for moving beyond the limitations of selfhood" (3). For example, seeing oneself as beautiful when dark skin is considered ugly is not just a practice of self-empowerment but a reimagining of the entire politics of beauty that upends a network of politics that emerge from dehumanizing definitions of beauty. It is watching Cynthia Erivo in *The Color Purple* standing on a stage alone, facing an audience singing "I'm beautiful / and / I'm / here" and not only *feeling* that she is beautiful after a lifetime of feeling and being told she is ugly but *knowing* that kind of self-love might have created a world other than what we currently have. To witness the self-love of Celie, as embodied by Erivo, or Whoopi Goldberg, or Fantasia Barrino, for that matter, is to glimpse that glimmer of something other than what we have. The attendant feelings emerging from a recognition of self-love are the resources for political action and structural transformation. Walking away from Erivo's moment thinking "Celie *finally* loves herself and has struggled to realize that about herself" while exiting the theater is to have missed the world-making revolution of her self-love and to reject the utopian power of noticing a woman who loves herself. It is not saying to ourselves, "Good for her" or "I wish I had that," but rather considering that a world where Celie *is* beautiful is possible. It is the essence of "the personal is the political" but framed as a utopian politics. Returning to Nash: "Black feminist love-politics crafts a political community that eschews the wounded subject that lies at the heart of identity politics. In its place, it crafts a collective marked by 'communal affect,' a utopian visionary future-oriented community held together by affiliation and 'public feeling' rather than an imagined—or enforced—sameness" (2011, 18–19).

The Black feminist love-politics Nash develops, ultimately, is precisely what is necessary for developing the kind of agency necessary for adequate work in Rhetoric and Composition. Such a utopian love-politics is everywhere throughout the pages of *Adequate*, but we name several practices here in order to make the connection between Nash and our development of agential adequacy here. It is adequate to

- form more pleasurable spaces of bonding over workplace burdens or traumas;
- develop more distributed mentorship that allow new folks to work less tirelessly;
- communicate the specificity of "enough" when we recognize it;
- resist finding solutions to vexing problems;
- create new models that reject accumulation of traditional success markers.

Building the kind of love-politics might also be recognizing that administration (not some nebulous "institution") does not recognize our humanity and that a reclamation via stories, complaint, or active resistance is a reclamation of the fundamental power that comes from recognizing ourselves as powerful and good. Because we are powerful, we can take on agential adequacy in ways that do not demand those who assume ownership over our work lives. Nash writes, "By insistently looking *away* from the state, love-politics practitioners perform frustrations, revealing their understandings of the limitations of a regime that is not committed to redressing their harms" (2011, 15). On a different scale, we want to turn away from administration to see what kind of work is possible when we look to ourselves to do the work. While many of us are in state institutions, this does not mean we look to management to solve our problems.

Utopian politics is not a sit-and-wait for something to happen. It is not simply enduring the present hoping others do the work of upsetting structures of inequity. It is a work that looks like building a better future without knowing precisely what that future looks like. It is the knowledge that whatever is happening now isn't working. The contributors here touch on the pragmatic, the possible, the achievable, and the impossible. The work of the possible is not solely the responsibility of us editors nor of the contributors.

Approach to the Creation and Organization of this Collection

We see the articulation of how this collection came together and our editorial approach as part of increased calls for transparency and vulnerability, and in the spirit of a distributed mentorship necessary for doing the work of creating such collections. The theoretical work done in the first half of this introduction was predicated on the following questions:

- Can we imagine work within the discipline if we take success, recognition, and hard work out of the equation?
- Instead of ceding laziness, unproductivity, and mediocrity as undesirable traits of those who don't care or who aren't committed to their jobs, what if we imagine these as agentive positions that allow us to actually do our jobs while remaining whole?

Included within the CFP was a sense of *how* we would be thinking about the ideas proposed. We remained open about the shape and structure of the collection, but in general things we were interested in and stated in the CFP included:

- examinations of unproductivity, quiet quitting, or failure to achieve as agentive choices;
- imaginations of a new set of affective relationships to our labor beyond our unlivable present;
- uses of temporality as an analytic frame to redefine the nature of academic work;
- critiques or reframing of keywords clustering around negative associations with labor including, but not limited to, imposter syndrome, exceptionality, replicability, mentorship;
- descriptions of imperatives (a la pedagogical, improvement, or production imperatives) that make imagining difficult;
- contributions we cannot imagine prior to you sending them our way.

In addition to circulating our call for proposals to email lists and on social media, we reached out to some folks in our professional circles by sharing the CFP with them directly. This process is common for edited collections where editors are empowered to select contributors in a variety of ways. In our call and in our response to authors who submitted proposals, we indicated that selection would be based on the stories that emerge when we place proposals in relation to each other. We offered to provide feedback on proposal drafts, and many people took us up on that offer. As our CFP said, our criteria for choosing pieces prioritized those that were clearly engaged with the theme of adequacy, those that were most clearly invested in (and were citational to) the discipline of Rhetoric and Composition, those that were clearly intersectional in their framing of labor, and those whose full pieces we could easily envision. As we reviewed, we also gave thought to how pieces would speak to each other, looking for throughlines between and among pieces. The pieces represented here were grounded in a kind of exciting theorizing that we hoped to engender in our original call and grounded in work necessary for continuing *in* the university. Many of the contributions will offer new ways to conceptualize things that must be done in the university at some points in our careers.

Three contributors had wonderful proposals, and we selected them for their boldness and creative ideas *and* because they offered insights to the concept of adequate that were not represented by others. We were deeply saddened by their need to back out of the project. While it is not uncommon for contributors to back out after they receive encouragement to develop proposals into full chapters, the reasons for these colleagues needing to back out tell us something important about the state of academic work. As editors, we believed it was important to mark the impossibilities for some of our colleagues. We extended deadlines, encouraged messy drafts, and did what we could to create a humane process. We believe it humane to make accommodations, and we asked some of our contributors directly: "What can we do to support you in the development of your chapter?" Ultimately, we had to accept contributors' choices to back out or say "no."

We also recognize that sometimes an invitation, though welcomed and considered deeply, is simply not the right time for our colleagues. Our research agendas do not align; internal pressures or service or other scholarship demands make saying "no" a necessity. An invitation is never a demand. Sometimes a cold email to a respected name in the field goes unanswered, which has everything and nothing to do with who we are. We wanted more contributors and more space to include more voices. At a certain point, we acknowledge that participation in an edited collection, for some, does not yield material benefits that would encourage colleagues to prioritize this work.

While academic presses have the right to choose external reviewers, we were encouraged to name several. As editors, we wanted to make sure that our list of external reviewers had scholarly engagements relevant to the concerns of this collection. Two other concerns guided our list. First, we are aware of who has been given space to contextualize this collection as a whole, and we thought carefully about how our reviewers might augment the printed considerations here. Second, we selected a list of external reviewers from folks we talked about the collection with and who were excited about it but could not submit proposals of their own. They asked us to be put on the reviewer list, and we have taken them up on their generosity here and have learned so much about how others not embedded within the project receive it.

In our acceptance letters, we asked our contributors to read and integrate the suggestions of the "Anti-Racist Scholarly Reviewing Practices: A Heuristic for Editors, Reviewers, and Authors" (Cagle et al. 2021). We wanted our contributors to work with minoritized scholars and engage the kinds of thinking these scholars encourage them to take. While the "Heuristic" is not the end all of antiracist work, we hoped that our contributors engaged with scholars of color to develop their ideas. We see many of our contributors not just citing BIPOC scholars but engaging their theories and thoughts.

Additionally, we noticed in drafts a tendency to articulate privilege in relation to some other imagined group of workers. Each and every one of the contributors to this collection recognize that they have some form of privilege that makes their lives less burdensome. As we noticed these moments in their chapters where they felt the need to assert their privileges, we asked them to remove those lines *unless necessary* for the point they are making. We did this for several reasons. One main reason is that it is our belief that unless you are making an argument about privilege and its consequences, to suggest that one group is less privileged than you can feel defensive or theatrical to many readers (Patterson 2018). So much of this collection is about asserting our rights to be adequate in an era of uncontrolled capitalism. We asked our contributors to trust their boldness, and we will defend their experiences and that boldness as worthy and important scholarly contributions. Another main reason is that privilege and disadvantage are complicated and relational, felt by everyone depending on the contexts in which rhetors and their audiences/writers and their readers interact. The arguments and stories herein are of a specific context. If we place any one of these contributors in a different context, their relationships to privilege and disadvantage shift.

Finally, with our editorial feedback we had four primary intentions: (1) Remind contributors to ground their work in whatever "adequate" can and might still mean and how authors might foreground that knowledge; (2) provide feedback that allows an author to strengthen his, her, or their prose; (3) be as generous in our feedback and as open to dialoguing with contributors as they want and time allows; and (4) approach responses to contributors as a dialogue, not a promise to accept whatever they submitted to us. We were open with contributors who needed to shift authorship or approaches, but we also made our own insistences. We encouraged all our contributors to ground, when necessary, the historic context in which they work. Our assumption here is that this book will outlast anyone reading it and its initial publication day, and so folks reading it twenty or thirty years from now should have citational access to what we all know to be currently true in 2022–2024. When it came to personal experiences, we trusted authors. Sometimes the need for citation bumped against the truth claims regarding a contributor's lived realities. On these moments, we tried to mark the difference and encouraged contributors to take a more "journalistic" approach that would help future readers see what we know to be valid in our present day. Our initial inline and end comments were invitations to dialogue. Whether contributors took us up on this offer was up to them, but we tried to answer every question and Zoom with everyone who wanted it. We recognize that continued dialogue might seem like more work for contributors to undertake. An offer was not always taken, and we hoped that our feedback was received generously, though we understand such generosity was neither a right of ours nor a demand we made of our contributors.

Our aim for *Adequate* from the beginning was to create an intellectual space to consider the difficult working conditions faculty face. The contributors in this collection stake their own claims about adequacy in the work of Rhetoric and Composition. They draw on a number of methods, methodologies, histories, and cultural experiences. And yet they understand adequacy as necessary for reimagining our work. Together, this work represents the dynamism of Rhetoric and Composition and the ways that the work we claim to take up as professionals might get done. As for any edited collection, readers are encouraged to take the paths that they see fit, reading as their interests carry them from one author to the next. We have organized the collection into three parts: "Theorizing Support Under Impossible Conditions," "Responding to Structural Inadequacy," and "Adequacy as a Path Toward Change."

In the first part, "Theorizing Support Under Impossible Conditions," contributors imagine possibilities for sustained, coalitional transformation and persistence in the face of an often hostile workplace. In "Solidarity as 'Living': A Theory of Relationality for Community Building as Women of Color in Academia," Eunjeong Lee, Amy J. Wan, and Sara P. Lopez Amezquita develop an adequate network of care as women of color in a cruel, unrelenting corporate structure full of racism, colonialist pressures for individualist success, and ever more output. In "Imagining a Critical, Coalitional Kindness: Moving Beyond Niceness to Envision a Discipline of Care and Cooperative Disagreement,"

Mara Lee Grayson critiques the "niceness theatrics" that saturate neoliberal corporate university structures. Beginning with Jewish rhetorical traditions rather than Protestant rhetorical traditions, Grayson theorizes "coalitional kindness" as an adequate response. Finally, Olivia Wood writes in "Rhetorical Theory and the Fight for a Living Wage" that the work of obtaining adequate wages is often undercut by the very rhetorical theory that undergirds what we do. Wood invites us to think more critically about subjectivity and contract negotiations. We must have a clearer sense of who management is to begin negotiating with them.

The essays in our next part, "Responding to Structural Inadequacy," offer close readings of specific institutional roles common in Rhetoric and Composition. In "A Dialogue on Un/Learning Institutional Knowledge in Bits and Doing *the Work* as Pre-Tenure Administrators," Kelin Loe, Ashanka Kumari, and Gavin P. Johnson describe "coalitional administration" as a process of interdependence that has helped them establish shared goals, values, and strategies toward defining adequacy as centering difference, social justice, and accountability. In "Embodying (In)Adequacy: 'Good Enough' as a Blow Against the Meritocratic Regime," Christina V. Cedillo, Vyshali Manivannan, Ada Hubrig, and Bernice Olivas illustrate how multiply marginalized faculty face nearly impossible living conditions exacerbated by the university's dehumanizing demands. In "Temporarily Adequate: Learning to Be Enough at the Writing Center," Lauren Silber, Malaika Fernandes, Tenzin Jamdol, Audrey Auerbach Nelson, Xiran Tan, and Shaoxuan Tian bring queer failure into their understanding of what can happen during the building of a university writing center and the work of writing consultation. In "A Labor of Love: A Generational Conversation About Success, Living Well, and All That," Jen Wingard and Rachelle A. C. Joplin discuss their own relationships to graduate mentorship in the context of a labor market with diminishing R1 faculty positions.

In the final part, "Adequacy as a Path Toward Change," contributors focus on their own specific locations to work through the messiness of carrying on in administrative capacities. In "Confrontations with Adequacy in Pandemic Teacher Training," Crystal Broch Colombini, Stephanie L. Kerschbaum, and Sara Webb-Sunderhaus share stories from their disparate yet connected experiences mentoring new teachers during COVID. Laurie A. Pinkert and Lauren Marshall Bowen level a powerful critique of faculty evaluations and major reviews in "Laboring Through the Lifecycle: Toward A Disciplinary Approach to Faculty Evaluation." Pinkert and Bowen argue that integration into the discipline should be a metric for success rather than an accumulation of publications.

They illustrate how their work on disciplinary lifecycling offers a framework for rethinking faculty evaluations. In "This Is Fine: Reflecting on (Missed) Opportunities and Adequate Moments of Departmental Collaboration, Labor, and Care," Brigitte Mussack weaves theories of dissonance and care work to consider what it means to produce training and documentation for contingent faculty in her program. Mussack's work illustrates the importance of remaining *in* dissonance and how care work functions as an entryway to it.

In addition to the lengthier chapters, three contributors offer short interludes. Sara Doan's, Katie Manthey's, and Ada Hubrig's interludes rest at the borders of a collection of ideas and offer provocations and perhaps invisible bridges for us to walk upon as we head to the next momentary stopping points. Finally, Seth Kahn and Tony Scott offer an afterword. As leading theorists of labor activism and political economic critique in Rhetoric and Composition, they provide a dialogue that emerges from a deep consideration with the ideas throughout.

Content warning: Several of the chapters and interludes in this volume contain references to depression, suicidal ideation, and other potentially upsetting material. We encourage our readers to make appropriate adjustments for themselves prior to engaging the chapters and interludes that follow. Some of our contributors have chosen to include their own content warnings; others have not. We ask readers to prepare themselves as needed.

As for thoughts that resolve the ideas in this introduction? We know many of the adequate gestures that we offer, the lines of reasoning that extend only so far, the less polished prose . . . It is in keeping with the spirit of adequacy that we, Timothy and Joshua, say, "This is good enough. This achieves much of what we want to do." We have done work that has built our friendship, and we have thought with as much care alongside our contributors as they have allowed and as we have allowed. We hope, always hope, that the work sits with you and you begin to, or recognize with greater clarity than before, that you can be adequate.

References

Adler-Kassner, Linda. 2017. "Because Writing Is Never Just Writing." *College Composition and Communication* 69 (2): 317–340.
Ahmed, Sara. 2017. *Living a Feminist Life*. Durham, NC: Duke University Press.
Ahmed, Sara. 2021. *Complaint!* Durham, NC: Duke University Press.
Berlant, Lauren. 2010. *Cruel Optimism*. Durham, NC: Duke University Press.

Bousquet, Marc. 2008. *How the University Works: Higher Education and the Low-Wage Nation.* New York: New York University Press.

Brandt, Deborah. 2015. *The Rise of Writing: Redefining Mass Literacy.* Cambridge: Cambridge University Press.

Cagle, Lauren E., Michele F. Eble, Laura Gonzales, et al. 2021. "Anti-Racist Scholarly Reviewing Practices: A Heuristic for Editors, Reviewers, and Authors." https://tinyurl.com/reviewheuristic.

Chaput, Catherine. 2009. *Inside the Teaching Machine: Rhetoric and the Globalization of the U.S. Public Research University.* Tuscaloosa: University of Alabama Press.

Cicchino, Amy, and Troy Hicks, eds. 2024. *Better Practices: Exploring the Teaching of Writing in Online and Hybrid Spaces.* For Collins, CO: WAC Clearinghouse.

Colombini, Crystal Broch. 2018. "Composing Crisis: Hardship Letters and the Political Economies of Genre." *College English* 80 (3): 218–246.

Combahee River Collective. 1977. "A Black Feminist Statement." In *The Second Wave: A Reader in Feminist Theory*, edited by Linda Nicholson, 63–70. New York: Routledge.

Comstock, Edward. 2023. "Toward a New Neurobiology of Writing: Plasticity and the Feeling of Failure." *College Composition and Communication* 74 (4): 695–730.

Connors, Robert. 1997. *Composition-Rhetoric: Backgrounds, Theory, and Pedagogy.* Pittsburgh: University of Pittsburgh Press.

Corrigan, Lisa M. 2023. "The Evisceration of a Public University." *The Nation.* 16 August 16. https://www.thenation.com/article/society/wvu-cuts-higher-education/.

Craig, Sherri. 2021. "Your Contract Grading Ain't It." *Writing Program Administration* 44 (3): 145–147.

Crowley, Sharon. 1998. *Composition in the University: Historical and Polemical Essays.* Pittsburgh: University of Pittsburgh Press.

Daniel, James Rushing. 2022. *Toward an Anti-Capitalist Composition.* Logan: University of Utah Press.

Flaherty, Colleen. 2016. "'Fake' Tenure?" *Inside Higher Ed.* March 10. https://www.insidehighered.com/news/2016/03/11/u-wisconsin-board-regents-approves-new-tenure-policies-despite-faculty-concerns.

Goodburn, Amy, Donna Lecourt, and Carrie Leverenz, eds. 2012. *Rewriting Success in Rhetoric and Composition Careers.* Anderson, SC: Parlor Press.

Hartline, Megan Faver. 2023. "Shaping Emerging Community-Engaged Scholars' Identities: A Genre Systems Analysis of Professionalization Documents that (De)Value Engaged Work." *College Composition and Communication* 74 (4): 592–617.

Hassel, Holly, and Cassandra Phillips. 2022. *Materiality and Writing Studies: Aligning Labor, Scholarship, and Teaching.* Carbondale, IL: National Council of Teachers of English.

Hesse, Douglas E. 2015. "The WPA as Worker: What Would John Ruskin Say? What Would My Dad?" *WPA: Writing Program Administration* 38 (2): 129–140.

Hiltzik, Michael. 2022. "'Quiet Quitting' Is Just a New Name for an Old Reality." *Los Angeles Times* August 25. https://www.latimes.com/business/story/2022-08-25/quiet-quitting-is-just-a-new-name-for-an-ancient-reality.

Hodgson, Ian, and Divya Kumar. 2023. "DeSantis Reshaped Florida Higher Education over the Last Year. Here's How." *Tampa Bay Times*. July 7. https://www.tampabay.com/news/education/2023/07/05/desantis-florida-higher-education-stop-woke-individual-freedom-tenure-new-college-diversity/.

Horner, Bruce. 2000. *Terms of Work for Composition: A Materialist Critique*. Albany: State University of New York Press.

Horner, Bruce. 2016. *Rewriting Composition: Terms of Exchange*. Carbondale: Southern Illinois University Press.

Horning, Alice. 2007. "Ethics and the jWPA." In *Untenured Faculty as Writing Program Administrators*. Anderson, SC: Parlor, 40–57.

Jordan, June. 2003. *Some of Us Did Not Die*. New York: Basic Books.

Kahn, Seth, and Amy Pason. 2021. "What Do We Mean by Academic Labor (in Rhetorical Studies)?" *Rhetoric and Public Affairs* 24 (1–2): 109–128.

Kynard, Carmen. "'All I Need Is One Mic': A Black Feminist Community Meditation on the Work, the Job, and the Hustle (& Why So Many of Yall Confuse This Stuff)." *Community Literacy Journal* 14 (2): 5–24.

Lorde, Audre. 1984. *Sister Outsider*. Berkeley, CA: Crossing Press.

Logan, Shirley Wilson. 1995. *"We Are Coming": The Persuasive Discourse of Nineteenth-Century Black Women*. Carbondale: Southern Illinois University Press.

Malenczyk, Rita, Susan Miller-Cochran, Elizabeth Wardle, and Kathleen Blake Yancey, eds. 2018. *Composition, Rhetoric, and Disciplinarity*. Logan: Utah State University Press.

Mannon, Bethany, and Privott, Georgia. 2023. "Evangelical Rhetoric in College Students' Writing Practice." *College Composition and Communication* 74 (4): 618–645.

McGee, Kate. 2023. "An Effort to Ban Faculty Tenure in Public Universities Has Failed in the Teas Legislature." *Texas Tribune*. May 27. https://www.texastribune.org/2023/05/27/texas-university-faculty-tenure-ban-fails/.

Menand, Louis. 2023. "The Rise and Fall of Neoliberalism." *New Yorker*. July 24. https://www.newyorker.com/magazine/2023/07/24/the-rise-and-fall-of-neoliberalism.

Miller, Susan. 1991. *Textual Carnivals: The Politics of Composition*. Carbondale: Southern Illinois University Press.

Miller-Cochran, Susan. 2018. "Innovation Through Intentional Administration: Or, How to Lead a Writing Program Without Losing Your Soul" 42 (1): 16.

Moten, Fred, and Stefano Harney. 1999. "The Academic Speed-Up." *Workplace: A Journal for Academic Labor* 4: 23–28.

Nash, Jennifer C. 2011. "Practicing Love: Black Feminism, Love-Politics, and Post-Intersectionality." *Meridians* 11 (2): 1–24.

Nash, Jennifer C. 2020. "Citational Desires: On Black Feminism's Institutional Longings." *Diacritics* 48 (2): nn76–91.

Nicolas, Melissa, and Anna Sicari. 2022. *Our Body of Work: Embodied Administration and Teaching*. Logan: Utah State University Press.

Patterson, GPat. 2018. "Entertaining a Healthy Cispicion of the Ally Industrial Complex in Transgender Studies." *Women and Language* 41 (1): 146–151.

Ratcliffe, Krista, and Rebecca Rickly, eds. 2010. *Performing Feminism and Administration in Rhetoric and Composition Studies*. Cresskill, NJ: Hampton Press.
Readings, Bill. 1996. *The University in Ruins*. Cambridge, MA: Harvard University Press.
Royster, Jacqueline Jones. 2023. *Making the World a Better Place, African American Women Advocates, Activists, and Leaders, 1773–1900*. Pittsburgh, PA: University of Pittsburgh Press.
Simpkins, Neil. 2023. "The Rhetorical Role of Syllabi in Student Conversations About Disability Accommodations." *College Composition and Communication* 74(4): 673–694.
Smith, David. 3 Nov. 2021. "How Did Republicans Turn Critical Race Theory into a Winning Electoral Issue?" *Guardian*. https://www.theguardian.com/us-news/2021/nov/03/republicans-critical-race-theory-winning-electoral-issue.
Spillers, Hortense J. 1987. "Mama's Baby, Papa's Maybe: An American Grammar Book." *Diacritics* 17 (2): 64–81.
Stolley, Amy Ferdinandt. 2015. "Narratives, Administrative Identity, and the Early Career WPA." *Writing Program Administration* 39(1): 18–31.
Strickland, Donna. 2004. "The Managerial Unconscious." In *Tenured Bosses and Disposable Teachers: Writing Instruction in the Managed University*, edited by Marc Bousquet, Leo Parascondola, and Tony Scott, 45–56. Carbondale: Southern Illinois University Press.
Strickland, Donna. 2011. *The Managerial Unconscious in the History of Composition Studies*. Carbondale: Southern Illinois University Press.
Walker, Alice. 1983. *In Search of Our Mother's Gardens*. New York: Harcourt Brace.
Welch, Nancy, and Tony Scott, eds. 2016. *Composition in the Age of Austerity*. Logan: Utah State University Press.

PART I

Sustaining Support Under Impossible Conditions

1
Solidarity as "Living"

*A Theory of Relationality for Community Building
as Women of Color in Academia*

EUNJEONG LEE, AMY J. WAN, AND SARA P. LOPEZ AMEZQUITA

The cycle of an academic year—the beginnings and ends of semesters, writing syllabi during breaks, doing service work and teaching, and finding time to research and write—revolves around the judgments of ourselves and our job performance or, more specifically, whether institutions will view us and our work as successful or merely *adequate*. As academics, the process of quantifying a year's activities and deciding what is significant enough to include in annual reports can make us feel like a triumph or failure—sometimes both.

This process of judging our work can be high stakes and agonizing, as it determines whether we are more than adequate, and can ultimately keep our jobs. And not all of us, especially those of us who have been traditionally marginalized in higher education, are judged in the same manner. What is considered "productive" work in one place, such as mentoring students or community engagement, becomes just "service" in another. In fact, we have often been confused and worried when institutions have obscured these judgments. We have also felt at risk when institutional colonial logics have worked to measure, categorize, and hierarchize our colleagues, their "competence," and productivity as a legitimate knower and successful worker, maintaining whiteness in academia (Ahmed 2012; Kynard 2020).

But what if we reimagine success and how it may be assessed? What if, instead of CV lines and other typical measures, our relations with one another and community building are our terms of success? While this might look like (in)adequacy from the eye of an institution, this is how we sustain alternative ways of being and knowledge-making that shift (or help us survive) the university's systematized colonial logics. Discussing the work we build collectively in solidarity as women of color and writing faculty, this chapter shares our theory of relationality for community building as a pathway for new ways of *living* and subverting the colonial logics of academia that privilege individual performance over everything else. We forward our theory of relationality in our work, recognizing that how we architect our time and disposition to work collectively involves our affective relationships and is fully dependent on our deliberate labor.

We explore how we, as racialized, immigrant-generation, multilingual women scholars, labor against and beyond the institutional terms and modes of being, knowing, and doing. We offer examples in which what looks adequate functions as our operational mode for living: shared writing groups, navigating coauthorship, managing job transitions, and other ways of sustaining our friendship and our bodies. In doing so, we question what constitutes adequate and purposefully defy the individualistic, quantifiable, productivity-oriented notion of success. Our collaborative approach moves against the pervasive whiteness and systematized colonial logics to sustain our own and our peoples' voices, values, and practices.

Interrelating narrative storytelling and community-oriented theory building, we look to capture the complexities of navigating, and sustaining ourselves and our relationships, in institutional spaces that were not built for us. In these tellings, the choices we make may sometimes look like success and at other times look (in)adequate, through the dominant view of noteworthy labor and success. Yet, the relationships we cultivate reorient us to work as a community. Our long-term collaboration is not just for publication to meet the institutional standards but also for affirming this way of living in solidarity and building humanizing spaces in the sometimes violent institution.

As we share our story of community building while "outmaneuvering" (Love 2019, 133) the traditional modes of success, we discuss what working can look like when we have accomplices and people who look like us on our side in academic settings. Our values of relationality, collaboration, and our priorities of joy, dignity, and well-being challenge the boundaries between community and institutions and problematize what adequate labor means, looks like, and can do.

Community as a Pathway for Living

It is no secret that academia operates with and from the individual-centered colonial logics. As Lorgia García-Peña (2022) explains in *Community as Rebellion*, "Grounded in a model of individual success that rewards white men ... academia promotes competitiveness, exceptionalism, and ownership of history and knowledge making" (25), and, therefore, building community is "almost antithetical to academia." The colonial and neoliberal institutional structure and culture together measure success as individual achievement. Yet, they do not define what is sufficient. Under this competitive system, the faster, the louder, and the more "branded" (i.e., top-tier publisher), the better. In fact, single-authored publication projects, and large private grants and fellowships that highlight the individual as part of the institution, are the preferred measure for knowledge and success. Such individualistic metrics shape norms in knowledge-making practices and processes, determining what is considered successful research, effective writing time, and productive management of our bodies in ways that "efficiently" approximate the colonial and neoliberal institutional tenure and promotion "clock." There isn't room for being just adequate within this kind of system.

Amy remembers both the joy and disconnect that came from starting her job at Queens College (QC):

> As someone who went to graduate school at an R1, I thought I understood the publishing expectations of the job—finish a book and you get to stay here. But as happy as I was that I was employed back in my home city, I spent most of my pre-tenure years panicking over navigating the narrowness of the path. And I felt the pressure of representation as one of the few BIPOC folks in the department and as the department's only specialist in composition and rhetoric. Adequacy didn't feel like an option.

While institutions claim they want us to "thrive" (individually), their models and structures of success are not designed for our well-being. This weighs heavy on those of us who are language-minoritized, immigrant-generation women of color, who often become what García-Peña calls "the One" (2022, 17) that the institutions, particularly predominantly white institutions (PWIs), often rely on for their mission of "Diversity, Equity, and Inclusion." The structure that relies on "the One," and the culture that treats us like "the One," even if we're not in reality, make it more challenging, and therefore even more crucial, to build community. Under this condition, success feels like "surviving, psychologically and physically" at times, as "death comes in multiple forms" (Flores Niemann et al. 2019, 5).

When her tenure-track position was about to start at QC, Eunjeong felt like an empty shell, after exhausting every drop of energy faking her confidence and competence and feeling alone for many years at PWIs. Being in community with Sara and Amy enabled her to name the void that her white therapist could not help with for the longest time, and to finally see herself outside the institutional terms of (in)adequacy:

> As a new assistant professor who was first-gen in many ways, I was already exhausted even before I began. After many years of "sticking myself back in" to achieve institutional "success," I felt I lost myself. Learning that Amy and Sara shared similar life experiences, I didn't feel like I was "sticking out" any longer. A gesture of inviting me to be in community felt like an oxygen mask.

Our collective form of moving and living in academia supports our well-being, cultivating the critical labor and learning necessary to build community. As García-Peña writes while amplifying bell hooks's emphasis and vision on community building and knowledge-making, "to critically rebel against the colonial racial-capitalist regime that pits us against each other through the narrative of exceptionalism," we must co-create. (25). As Bettina Love (2019) argues, community building requires "action and solidarity" (132), not just theory, and, therefore, demands new ways of *living*. In this manner, we find ourselves in tune and in solidarity with BIPOC women scholars who have forwarded this form of community-oriented living as the antidote for multiple forms of deaths in institutional and academic spaces (Browdy et al. 2021; Flores Niemann et al. 2019; García-Peña 2022; Love 2019). By consistently questioning and (re)imagining "a relation, a network, and an ethos with various potentials for transforming what and whom the university can be for" (Boggs et al. 2019), we forge new possibilities for living beyond the typical judgments of (in)adequacy and their counterpart of exemplary. We, thus, turn to our community building to thrive and to live well—on our own terms—despite the white supremacist institutional spaces.

Co-Conspirators and Having Something at Stake

Important in community building is recognizing different positionalities and relational practices people bring and come to inhabit. Pointing out the difference between allies and co-conspirators, for example, Love (2019) explains how ally-ship is "performative or self-glorifying," as allies "do not have to love dark people, question their privilege, center their voice, build meaningful relationships with folx working in the struggle, take risks, or be in solidarity with others" (117). In contrast, Love argues, a co-conspirator works toward "authentic relationships of solidarity and mutuality, which are not possible when we try to avoid or transcend power imbalances" and "social change work... rooted in collaboration, humility, and accountability" (118). She emphasizes the active doing of the work—being present, in solidarity, and building relationships, despite the struggles, stakes, and risks. That is, co-conspirators understand that being in solidarity with others can (and does) compromise their privilege or positionality. In being co-conspirators, we must change our way of moving and relating in our world.

In this sense, becoming co-conspirators means shifting away from the institutional logics and building with others—in solidarity. Carmen Kynard (2020) critically asks, "What institutional practices are we interrupting? ... What institutional practices and actors are we sustaining? And at whose detriment?" (18). For us, this means working collectively to reimagine how we can work and relate differently. So when we worry about performing only adequately in the eyes of the institution, we have each other to assure that there is value in the labor we choose to do. We help each other tune in to the questions that have not been centralized, and seek answers in ways that become sustainable. In this way, community building in solidarity means creating something else that can hold us within and beyond the institutional space. After all, the stakes of this form of building and solidarity as living while working in academia are those of supporting our survival and well-being in a hostile and/or marginally inviting space. And because we have witnessed and experienced ourselves how positionalities are intersected with different forms of privilege, marginalization, and discrimination, we view and appreciate our community-oriented living as mindful and deliberate practice.

For Amy, part of what makes it easier to navigate and create a place in the institution is when she sees herself in community with the people surrounding her everyday—whether students or the people she is writing with right now. When she first started at QC, she was one of one, perhaps not "the one" in the way García-Peña defines, but a single person in the field, in a department of mostly white literature scholars. The two other BIPOC junior faculty who were there when she started left within two years of the start of her job. She felt like she was racing to meet every milestone:

I liked and appreciated my job and the students I got to teach every day, many of whom looked like me. But I also felt the pressure of performing in ways that were not always healthy. I kept quiet when I should have had the confidence in my own expertise to speak up. This is not to say I was silenced by others but more that I silenced myself to make sure I could keep my job—a quiet and tense navigation that always kept me on edge.

As someone growing up minoritized in the US, I was familiar with this navigation because I have been doing it for my entire life. I published what I needed to do to get tenure, but I wasn't sure of myself. When Eunjeong and Sara were hired, I felt pressure to make sure they were happy, and I sought ways to offer them support and mentoring. I felt like it was my responsibility to do so, and I didn't want them to feel alone in navigating the institutional space like I did. But as they became more intertwined in my work and non-work life, the relationship we developed was not one in which I was the person responsible for them but one in which we were answering to one another. Their presence made me feel like I was not a lone voice anymore and reassured my perspective that supporting students should mean affirming their voices and did not rely on tired deficit or white savior narratives.

For Eunjeong, institutional success was supposed to be a reward for all the sacrifices that she made at the expense of herself and life. But Sara's and Amy's presence helped her to see herself and her labor away from the neoliberal logic of cost-effectiveness and "worth," actively affirming herself, not as a worker who could be either adequate, exemplary, or a failure but as a whole person:

> Being in community with Sara and Amy taught me what it means to care collectively as a human being, against the culture and logics of the colonial university that defines our relation as a co-worker. They cared about my time, history, future, and my well-being on and off campus—they apologized for messaging me about work at night or on the weekend, told me to go home to rest rather than attending a department event when I was sick, offered a space to talk, laugh, and cry, among many others. While these acts might seem like a small gesture of kindness, I know kindness in the colonial institution always costs something—their own time, schedule, energy, and the institutional standards and pathways to success. Our community and relational practices have shown me a different way of living that protects—not sacrifices—me as a full human, not a faceless, anonymous body that constitutes the university.

For Sara, building community has been a long-engaged modus operandi. She cannot recall exactly when this became part of her nature, but Sara can name almost every instance in which having and building community made her feel alive, emboldened, and open to being vulnerable. Perhaps for that reason, Sara has always been suspicious of institutions, even if the people in them are well intentioned. When Sara started her position at QC, she noticed the institution's insistence on "knowledge production" as solely focused on the single-authored monograph. Just in her first year, Sara lost track of the many times people asked her "what her book was about" and "what presses were being considered." She also noticed that many colleagues discussed "success" and "achievement" in ways that distanced themselves from their students, their pedagogy, their communities, and their "service" work. They often cited periods and topics of study but rarely connected that to classroom conversations with students, and when they did talk about their teaching, their conversations rarely pointed to education as an area of knowledge production. To some extent, these observations and her fear of the tenure clock, as well as the many solidarity practices she gained with and from immigrant young adults in the immigrant rights movement, led Sara to cultivate ways of doing things differently—to work with colleagues she could trust to rethink some of these systemic practices:

> When I got my position at QC, I felt like in many ways I was stepping into my own dream. I was coming back home—to the place that shaped me, surrounded by people who manifested many of the cultural and linguistic practices that drove me to getting a PhD. And most importantly, I felt like I could continue my educator pathway working and learning with students who—as I have always believed—capture the brilliance, tenacity, and richness of our world. But to a great extent taking this position placed me on the side of the institution. I realized that many of the hurdles and pains I went through as an immigrant-generation undergraduate student could (and have been) extended by the institution I am now a part of. Upon finishing my PhD, I also came from Kentucky with a new love and appreciation for what building community could mean in a predominantly white and rural space, and I longed [for] and wondered what that could look like in my dream place. Perhaps, because we were "the" few writing people, and perhaps because we shared many similar experiences as immigrant-generation women of color in academia, and perhaps because Amy purposefully sought us to support us and engage with our research, it didn't take long before I began to feel that I could be myself and push some boundaries.
>
> I remember how difficult the first year on the tenure track was in that I was consumed with worry about producing knowledge. This worry kept me overworking and tired, abandoning many of the cultural and community practices I had long engaged in. And I don't exactly remember the first

time it happened, but I do remember making a habit of going to Eunjeong's office, saying nothing, and breathing in and out, and feeling a sense of keenness and being able to just name those worries. I also remember how in these shared moments of vulnerability, and solidarity, we saw each other on this similar pathway, and we began to rethink what knowledge production could look like. We began to formulate new options, and our conversations from our interest in supporting our immigrant and racialized communities' ways of knowing soon turned to writing together in each other's offices. We wrote to express our frustrations and dreams, not to produce. Furthermore, because Amy was consistently present for both of us, and checking in on us, we began to share those conversations with her, and our conversations also evolved to writing together, realizing that we were intersecting in different ways, and could elevate each other's expertise, vision, and research by working collaboratively, collectively, and in solidarity.

In these moments of building relationships with one another, all of us chose to live in ways that held each other up. We chose to prioritize each other's well-being, all in the face of an institutional logic that is hostile, sometimes violently and sometimes gently prodding individuals up the ladder on their own. We chose to protect and sustain each other from the multiple forms of deaths and diseases that are too common in institutional and academic lives, to build a space and time that is worthy of living together. Our choice to refuse the institutional pathways of success and embrace "adequate" is grounded in our desire to live and work differently in solidarity.

Collaborative Living as Deliberate Practice

When an institution operates on the culture of "the One," you feel like you have to operate as the one and succeed on institutional terms. After all, to do what the institution deems as just adequate is not about individual accomplishments but about what is being judged and how, which is often by the individualistic standards. The culture of the One dominates the standards and reiterates what is adequate and what is below it. Even when you're not the One, or even if we seemingly have "diversity," the culture is picked up and recirculated by people who should really fight. To not do that and build community take deliberate practice—against the institutional values and rhythms, to make something new, to be and work in community, to prioritize care and humanity, as a way of living. This means being ok with what the institution considers adequate as opposed to the institutional success and culture of hyperproduction and activity.

Collaboration can be one such example. Community building takes community-oriented disposition and value but also working collectively, which the institution does not often recognize as expertise and conscientious labor. The three of us have worked together over many years, have built up trust as we've written and negotiated the terms of that writing together. For example, deciding the order of the authors in academic publication can be tricky because it implies the individualistic, top-down-oriented corporate work structure where one leader often decides or oversees the work, and the rest does less work (though this is not always the case). As we understand that our community-oriented work and publications are subject to such standards and terms of "success," we have navigated authorship decisions, considering how the inequitable authorship structure impacts us differently as pre-tenure and tenured faculty, as well as the labor and expertise that the focus of the piece relied on.

We also make conscientious efforts to represent our writing voices as interwoven. Always nervous about her writing voice, Eunjeong has learned so much from Amy's and Sara's way of "workin' language" (Alvarez et al. 2022)—how we cultivate each other's voices, conscientiously recognize the intellectual lineage before us, and situate our work in the scholarly conversation built by other BIPOC scholars. In this sense, our collaborative writing isn't just documentation of our collaborative knowledge building but also an extension of how we orient to each other as a community and to other scholars who have taught us to center language-minoritized and racialized multilingual communities. As Amy shares here, this orientation might mean being okay with fewer CV lines, or publications in community venues over flagship journals, which takes deliberate and insistent resistance against the common institutional pathways of success:

> If you look at my CV, I don't publish as much as other people who are at the same stage of their career. This is not a quality over quantity choice but a choice about how I spend my time. In addition to not being listed as first author as often as Eunjeong and Sara because they are still pre-tenure, a lot of my work time is dedicated to the students at Queens and to being in dialogue with my colleagues here. My priorities are to build lasting structures that will impact the material conditions of our students and the people I work with. My publications, such as they are, reflect this engagement.

For us, working and living collectively have also meant sharing many of the health and family crises that have happened to us over the years. It has meant that we work on pieces at different times and with different kinds of contributions, prioritizing our health and well-being foremost. Throughout the pandemic, we met regularly for our collaborative projects. But these meetings were not just about work. We checked in, and still do, with each other, sharing how we are doing, the joy and sorrow we are feeling, virtual hugs, affirming a sense of connection. We encourage each other to rest, breathe, and take time for joy, including our time with our families. We share what we have learned and gained throughout the years and pass on these knowings to our most junior colleagues, not as a form of pressuring the "get the work done" practice (although that is obviously also at stake) but to show up and cherish each other as people and because we want to sustain each other and to be well. We continue to encourage these practices that center our body and humanity in our shared writing group. Like Amy says, we've "got each other's back," and this sense and practice of solidarity are at the center of our living:

> At the end of the day, I feel responsible and accountable to Eunjeong and Sara and to the other people I feel in community with. To our students. Not to the college, who wants to measure them by their GPAs and graduation rates and us by the numbers of publications and citations we have. When I have a decision to make, I always try to put in the labor of thinking hard about who benefits in both concrete structural ways and in light of people's identities and well-being. I am not motivated by what will look good on a CV and instead actively look toward what will matter to the people around me. It's a careful dance and one in which you must actively quiet your ego! This way of doing things almost never yields a long list of publications or boosts your standing in the field but it is really a matter of survival. I don't think I could live any other way.

Choosing adequacy over institutional pathways of success is possible through a community who is willing to affirm and support such living. Therefore, part of the labor to be adequate is figuring out those you'd like to be in community with and where your people are. Eunjeong talks about her mistakes of naively assuming and trusting people to want the same kind of community, solidarity, and advocacy against the colonial university structure and academic culture, and how making this community building visible was a deliberate practice:

> When I first decided to leave QC, choosing my immigrant families over my job seemed obvious, given their deteriorating health and precarious life circumstances. But I felt inadequate. Some friends advised me not to go on the job market so soon. What felt harder, however, was moving away from my community. Yet, I firmly stood by what my community taught

me—our life matters as much as, if not more than, our job. They graciously supported my decision to prioritize my personal life as a colleague and a friend. Sara passed on job postings, and Amy wrote a recommendation letter. And they sustained me beyond my time at QC till now, reminding me to care for my body foremost.

While the deliberate community-oriented living allowed me to feel more, it also made me feel less human in different institutional spaces. I showed up vulnerable, candid, yet critical of the structure, only to realize that my vulnerability can make people feel uncomfortable, and that also can further marginalize me as someone "too naïve," "too caring," "too emotional." I feel conflicted. While I truly believe in the power of collective action, I feel exploited when my labor, but not my full self, is wanted to fulfill the superficial mission of DEI.

In my performance review, I received suggestions to put the article titles only without my coauthors' names, to highlight my contribution. To the institution, my collaboration is just easy work, rather than a deliberate knowledge-making in solidarity and community building practice. I refused; this is our work together. But also, even if it is "my" idea, that idea couldn't have come about without the dialogue. I'm torn that I have to quantify collaborative work, as if it is always possible to delineate mine versus yours—the colonial logics of ownership that Patel (2016) warns against. I learned to read, sense, and build community through our solidarity and friendship, yet that literacy also makes me feel less human in other spaces.

Institutional logics, as Eunjeong describes in her narrative, operate based on individual ownership as success, and while this works well for the institution, it does not guarantee or grant any further protection to the well-being of the human/s who contributed to such production. Additionally, this logic foments a culture of fast production, which relegates management of "one's" production to the individual. But managing a life that includes work is busy and complex enough, and in some circumstances our health conditions also influence such difficulties. For Sara, managing her health is a top priority that demands several forms of support—several of which academia is not designed for.

I have preexisting conditions, with more than one autoimmune disorder, and over the years the symptoms related to these conditions, as well as increased levels of stress and lack of rest, have started to catch me up. Success in academia often correlates and/or intersects unhealthy habits such as overworking, staring at screens for long periods of time, and sacrificing personal relationships and spaces—to get things done. Because I am committed to living in a way that feels sustainable and joyful—and can keep me alive, I have started resisting these ways of operating, and I am grateful to Amy and Eunjeong for their insistent affirmation that I take this approach, that we take this approach. I have found comfort in hearing them say that it is okay to step back from work and focus on other things that fulfill my life; more than that, I have learned that I can go to them not just to share my woes but the practices that are adding livelihood to my life, like dancing. And I have found that I do not have to feel shame in saying that I need rest.

The ways of living we discuss here solely depend on deliberate labor against (i.e., resistance) the default mechanisms for traditional success. Beyond the inner workings of the college itself, beyond helping each other reach those traditional modes of success through publications while staying true to our values, at the end of the day, we are here for each other. We have space to discuss the racist things said during a meeting, a discriminatory practice experienced in the copy room, a difficult family problem, even space to strategize about how to advocate for our students in a meeting or to move forward with the next thing we want to do. This is a deliberate space of noncompetition and collectivity in ways that are not measured by those traditional means, and another form of labor that takes time, thoughtfulness, and expertise. How we act with one another cannot be written up and put in a promotion file. Yet, we are also building for our incoming and future junior BIPOC colleagues—because we understand this isn't just about us.

To do so, we need to listen to voices other than the institution's as we make decisions about what we prioritize, what and how we spend our time on, and how we relate to each other. As we've shown, the institutional message of needing to be more than adequate can be heard as one of many, if your priority is building a community. Doing this also means having space to be vulnerable with one another. We express this vulnerability here so readers can understand what it takes to build this kind of community, but it's important to know that we haven't expressed it all. We are being mindful to ensure that all our vulnerabilities are not offered up in an article to be consumed in the way academic knowledge is consumed. We haven't given you everything here.

Living Beyond Adequacy

While writing this piece, Eunjeong asked, "Are you only accepting the part of the person who is producing labor?" To be able to answer "no" to that question is what we actively resist through living in community. Living in community is not about establishing a structure and assuming it will happen, as we see that as an extension of the institutional operation and standards with the assumptions of the monolithic bodies and labor conditions. Rather, living in community means being *present in* and choosing and acting for the community, against the capitalist system and culture that tell us that choosing *us* or *our* well-being over *me* or *mine* is not wise and put me at a risk of falling short or behind.

Beyond meeting those institutional benchmarks of success, our discussion of living in solidarity offers a mode of living that collectively counters and affirms our active presence outside the institutional logics that narrowly define and center judgments of individual (in)adequacy. It encourages us to determine our own terms of success, centering values of anticolonial, anticapitalist ways of being. As Sara has reminded us in our process of writing, this shift also means rethinking the matrix of success of our own academic publications away from the traditional measure, such as Journal Impact Factors, and turning to and celebrating how our work has reached and impacted our students—one of the communities we imagine learning with. Similarly, we work to approach our careers by centering joy, or what sustains us as humans. Joy helps us be more conscious of the kind of academic work we want to do and how to do it differently—this is what's coming from our relational practice. In this sense, our relations with one another and community building are our terms of success. While this might look like adequacy from the eye of the institution, it is through our relations and community building that we cultivate and sustain alternative ways of being and doing knowledge making that shift the colonial logics of the university.

The practices we have learned throughout our friendship give us hope that building community and transformation is possible within the fissure of the colonial structure in the university and academia. We are cautious but also confident in thinking that we have worked to see our core not in our work but in our life and our being and different ways of knowing and doing the work. And at the bottom of this practice lies our refusal (Grande 2016) to see ourselves and each other through the same lens through which the university often sees us—always functioning at its optimal capacity, managing time and body to work tirelessly for the maximum production at the maximal efficiency and effectiveness, for recognition and promotion of self and the university, for their empty words, "we want you to succeed," at the expense of everything else.

And sometimes, the sense and praxis of solidarity that we have built together has allowed us to feel and practice alongside one another in ways that don't appear on our CVs, other than the series of articles or book chapters we have worked on together. While these may look like "success" in the traditional sense, the success that we are prouder of is invisible—the kind of living and solidarity that helped us sustain ourselves and our often slow yet steady fight against the colonial terms of being, knowing, and doing. If the university and academia call this inadequate, we are happy to live with our practices of "inadequacy" and to collaboratively build, work, and otherwise be in community and solidarity with our peoples. This is our way of living well—our way of forging a new path—not just for the three of us but for our future colleagues and community members as well.

References

Ahmed, Sara. 2012. *On Being Included*. Durham, NC: Duke University Press.

Alvarez, Sara. P., Amy J. Wan, and Eunjeong Lee. 2022. "Workin' Languages: Who We Are Matters in Our Writing." In *Writing Spaces: Readings on Writing*, vol. 4, edited by Dana Lynn Driscoll, Megan Heise, Mary K. Steward, and Matthew Vetter, 1–17. Anderson, SC: Parlor Press.

Boggs, Abigail, Eli Meyerhoff, Nick Mitchell, and Zach Schwartz-Weinstein. 2019. "Abolitionist University Studies: An Invitation." *Abolition Journal*. Accessed January 28, 2023. https://abolitionjournal.org/abolitionist-university-studies-an-invitation/.

Browdy, Ronisha, Esther Milu, Victor del Hierro, and Laura Gonzales. 2021. "From Cohort to Family: Coalitional Stories of Love and Survivance." *Composition Studies* 49 (2): 14–30.

Flores Niemann, Yolanda, Gabriella Gutiérrez y Muhs, and Carmen G. González. 2020. "Introduction." In *Presumed Incompetent*, edited by Yolanda Flores Niemann, Gabriella Gutiérrez y Muhs, and Carmen G. González, 3–9. Logan: Utah State University Press.

García-Peña, Lorgia. 2022. *Community as Rebellion*. Chicago: Haymarket Books.

Grande, Sandy. "Refusing the University." In *Toward What Justice? Describing Diverse Dreams of Justice in Education*, edited by Eve Tuck and K. Wayne Yang, 47–65. New York: Routledge, 2018.

Kynard, Carmen. 2020. "'All I Need Is One Mic': A Black Feminist Community Meditation on the Work, the Job, and the Hustle (& Why So Many of Yall Confuse This Stuff)." *Community Literacy Journal* 14 (2): 5–24.

Love, Bettina. 2019. *We Want to Do More than Survive: Abolitionist Teaching and the Pursuit of Educational Freedom*. Boston: Beacon Press.

Patel, Leigh. 2016. *Decolonizing Educational Research: From Ownership to Answerability*. New York: Routledge.

2
Imagining a Critical, Coalitional Kindness

Moving Beyond Niceness to Envision a Discipline of Care and Cooperative Disagreement

MARA LEE GRAYSON

Rhetorics of scarcity, real or manufactured, tend to dominate in times of crisis (Scanlan et al. 2010). Yet, with human rights and academic freedom under increasing threat in the United States, in places where critical curricula remain, denial and minimization seem to comprise the modus operandi of our academic institutions. If complacency is the prevailing mood, however, it is not the prevailing discourse. Instead, the rhetoric is one of (unearned) victory. In the public California institution where I work, for example, I regularly receive emails celebrating the school's commitment to equity, despite recent incidents of racism on campus (Guzman-Lopez 2023) and statewide investigations of the university system's long-standing pattern of sweeping sexual harassment under the rug (Nguyen 2023). Not long ago, during a workshop on culturally sustaining pedagogy, the facilitator concluded a critique of Texas state legislation by stating: "I'm very grateful I'm in California."

    I am not suggesting that one should not be grateful for the privileges afforded by their place of residency. I am suggesting that when unaccompanied by self-critique, directing criticism outward may be understood as both a coping mechanism and a form of damage control: "Critique . . . allows people to sustain an idea of themselves as being critical while being silent about 'those things happening here.'... You can burn it down as long as it is somebody else's house" (Ahmed 2021, 217). In other words, the prevailing discourse can be summed up as something like this: "Sure, things are bad *over there*, but they're fine *here*." I have noted a similar dynamic on the now-defunct Writing Program Administrators Listserv (WPA-L), which, in the years leading up to its discontinuation, was a hotbed not only for contentious conversations but for the allowance of discriminatory perspectives to be voiced with the same weight as more equitable points of view, if not greater weight.[1] Writing about an incident during which "whataboutism" was deployed to derail a conversation about disciplinary racism on the WPA-L (Grayson 2023), I cited sociologist Crystal Fleming's astute observation: "Racism is always someone else's crime" (Fleming 2018, 46).

Intriguingly, efforts to develop a moderation structure that would, ideally, create a safer environment for disciplinary discourse resulted in an overhaul of the WPA-L that limited posts to announcements, thus restricting any and all discussion. Though I participated in these efforts, I personally am disappointed that the revision of the WPA-L eliminated community interaction for what feels like, if not a top-down structure, certainly an impersonal one. Moreover, it troubles me that in a discipline populated by writers, writing scholars, rhetoricians, and teachers, we can't seem to figure out how to have a cooperative conversation. The problems we face as researchers, educators, and workers may be situated within our local contexts, but they are rarely unique to those contexts. In other words, shouldn't we have a space, even a flawed one, that enables discourse about the problems that affect us across institutions?

It's not shocking that in a disciplinary community that is geographically, experientially, and ideologically diverse (though arguably not nearly as diverse as it ought to be), conversation grows contentious. But instead of working on building better conversations—or becoming better conversationalists—we seem to retreat. Though one might argue that rhetoricians and compositionists ought to know better, we wind up relying on the same incomplete concepts and buzzwords that our institutions do when they call on us to be collegial, practice and promote civility (Ward 2017), and build cultures of care,[2] without defining *care* or explicating what it means to care for ourselves and one another.

When terms are undefined, rather than admit uncertainty, we default to the status quo. Thus, "care" is interpreted through existing frameworks and

---

1. More information about the history of the WPA-L can be found in Zachary Beare (2017). More information about the specific discussions noted can be found in Mara Lee Grayson (2023) and Iris Ruiz et al. (2023).
2. From my university's strategic plan.

ideologies, such as the problematic notions of Niceness[3] that prevail in educational spaces. Such notions, while seemingly unassailable—*who can argue against being nice?* one might wonder—are rooted in and uphold ethnocentric norms of communication and behavior that further marginalize and discount the ways of knowing of nonwhite, non-Christian, non-western people (Castagno 2014; Galman 2019; Grayson 2023; Villarreal et al. 2019; Wegwert and Charles 2019; Yoon 2012). Niceness forms the foundation not of the culture of care but of the "pseudocommunity" wherein "the illusion of consensus" prevails, regardless of what inequities lurk beneath (Grossman et al. 2001, 962).

Speaking from my own positionality as a neurodivergent, white-privileged, Jewish woman, I must admit that these easy fixes feel especially unnatural to me, perhaps because they almost directly contradict the ethos and aims of Jewish rhetorics, wherein "contradictions and unanswered questions are preferable to falsities and questions never asked" (Grayson 2023, 155). My experience as neurodivergent contributes to the confusion I feel in the face of performativity. For example, though I spend much of my research and writing time theorizing this performativity, I do not always pick up on the social cues that tell me, in the moment, that an exchange is indeed performative. I also tend to be blunt and talkative, behaviors that while generally acceptable in Jewish discourse, I have learned are far less welcome in professional spaces crafted in the images of hegemonic middle-class whiteness and Anglo-Saxon Protestant Christianity.

While I acknowledge that my ways of meaning making are not normative for or applicable to everyone, I do think the discourses and cultural rhetorics to which I am accustomed have more to offer our discipline and profession than the ableist white cultural hegemony that defines the contemporary academy would have us believe. For example, as peoples who for thousands of years have had to negotiate their marginalized and exilic positionings, Jewish cultures, generally speaking, embrace uncertainty and complexity. Accordingly, Jewish rhetorics may help us understand the cooperative dimensions of disagreement (Horn 2021; Schiffrin 1984; Tannen 1981) and the connections between literacy and empathy (Greenbaum 2008; Moskow and Katz 2008). And the "care work" (Piepzna-Samarasinha 2018) that disabled folx do to support one another can teach us all about how we can affirm one another's identities and remind "each other that we are more than the sum of our damn CV lines and . . . what our bodyminds are going through are real and legitimate" (Hubrig 2022, 34).

---

3. Like Angelina E. Castagno and others, I capitalize the term "Niceness." I make this choice to demonstrate its constructedness and systemic power.

Drawing upon the Jewish rhetorical embrace of uncertainty and defining success by process rather than product, in this chapter, I consider the limitations of "niceness" as a framework for care in the neoliberal academy. In such spaces, the surface-level theatrics of Niceness have been presented as an adequate solution to socially, culturally, and institutionally situated interpersonal challenges. I argue that Niceness theatrics are not only inadequate but dangerous, for they obscure what ought to be our most foundational starting point for interacting and working together: the acknowledgment that, beneath our different lived experiences, there is a shared humanness that necessitates caring in a more coalitional way. Eschewing the need for efficient solutions, I explore how replacing Niceness with greater care and cooperative disagreement may help us recognize one another's humanity—an adequate goal that, though it ought to be the bare minimum for interpersonal interaction in professional spaces, is one we too rarely achieve. Toward that end, I explore what I call a *critical, coalitional kindness* as a framework for success in rhetoric and composition and in academia more broadly.

Contexts for Care in the Academy

In rhetoric and composition and in other disciplines, though we have lauded the benefits of collaboration across identity groups (Ore et al. 2021), we have still struggled to build broader "networks of trust and mutual support" (Kahn and Lynch-Biniek 2022, 18) that enable coalition across ranks and identities. In "From Activism to Organizing, From Caring to Care Work," Seth Kahn and Amy Lynch-Biniek note two problems common to faculty organizing: the tendency for the bulk of the labor to fall on those in the most precarious positions "while those of us with privilege and security often do little to support their efforts," and the need for support and institutional policies that ensure such labor is "central to everyone's professional responsibilities" (2). Drawing upon Leah Lakshmi Piepzna-Samarasinha's framing of "care work" *as* work, that is, as labor, Kahn and Lynch-Biniek contend that we "need to pay more attention to how we care or are cared for" especially in the contexts of "white supremacist, neoliberal, hegemonic regimes that work so hard to make sure we don't care for each other" (6).

In the context of the university, academic care work often entails recruitment and retention efforts and administrative and service labor "for which people are evaluated and disciplined for underperforming, but not credited for performing well" (Kahn and Lynch-Biniek 2022, 7). This may indeed be the type of "care" university presidents mean when they boast their dedication to "care" of faculty and students in their new strategic plans, especially in colleges and universities that emphasize teaching and service over research, and clearer policies delineating the nature and value of such academic care work can contribute to more equitable workplaces—at least where labor is concerned.

Of course, policies do little if there is no commitment to enforcing them. Though Kahn and Lynch-Biniek suggest that "building networks of solidarity devoted to care work helps to mitigate that risk" (2022, 18), building solidarity among workers requires, well, solidarity, or at least a desire for solidarity, which I am not sure is as widespread among our colleagues as many of us would like it to be. While it is suggested that strong solidarity networks can protect those "most threatened by retaliation" (11), my own experiences being thrown under metaphorical buses for challenging institutional inequity (and the similar experiences of too many others in the field) tell me that many faculty members are less interested in solidarity with their colleagues than they are in solidarity with whiteness, cis-heteropatriarchy, ableism, and other systems of oppression, if not the institutions that uphold them.

Research has demonstrated that institutionalized equity work does little to effect organizational change when the ideologies that underlie the work are incomplete or inequitable themselves (Dugan 2021; Smolarek and Martinez Negrette 2019). Likewise, if the notions of care that underlie our organizing or equity work are inequitable, we are limited in the care we will receive from or provide our colleagues. For that reason, I am interested in other notions of care, those that have less to do with service labor and the *work* of care work than with the conditions for care in the academy and the ideologies that impact interpersonal interaction—and therefore, as anyone who has worked in a dysfunctional workplace knows, virtually everything else—in academic workplaces.

Specifically, I am interested in how we interpret the notion of care in white hegemonic spaces and how that interpretation prevents broader coalition among faculty as workers. For example, I saw leaders of my own faculty union silence spirited disagreement among workers during the planning stages of contract negotiations. It isn't surprising that members of a large statewide university system whose costs of living, institutional ranks, and salaries differ might disagree on the most important aspects of a new contract, and, as colleagues, we ought to care enough to hear one another out. Yet, such arguably necessary disagreements may be shut down in favor of false politeness and gestures toward equity that don't achieve the ends they claim to seek. Perhaps viewing disagreement and discussion as inadequate methods of collective bargaining, even well-intentioned people may overlook the ways such discourse presents perfectly adequate opportunities for understanding and coalition. Without those opportunities to really hear one another's differing perspectives, and the lived experiences that inform them, too often we simply become intransigent with regard to our own.

It is no secret that the academy and its institutions, like all systems of schooling, reflect hegemonic whiteness, masculinity, Christianity, ability, and heteronormativity. Accordingly, academic institutions can be sites of harm and trauma for marginalized individuals, yet, as I have noted elsewhere, existing models of mental health uphold "the White psyche and body as normative and universal, even when traumatized, while simultaneously overlooking and marginalizing the traumatic experiences of people of color" (Grayson 2022, 416). Racism, sexism, and other systemic oppressions contribute to experiences of trauma and present barriers to diagnosis and treatment of trauma-based stress (Sibrava et al. 2019) and neurodivergence (Birdwell and Bayley 2022). In academia, especially, which prizes (white, western, masculinist, abled) notions of reason and rationality, expressions of emotion and ways of thinking that differ from the norm are rejected (Price 2011). This context may illuminate the limitations and inequities of dominant frameworks for demonstrating care or attending to our students' and colleagues' experiences of harm.

Inequitable Etiquette: What's the Problem with Being "Nice"?

All etiquette is culturally and socially situated, and, as educators in the United States, we have been acculturated in what Irene Yoon has identified as a "white-centered professional culture" (Yoon 2012, 589). It is from this culture that Niceness emerges, and it is this culture that Niceness sustains. In her introduction to the edited collection *The Price of Nice: How Good Intentions Maintain Educational Inequity*, educational scholar Angelina E. Castagno identified Niceness as "an analytic category that encompasses a wide range of practices and discourses" and is "pervasive in educational settings" (Castagno 2019, xiv). Scholars who critique Niceness in educational institutions have connected Niceness to whiteness (Bissonnette 2016; Castagno 2014, 2019; Sierk 2019; Tevis et al. 2023; Wegwert and Charles 2019), Christianity (Grayson 2023; Villarreal et al. 2019), "middle-classness" (Wegwert and Charles 2019, 93), and cisgender femininity (Galman 2019; Tevis et al. 2023; Wegwert and Charles 2019).

It is conventionally understood that "to be nice is to be pleasing and agreeable" (Castagno 2019, x) and to behave in "socially acceptable" ways (Mac 2019,

55). On the individual level, performing "Niceness" requires adherence to indirectness and nonconfrontation, norms of communication that are raced, classed, and gendered (Galman 2019). Individuals who are nice "do not point out failures or shortcomings in others but rather emphasize the good, the promise, and the improvement" in others (Castagno 2019, x). Although Niceness is often linked to good intentions, its etymology helps to illuminate its potential for harm. The English word *nice* is derived from Latin and French words that translate, respectively, to "ignorant" and "not to know." Accordingly, the nice person does not merely emphasize the good; the nice person also intentionally avoids "potentially uncomfortable or upsetting experiences, knowledge, and interactions" and reframes "potentially disruptive or uncomfortable things in ways that are more soothing, pleasant, and comfortable" (x).

Niceness, then, involves a turning away from, a writing over, and a refusal to see or engage with the more troublesome aspects of education, such as the gendered whiteness endemic to public schooling and higher education (Tevis et al. 2023). Niceness as an analytical category helps us better understand the insidious and pervasive means by which white racial equilibrium is maintained in all educational spaces, even outside the context of race talk. We might say that Niceness describes the underlying etiquette of educational spaces, the "conventional requirements or expectations for social behavior" (Sullivan 2014, 26) that maintain racialized social order. As literacy educator Jeanne Dyches Bissonnette has suggested, Niceness in teacher education programs makes space for future teachers to "offer 'nice', liberal-oriented insights without truly engaging in the complex, arduous, self-reflection processes culturally responsive teaching requires" (2016, 10).

In our explication of the "white women's rituals" that transact whiteness in social justice education, Tenisha Tevis, Naomi Nishi, and I identified the weaponization of Niceness as a social ritual through which white women transact whiteness in exchange for power in educational spaces. In spaces defined by whiteness, "the white norms of 'niceness' are seen as rational, whereas anyone who challenges those norms, such as by naming racism overtly or by speaking directly, firmly, or passionately, is seen as irrational. The 'angry' antiracist becomes the irrational aggressor, and the 'nice' white woman the rational victim" (Tevis et al. 2023, 69). In this way, Niceness represents "a will to power through the strategic performance of vulnerability and powerlessness" (Grajeda 2022, 14).

Importantly, as "both an institutional norm within schools and an embodied practice among educators" (Castagno 2019, xix), Niceness operates not only on individual and interpersonal levels but on the institutional level as well. On the institutional level, Niceness informs systems of academic labor and teacher evaluation (Weatherston 2019), the types of (dis)engagement with social justice encouraged by school culture and officials (Ben et al. 2019; Smolarek and Martinez Negrette 2019), and norms of communication and behavior that disproportionately harm marginalized and minoritized faculty members and students (Ben et al. 2019; Villarreal et al. 2019). By silencing criticality, Niceness reinforces the anti-intellectualism of contemporary neoliberal higher education (Bissonnette 2016; Wegwert and Charles 2019) and maintains status quo white supremacy (Ben et al. 2019; Tevis et al. 2023) while simultaneously evading critique (Castagno 2019).

Niceness is indeed difficult to critique, in part because "Niceness is incredibly attractive" (Castagno 2019, x). For those who benefit from Niceness, it is arguably easier to be "nice" than to engage deeply and critically with issues related to inequity that have no simple solutions. Students of color and others whose culturally situated practices do not align with Niceness may "strategically deploy Niceness, even subconsciously, as a method of navigating lonely or hostile environments" (Bustamante and Solyom 2019, 163). Niceness is also difficult to critique because within white contexts wherein educators "cling to niceness, believing that their allegiance to the construct highlights their humanity and improves their pedagogy" (Bissonnette 2016, 13), Niceness masquerades as care but is wholly inadequate in sustaining it. I suggest that the problem of Niceness lies in two mutually sustaining yet seemingly paradoxical dynamics: One is that Niceness is individualistic and arhetorical; the other, that Niceness is systematic and rhetorical.

Niceness Is Individualistic and Arhetorical

Niceness, we might say, is subject based. Our semantic framing positions Niceness as an innate or ingrained quality and renders Niceness almost intransitive as an action. Individuals are told to *be* nice, as though Niceness behaviors are intrinsic (or not) to one's nature. If Niceness is innate, some of us are born with or into it—and some of us are not. Niceness, therefore, is intrinsically exclusionary, similar to how beauty, in a gendered society and the "violent sociocultural regime" of whiteness, is a form of capital that functions to "exclude blackness" (McMillan Cottom 2019, 45) and therefore "requires a performance of gender that makes some of its members more equal than others" (62).

This gendered performance is at the root of Niceness. As Sally Campbell Galman explains, one of the predominant archetypes of the "teacher" is the "original nice White girl next door . . . She is young, pretty, and nice, almost certainly White, and focused on nurturing children" (2019, 72). While Galman is speaking specifically of the expectations for schoolteachers, not university faculty, the same archetypes follow women into postsecondary education, where the dominant concept of the professor is a white man and wherein women are expected to embody and perform the same roles expected of schoolteachers. Those expectations are often reflected in service assignments and course evaluations (Weatherston 2019). Galman notes that the archetypal teacher's "beauty directly reflects her good character," just as ugliness reflects meanness among "toothless fairy-tale witches or hook-nosed, swarthy Disney villainesses" (Galman 2019, 72). Such racialized tropes make clear that one does not intrinsically possess the "good character" of Niceness if one is Jewish ("hook-nosed") or dark-skinned ("swarthy"), poor, or disabled ("toothless").

If we assume that one can *be* nice, Niceness is individualistic, in that it operates on the level of the individual and their nature, but it lacks individuation, in that it does not adapt to the needs of individual persons or rhetorical contexts. Consider, for example, the critique posed by Joseph C. Wegwert and Aidan/Amanda J. Charles of the so-called Golden Rule ("Do unto others as you would have them do unto you"): "The dictate of the Golden Rule centers on the individual and naturalizes the privileges and preferences of dominant groups . . . [T]his ethic calls for a process of normalization" (2019, 101–102). In educational contexts, wherein the majority of teachers are white (Tevis et al. 2023), it is the lives, attitudes, and preferences of teachers that are normalized (Wegwert and Charles 2019, 102). To Wegwert and Charles's critique, I'll add that, though the concept predates Christianity, the label "the Golden Rule" was first deployed in the context of Christianity (Gensler 2013). Thus, our framing of the Golden Rule *as* "the Golden Rule" is at root a Christian framing, demonstrating its hegemonic aims and its limitations.

The Golden Rule, conceptualized as an ideal, universal approach to interpersonal interaction, requires us to "think of our neighbors and their needs through the lens of our own individual experiences, preferences, and desires" (Wegwert and Charles 2019, 102). The Golden Rule, however, does not require we care enough about our neighbors to understand or even acknowledge their experiences, preferences, and desires. Thus, we might argue that Niceness enacted within this framing is both individualistic and arhetorical, divorced from any concept of audience.

Moreover, given the cultural situatedness of the Golden Rule, only abled, middle-class, white, Anglo-Saxon Protestant people can *demonstrate* the intrinsic

Niceness it encourages. Those who do not share these identities—those for whom these preferences, desires, and norms of communication are not actually normative—must instead theatrically *represent* or *portray* Niceness, meaning that the process of normalization encouraged by frames like the Golden Rule is in fact a process of acculturation. This is merely one way in which we may come to understand Niceness not as a character trait but as a rhetorical system for the maintenance of status quo whiteness.

Niceness Is Systematic and Rhetorical

Though Niceness may lack individuation, niceness is deeply rhetorical. Like whiteness, Niceness is too easily "assumed to be about individuals" when it is, in fact, a collection of behaviors and expectations that can be performed by anyone, regardless of race (Sierk 2019, 38). Marginalized or minoritized students or faculty members may internalize ideals of Niceness and whiteness (Bustamante and Solyom 2019; Sierk 2019) or feel compelled to perform Niceness in professional settings to sustain enrollment or employment (Ben et al. 2019; Bustamante and Solyom 2019; Villarreal et al. 2019).

While students and faculty members of color may labor to adapt to the inequitable discursive and behavioral norms of whiteness and Niceness, neurodivergent students and faculty members may not easily identify the norms *as* norms, and therefore may struggle to understand neurotypical interpersonal and professional communication (Mitchell et al. 2021). Because neurotypical people are unlikely to recognize or empathize with neurodivergent ways of communicating (Mitchell et al. 2021) and because Niceness prevents potentially awkward conversations, people who understand the norms are unlikely to explain them to those who don't. Instead, the neurodivergent person serves as a warning to their classmates and colleagues. As Jared David Berezin recalls of being seated apart from his classmates as a seventh grader with ADHD: "I performed my disability—my deviation from the norm—in a removed, yet visible space. In doing so, I demonstrated for the 'normal' students the consequences, namely segregation and loneliness, of not performing the 'normal' expectations in the field" (2014, n.p.). Berezin's needs and humanity were not seen by his teacher or classmates; instead, his bodymind was rhetorically used in his classroom to send a message to other students about the dangers of difference.

Similarly, despite attempts at adaptation, Niceness is often weaponized against marginalized and minoritized students and faculty members. In prior work, I have described how Jewish faculty members are admonished to "be nice" without explication of the particular expectations held of them (Grayson 2023). To highlight white women's weaponization of emotion in higher education, Mamta Motwani Accapadi recalls how a woman of color was "reprimanded for her 'angry tone'" after a meeting because a white woman cried during the meeting and complained to her supervisor (2007, 211). When the evasive, nonconfrontational behaviors of Niceness in educational spaces are performed by white women, "there is a strategic and self-preserving element in play... none of this is innocuous" (Galman 2019, 73). As my colleagues and I have noted, white women "transact whiteness for their own version of power, within the contexts of white patriarchy" (Tevis et al. 2023).

Niceness maintains the gendered whiteness of educational spaces in part through the avoidance of productive discourse about racism. Honesty is paramount to race talk and explorations of hegemonic whiteness, and "without such honest dialogues the hope for antiracism or the deconstruction of whiteness will remain aspirational" (Nishi et al. 2016, 4). Niceness, however, makes this virtually impossible because "niceness requires that racism is acknowledged only in acts that intentionally seek to discriminate against individuals" (Sierk 2019, 46). As a result, "allegations of racism directly challenge Niceness and are easily discredited along the lines of intentionality" (45), and the broader structures and ideologies that maintain whiteness and racism in educational institutions are ignored. What's worse, as Cynthia Diana Villarreal and colleagues found in their study of faculty experiences at a Christian-affiliated university, through processes of socialization, "racially minoritized faculty also learned that there were consequences for those who challenged or held colleagues accountable for their racist behaviors" (Villarreal et al. 2019, 133).

In other words, Niceness serves both to explain away more insidious dynamics of racism, sexism, and ableism, and to acculturate and silence minoritized faculty members and anyone else who challenges the status quo. On structural and institutional levels, Niceness rhetorically operates *through* individuals to maintain whiteness. In this way, "Niceness is a shield, protecting the status quo by subverting and sublimating the voices, presence, needs, history, and experiences of marginalized peoples" (Ben et al. 2019, 145). As appealing as Niceness may seem on the surface, even to some who are harmed by it, Niceness does little to bring people together but "often damages the social fabric by enjoining conformity to the terms of unjust social arrangements" (Ward 2017, 118). Niceness, then, can be understood either as a failed coalitional strategy—one that is woefully inadequate to achieving real coalition in current social, political, and economic contexts—or as a strategic obstacle to coalition, erected with intention and designed to fail.

Toward Critical Coalitional Kindness

If we admit that Niceness is unproductive at best and oppressive and violent at worst—an admission that is already, in academic disciplines and higher education institutions, designed to maintain the status quo, no easy feat—we must identify a better framework for difficult interpersonal dialogue, one that neither silences nor shields and encourages critical but supportive discourse. It helps to recognize first that the opposite of Niceness isn't meanness—it's "open, critical, and provocative instruction, conversation, and reflexivity" (Bissonnette 2016, 19) and the creation of "spaces where deficit ideologies can be unlearned and replaced with ideologies of justice and equity" (Castagno 2019, xxii). Because calls for Niceness in unjust contexts "attempt to de-legitimize the expression of important attitudes—such as anger and indignation—that can be just and appropriate responses to relationships, practices, and institutions" that are undemocratic (Ward 2017, 118), we might also find the opposite of Niceness in "our willingness to work together amid contentious disagreement to keep democracy intact, and to resist domination" (134).

It is in the spirit of this willingness that I offer what I call *critical, coalitional kindness* as a framework for engagement and, indeed, care. While Jewish rhetorical practices are far more natural for me than the whitely norms of Niceness, my personal affiliation is not the primary reason I draw upon Jewish cultural rhetorics in my conceptualization of this framework. I draw upon Jewish rhetorics in large part because, in the popular imaginary, Jewish people are decidedly not "nice." The not-Niceness is evident in dominant narratives and stereotypes of Jewish people as "pushy" (Tannen 1981) and in those "hook-nosed" Disney archetypes of villains and villainesses. Jewish not-Niceness isn't mere stereotype, however. In the existing conception of Niceness, we *aren't* nice because, by and large, Jewish rhetorical practices do not align with the practices of Niceness. Despite this misalignment, in the popular imaginary, Jewish people are expected to perform whiteness (Grayson 2023), which makes our inability or unwillingness to reproduce white modes of discourse especially disruptive to the status quo.

The critical, coalitional kindness I envision draws upon the Jewish philosophy of *Tsedek*, or justice, and Jewish rhetorical practices of argumentation and cooperative disagreement. I am particularly cognizant of Jewish rhetoric scholar David Frank's point that if we value pluralism and disagreement rather than "consensus enforced through rules or secured through schism and polarization" (2004, 71) and aim for "and a vision of reason capable of hosting antimonies" (85), we cannot "suggest that Judaic thought is intrinsically better" than other traditions (71). The framework I suggest, then, is really a reminder that we have work yet to do in building that pluralistic society and discipline, and an offering of a path forward.

The Jewish tradition of argument—articulated in the Torah, the first five books of what is often, via Christian appropriation, labeled the "Old Testament," and the Talmud, the Jewish compendium of reason and rabbinical scholarship—promotes agency and collaboration (Waisanen et al. 2015); allows for dissent (Charney 2014; Frank 2004), "conscious scrutiny and criticism" (Frank 2004, 75); holds the potential for change, even of oneself or one's own thinking (Metzger 2014); does not require consensus or resolution (Bizzell 2014; Horn 2021) but is committed to speech as action; and is rooted in *Tsedek* (Frank 2004). Unlike classical understandings of justice, *Tsedek* emphasizes equity, mercy, peace, and compassion. Accordingly, perhaps, Jewish tradition not only allows for but encourages ad hominem reasoning, such as the *argumentum ad Deus*, "an argument asking God to be consistent with God's stated values" (75). This particular approach may help us understand the Jewish imperative to challenge the status quo and, thus, presents an antidote to the Niceness that serves the status quo even while professing commitments to change.

Further, while the Christian tradition and the whitely tradition of Niceness, wherein, respectively, contrition before divine authority and agreeableness are both valued and expected as signs of love and respect, in Jewish rhetoric, argumentation precludes neither love nor respect—and is, in fact, demonstrative of both. Consider, for example, cooperative disagreement, a discursive practice of sustained, sociable argument, often about topics that might not seem polarizing or even serious, that signals intimacy rather than discord (Schiffrin 1984). As such, cooperative disagreement as part of interpersonal communication establishes community and fellowship, and serves as a reminder that disagreement, even when contentious, need not be feared.

In keeping with these traditions, I offer the following as characteristics or dispositions of critical, coalitional kindness:

1. **CRITICALITY OF SOCIETY AND SELF, WITH EMPHASIS ON THE (MIS)ALIGNMENT BETWEEN LANGUAGE AND PRACTICE.** To practice coalitional kindness, we must be critical, including of ourselves, and challenge hypocrisy, even when we are the ones acting in ways that do

not align with our stated values. In Jewish tradition, language leads to, stems from, and *is* action. Thus, a misalignment between what we say we value and how we behave demands intervention. This means that we must call out status quo injustice, point out—even ad hominem—when people and institutions act in ways that run counter to their stated values, and question our own actions and motivations. Like the "fundamentalists and extremists [who] often lack the ability to laugh at themselves" (Waisanen et al. 2015, n.p.), however, very often we enter what should be deliberative discourse without the willingness to consider that we too are fallible and that our own perspectives may be incomplete. This unwillingness may stem from the (white, western, Christian) belief in a singular Truth, an orientation the next disposition seeks to address.

2. **SUSPENSION OF THE NEED FOR SINGULAR RESOLUTION.** Like Jewish traditions, which teach us that "the process of argumentation is often more important than Truth" (Frank 2004, 85), a critical, coalitional kindness emphasizes the question over the answer. We might begin by acknowledging that disagreement among human beings is expected and therefore ought to be valued. To better understand the arguments put forth by different human beings, we might consider the Talmudic approach in which, as Patricia Bizzell explains, rather than waiting for you to finish speaking in order to object, "your interlocutor listens patiently and asks only a few questions to make sure you have quite said everything you want to say, before venturing his or her own opinion." Importantly, Bizzell clarifies, the idea here is not "utter relativism" but the belief that "from the plethora of positions, new insights emerge" (2014, 144).

3. **VALUING COLLABORATION AND THE OTHER.** When we value argument, we must also value those with whom we argue. Too often when we do engage with one another via disagreement (such as, e.g., on the now-defunct WPA-L), we value the argument over the people engaged with and impacted by it. What gets lost in such arguments is that some of us are actually hurting and need to be heard not only for our perspectives but for our humanity, not only as thinkers but also as human beings. Accordingly, a critical, coalitional kindness must value empathy over comfort. It can be uncomfortable to be vulnerable. It can be uncomfortable to ask for help, just as it can be uncomfortable to provide it. As Piepzna-Samarasinha has pointed out in relation to care work, the notion of "'community' is not a magic unicorn . . . the only way we will do this is by being fucking real, by not papering over the places where our rhetoric falls fat, where we ran out of steam, or where shit

is genuinely fucking hard" (Piepzna-Samarasinha 2018, 35). Empathy exists not in the total amelioration of discomfort but in, at least for starters, the acknowledgment of discomfort, and, if I can borrow Piepzna-Samarasinha's words, shared in reference to disability solidarity, "the reality that sometimes we all need care, simultaneously" (65).

Building Care Through Critical, Coalitional Kindness

From a semantic perspective, *care*, or *caring*, requires an object. From a human perspective, however, the syntactic need for an object that is cared about or cared for, can *objectify*, as happens when, for example, the disabled bodymind is subjected to "able-bodied people begrudgingly 'helping'" (Piepzna-Samarasinha 2018, 49), when special education instruction is guided by "paternalistic benevolence" (Mac 2019, 63), or when white saviorism masquerades as social justice (Tevis et al. 2023). Regardless of the professed intent of the carers, for those who have experienced such care, "care meant control" (Piepzna-Samarasinha 2018, 37).

From some ethical and theological perspectives, caring can be understood as a response to values, or the value placed on something. Whereas one might profess a commitment to an ideal "without engaging the attitudes and passions that move them to realize the ideal . . . caring, by contrast, engages the will reliably over time" (Ward 2017, 124). It is care, then, that motivates us to move beyond performative gestures and speech toward action. Of course, we each prioritize differently, and what we care about shall, accordingly, differ. But as a community of compositionists and rhetoricians, however loose and diasporic, we should all care about communication and the future of our discipline, whatever we wish that future to be.

Critical, coalitional kindness reminds us that justice and empathy are more important than rank, title, or hierarchy, and that depth of understanding is more important than consensus. It reminds us that our actions ought to align with our values—and that we should expect to be challenged when they do not. Practicing critical, coalitional kindness demonstrates that we care enough—about each other, the subject at hand, and justice—to argue, to possibly be uncomfortable and to possibly be wrong but also, perhaps, to learn and grow by virtue of others' and our own critical engagement, including with ourselves, and to find community by engaging other people empathetically toward justice.

References

Accapadi, Mamta Motwani. 2007. "When White Women Cry: How White Women's Tears Oppress Women of Color." *College Student Affairs Journal* 26(2): 208–215.

Ahmed, Sara. 2021. *Complaint!* Durham, NC: Duke UP.

Beare, Zachary. 2017. "Apologies for Cross Posting: Composing Disciplinary Affects and Conflicts on the WPA Listserv." PhD diss., University of Nebraska, Lincoln.

Ben, Colin, Amber Poleviyuma, Jeremiah Chin, Alexus Richmond, Megan Tom, and Sarah Abuwandi. 2019. "The Self-Contained Scholar: The Racialized Burdens of Being Nice in Higher Education." In *The Price of Nice: How Good Intentions Maintain Educational Inequity*, edited by Angelina E. Castagno, 145–160. Minneapolis: University of Minnesota Press.

Berezin, Jared David. 2014. "Disabled Capital: A Narrative of Attention Deficit Disorder in the Classroom Through the Lens of Bourdieu's Capital." *Disability Studies Quarterly* 34(4).

Birdwell, M. L. N., and Keaton Bayley. 2022. "When the Syllabus Is Ableist: Understanding How Class Policies Fail Disabled Students." *Teaching English in the Two-Year College* 49 (3): 220–237.

Bissonnette, Jeanne Dyches. 2016. "The Trouble with Niceness: How a Preference for Pleasantry Sabotages Culturally Responsive Teacher Preparations." *Journal of Language and Literacy Education* 12 (2): 9–32.

Bizzell, Patricia. 2014. "Rabbi Moses ben Nachman, Sophist?" In *Jewish Rhetorics: History, Theory, Practice*, edited by Michael Bernard-Donals and Janice F. Fernheimer, 131–146. Waltham, MA: Brandeis University Press.

Bustamante, Nicholas, and Jessica Solyom. 2019. "Performative Niceness and Student Erasure: Historical Implications." In *The Price of Nice: How Good Intentions Maintain Educational Inequity*, edited by Angelina E. Castagno, 161–181. Minneapolis: University of Minnesota Press.

Castagno, Angelina E. 2014. *Educated in Whiteness: Good Intentions and Diversity in Schools*. Minneapolis: University of Minnesota Press.

Castagno, Angelina E. 2019. "Introduction: Mapping the Contours of Niceness in Education." In *The Price of Nice: How Good Intentions Maintain Educational Inequity*, edited by Angelina E. Castagno, ix–xxiv. Minneapolis: University of Minnesota Press.

Charney, Davida. 2014. "Taking a Stance Toward God: Rhetoric in the Book of Psalms." In *Jewish Rhetorics: History, Theory, Practice*, edited by Michael Bernard-Donals and Janice F. Fernheimer, 1–15. Waltham, MA: Brandeis University Press.

Dugan, Jamila. 2021. "Beware of Equity Traps and Tropes." *Educational Leadership* 78 (6): 35–40.

Fleming, Crystal M. 2018. *How to Be Less Stupid about Race: On Racism, White Supremacy, and the Racial Divide*. Boston: Beacon.

Frank, David. 2004. "Arguing with God, Talmudic Discourse, and the Jewish Countermodel: Implications for the Study of Argumentation." *Argumentation and Advocacy* 41: 71–86.

Galman, Sally Campbell. 2019. "Nice Work: Young White Women, Near Enemies, and Teaching Inside the Magic Circle." In *The Price of Nice: How Good Intentions Maintain Educational Inequity*, edited by Angelina E. Castagno, 70–88. Minneapolis: University of Minnesota Press.

Gensler, Harry J. 2013. *Ethics and the Golden Rule*. London: Routledge.

Grajeda, Erika D. 2022. "'Karenism' and the Problem of White Women: Reflections on Quotidian Forms of White Vigilantism in the Classroom." *Journal of Men's Studies* 30 (3): 363–382.

Grayson, Mara Lee. 2022. "The Trigger Warning and the Pathologizing White Rhetoric of Trauma-informed Pedagogy." *Rhetoric of Health and Medicine* 4(4): 413–445.

Grayson, Mara Lee. 2023. *Antisemitism and the White Supremacist Imaginary: Conflations and Contradictions in Composition and Rhetoric*. New York: Peter Lang.

Greenbaum, Andrea. 2008. "Talmudic Rhetoric: Explorations for Writing, Reading, and Teaching." In *Judaic Perspectives in Rhetoric and Composition*, edited by Andrea Greenbaum and Deborah Holdstein, 151–169. New York: Hampton Press.

Grossman, Pamela, Samuel Wineburg, and Stephen Woolworth. 2001. "Toward a Theory of Teacher Community." *Teachers College Record* 103: 942–1012.

Guzman-Lopez, Adolfo. 2023. "Even at 'the Most Diverse' Cal State School, Students and Faculty Press for Better Discussions of Race." LAist. April 2023. https://laist.com/news/education/diverse-california-state-university-csu-dominguez-hills-race-racism-safe-space.

Horn, Dara. 2021. *People Love Dead Jews: Reports from a Haunted Present*. New York: Norton.

Hubrig, Ada. 2022. "On 'Crip Doulas,' Invisible Labor, and Surviving Academia While Disabled." *Journal of Multimodal Rhetorics* 5 (1): 33–35.

Kahn, Seth, and Lynch-Biniek, Amy. 2022. "From Activism to Organizing, from Caring to Care Work." *Labor Studies Journal* 47 (3): 320–344.

Mac, Sylvia. 2019. "Niceness in Special Education: An Ethnographic Case Study of Benevolence, Goodness, and Paternalism at Colina Cedro Charter High School." In *The Price of Nice: How Good Intentions Maintain Educational Inequity*, edited by Angelina E. Castagno, 54–69. Minneapolis: University of Minnesota Press.

McMillan Cottom, Tressie. 2019. *Thick and Other Essays*. New York: New Press.

Metzger, David. 2014. "Maimonides's Contribution to a Theory of Self-Persuasion." In *Jewish Rhetorics: History, Theory, Practice*, edited by Michael Bernard-Donals and Janice F. Fernheimer, 112–130. Waltham, MA: Brandeis University Press.

Mitchell, Peter, Elizabeth Sheppard, and Sarah Cassidy. 2021. Autism and the Double Empathy Problem: Implications for Development and Mental Health. *British Journal of Developmental Psychology* 39(1): 1–18.

Moskow, Michal Anne, and Steven B. Katz. 2008. "Composing Identity and Community in Cyberspace: A 'Rhetorical Ethnography' of Writing on Jewish Discussion Groups in the United States and Germany." In *Judaic Perspectives in Rhetoric and Composition*, edited by Andrea Greenbaum and Deborah Holdstein, 85–108. New York: Hampton Press.

Nishi, Naomi W., Cheryl E. Mathias, Roberto Montoya, and Geneva L. Sarcedo. 2016. "Whiteness FAQ: Responses and Tools for Confronting College Classroom Questions." *Journal of Critical Thought and Praxis* 5 (1): 1–20.

Nguyen, Alexander. 2023. "Audit Exposes Flaws in Cal State University's Handling of Sexual Assault Cases." KPBS. May 26. https://www.kpbs.org/news/education/2023/05/26/audit-exposes-flaws-in-cal-state-universitys-handling-of-sexual-assault-cases.

Ore, Ersula, Kim Weiser, and Christina V. Cedillo, eds. 2021. "Symposium: Diversity Is Not Justice: Working Toward Radical Transformation and Racial Equity in the Discipline." *College Composition and Communication* 74(2): 601–620.

Piepzna-Samarasinha, Leah Lakshmi. 2018. *Care Work: Dreaming Disability Justice*. Vancouver, BC: Arsenal Pulp Press.

Price, Margaret. 2011. *Mad at School: Rhetorics of Mental Disability and Academic Life*. Ann Arbor: University of Michigan Press.

Ruiz, Iris D., Latina Oculta, Brian Hendrickson, Mara Lee Grayson, Holly Hassel, Mike Palmquist, and Mandy Olejnik. 2023. "'Help, I Posted': Race, Power, and Disciplinary Shifts, and the WPAListservFeministRevolution." In *Systems Shift: Creating and Navigating Change in Rhetoric and Composition Administration*, edited by Genesea M. Carter and Aurora Matzke, 73–98. WAC Clearinghouse.

Scanlan, Stephen J., J. Craig Jenkins, and Lindsey Peterson. 2010. "The Scarcity Fallacy." *Contexts*: 34–39.

Schiffrin, Deborah. 1984. "Jewish Argument as Sociability." *Language in Society*, 3(13): 311–335.

Sibrava, Nicholas J., Andri S. Bjornsson, A. Carlos I. Perez Benitez, Ethan Moitra, Risa B. Weisberg, and Martin B. Keller. 2019. "Posttraumatic Stress Disorder in African American and Latinx Adults: Clinical Course and the Role of Racial and Ethnic Discrimination." *American Psychologist* 74 (1): 101–116.

Sierk, Jessica. 2019. "Being Nice to the Elephant in the (Class)room: Whiteness in New Latino Diaspora Nebraska." In *The Price of Nice: How Good Intentions Maintain Educational Inequity*, edited by Angelina E. Castagno, 37–53. Minneapolis: University of Minnesota Press.

Smolarek, Bailey B., and Giselle Martinez Negrette. 2019. "'It's Better Now: How Midwest Niceness Shapes Social Justice Education." In *The Price of Nice: How Good Intentions Maintain Educational Inequity*, edited by Angelina E. Castagno, 218–237. Minneapolis: University of Minnesota Press.

Sullivan, Shannon. 2014. *Good White People: The Problem with Middle-Class White Anti-Racism*. Albany, NY: SUNY Press.

Tannen, Deborah. 1981. New York Jewish Conversational Style. *International Journal of the Sociology of Language* 30: 133–149.

Tevis, Tenisha, Naomi Nishi, and Mara Lee Grayson. 2023. *White Women in Educational Spaces: The Gendered Transaction of Whiteness*. London: Palgrave.

Villarreal, Cynthia Diana, Roman Liera, and Lindsey Malcom-Piqueux. 2019. "The Role of Niceness in Silencing Racially Minoritized Faculty." In *The Price of Nice:*

How Good Intentions Maintain Educational Inequity, edited by Angelina E. Castagno, 127–144. Minneapolis: University of Minnesota Press.

Waisanen, Don, Hershey H. Friedman, and Linda Weiser Friedman. 2015. "What's So Funny About Arguing with God? A Case for Playful Argumentation from Jewish Literature." *Argumentation.* https://academicworks.cuny.edu/bb_pubs/1142/.

Ward, Ian. 2017. "Democratic Civility and the Dangers of Niceness." *Political Theology* 18 (2): 115–136.

Weatherston, Kristine T. 2019. "Evaluating Niceness: How Anonymous Student Feedback Forms Promote Gendered and Flawed Value Systems in Academic Labor." In *The Price of Nice: How Good Intentions Maintain Educational Inequity*, edited by Angelina E. Castagno, 110–126. Minneapolis: University of Minnesota Press.

Wegwert, Joseph C., and Aidan/Amanda J. Charles. 2019. "The Perfect Storm of Whiteness, Middle-classness, and Cis Femaleness in School Contexts." In *The Price of Nice: How Good Intentions Maintain Educational Inequity*, edited by Angelina E. Castagno, 91–109. Minneapolis: University of Minnesota Press.

Yoon, Irene H. 2012. "The Paradoxical Nature of Whiteness-at-Work in the Daily Life of Schools and Teacher Communities." *Race, Ethnicity and Education* 15 (5): 587–613.

3
Rhetorical Theory and the Fight for a Living Wage

OLIVIA WOOD

Almost nowhere—if anywhere—in the United States does the local minimum wage meet the local cost of living. Where I live, in New York City, the minimum wage is $15/hour, but a living minimum wage for a typical single adult with no children is $25.65/hour, or about $53,000 per year (MIT Living Wage Calculator 2023). Adjunct lecturers and graduate assistants at my university aren't paid anywhere near that much, and the problem is similar across US higher education: Real wages are declining across job titles (AAUP 2023), permanent full-time positions are few and far between, and a significant portion of our workforce doesn't earn enough money to make ends meet yet must find ways to make ends meet anyway.

Not coincidentally, higher education is experiencing a huge surge in labor organizing, primarily among contingent faculty and graduate student instructors, very often spearheaded by workers in the humanities. Since 2022, more than 35,000 student workers and 4,000 faculty have won union elections (Herbert et al. 2023), with many more filing for representation, and important higher education strikes have happened at Columbia, the University of California, the University of Michigan, the New School, and the University of Illinois at Chicago, among others. Undergraduate workers are also organizing more and more—residence hall workers at Tufts, Barnard, Columbia,

Fordham, and elsewhere; computer science TAs at Brown; and campus workers at Temple University, the University of Oregon, California State University, The New School, and more.

Strikes and new organizing can be the result of increasing class consciousness in the sector, and also part of a domino effect: At Fordham University, the contingent faculty went public with their intent to unionize in 2016, then the graduate workers in 2021, and then the Fordham RA Union in early 2023, only a week after the contingent faculty ratified our second contract and called off our planned strike. The same happened at the New School, with undergraduate student workers filing to join the graduate worker union soon after the adjunct faculty strike of 2022, and resident advisors at Barnard and Columbia filed in the wake of the 2021 Columbia strikes. These struggles are especially relevant for us in the field of Rhetoric and Composition, because due to the nature of first-year writing, a very large proportion of our courses are taught by contingent faculty and graduate workers.

At the same time, much of the history of rhetorical theory (and well-intentioned professional wisdom) is directly antithetical to labor organizing. Many ideas about persuasion, rhetorical consent, and coercion are very important in rhetorical situations between peers, in teaching scenarios, or in other situations in which a structurally empowered rhetor would like to minimize the impact of their structural position on a rhetorical situation. It is my contention that these same theories, when applied to labor movement contexts, predispose Rhetoric and Composition workers to play nice with the boss, respect the point of view of our exploiters, delude ourselves that they will pay us better if we can just convince them that we deserve it, and overall take a rhetorically conservative approach at and beyond the bargaining table. These tactics mean weaker unions, weaker contracts, and lower wages. Theoretical attention to "unpaid labor," while an important response to an industry culture of overwork and invisibilized labor, can also result in an aversion to workplace organizing and other kinds of activism, especially agitational writing, which is sometimes hard to distinguish from public humanities work we might do for our jobs.

This chapter will discuss the limitations of some rhetorical theories in the context of class struggle while drawing on personal examples from the collective bargaining table and other experiences from my last five years in the higher education labor movement. Specifically, I'll focus on two strands of thought: (1) the discussion following Edward P. J. Corbett's 1969 article "The Rhetoric of the Open Hand and the Rhetoric of the Closed Fist," about working-class and protest rhetorics, and (2) the legacy of feminist rhetorical theory and its approaches to coercion and openness. For the purposes of this chapter, "adequacy" in rhetoric and composition is figured as success in winning (adequately) higher wages, lower workloads, better benefits, and other job protections for ourselves and for our colleagues across all colleges and universities. We might understand "adequacy" as being just "good enough" to keep our jobs, along the lines of "quiet quitting" or "acting your wage," but I want to invert the concept into a positive call for action: What pay and working conditions do we want to consider genuinely adequate for our needs, and not just "better than other jobs"? And what are we willing to do to achieve these adequate working conditions? A common refrain in the labor movement is, "a rising tide lifts all boats"—wins at one workplace do place pressure on other employers to raise wages enough to remain competitive and inspire workers in other places to push for more. Fighting this fight is service to the discipline—and to each other.

"The Rhetoric of the Open Hand and the Rhetoric of the Closed Fist"

In 1969, shortly after student activists at Columbia University occupied their campus in 1968, *CCC* published Corbett's essay "The Rhetoric of the Open Hand and the Rhetoric of the Closed Fist." Corbett repurposes Zeno of Citium's analogies of the hand and fist to describe the two styles of persuasive discourse he observed at that time: "The open hand might be said to characterize the kind of persuasive discourse that seeks to carry its point by reasoned, sustained, conciliatory discussion of the issues. The closed fist might signify the kind of persuasive activity that seeks to carry its point by non-rationale, non-sequential, often non-verbal, frequently provocative means" (288). He provides the Black Power movement and the student movement as examples of this rhetoric, contrasting it with the kinds of discourse students are expected to learn and produce in writing classrooms. He acknowledges that closed fist rhetoric and its more "coercive" tactics may be necessary sometimes, but he feels "apprehensive" when he sees students "abandoning the reasonable and reasoning approach" (293) and fears that the younger generation is embracing irrationality, to the detriment of society.

In the present day, I have the impression that teachers of Rhetoric and Composition, overall, have much more sympathy for closed fist rhetorical tactics than Corbett did, and increased scholarly and pedagogical attention has been paid to activist techniques. But these sympathies are typically applied to what we research,[1] what we teach,[2] and what we support our students in doing—the sympathy is less evident in our own actions as workers. Some reticence comes from fear of reprisal—a real threat that should be taken seriously. But my contention is that as rhetoricians, we also have an underlying ideological bias toward the rhetoric of the open hand; our job is, very often, to teach essay writing, to teach speech writing, to teach argument and the analysis of argument, and to write in long-form, expository genres that lay out each argument and piece of evidence in a sequential and dispassionate way. These genres are *necessary* for our *jobs*, but they are not *adequate* for our needs as *workers*.

From March 2022 through January 2023, I served on the bargaining team for Fordham Faculty United (FFU), the union representing contingent faculty and postdoctoral researchers at Fordham University. Prior to each semester of AY 2022–2023, we debated whether and how to encourage our colleagues to discuss the union with our students. While some faculty were hesitant to discuss the union during class for fear of retaliation from department chairs or higher-level administrators, others were *ideologically* opposed to doing so, arguing that it's inappropriate for teachers to discuss labor issues and make arguments relating to their own personal interests with students, that teachers' jobs are to teach the curriculum and nothing else. One person also argued that discussing the union during class would harm our credibility "in the public square" because it would make us look unprofessional and selfish.

Choosing not to discuss the union during class out of fear of reprisal is very understandable, and some instructors have more flexibility regarding content than others. However, the ideological argument against discussing the union—even just to let students know there might be a strike and we would appreciate their support—shows philosophical investments in dispassionate discourse and the idea of academic work as "above" and apart from material conditions.

These investments also manifested in a tactical discussion when the union attended Fordham President Tania Tetlow's inauguration. We assembled in front of the library, marched across campus to the ceremony, and chanted near the procession staging ground. I argued that during the ceremony, we

---

1. E.g., Seth Lee and JongHwa Kahn (2020); Leigh Gruwell (2022); Risa Applegarth (2024); Lisa Phillips et al. (2024), and the recent Rhetoric Society of America conference themes, "The Charge for Change" (2022) and "Just Rhetoric" (2024).
2. For instance, the Rhetoric and Public Advocacy minor offered at the University of North Carolina at Greensboro, implemented in AY 2018–2019.

should chant through Tetlow's speech—or stand in a group with our signs near the front just outside the roped-off area so that we'd be visible to all of the attendees, all examples of the "body rhetoric" (Corbett 1969, 291), "group rhetoric," (292) and disruptive, "coercive" (293) tactics that Corbett describes as characteristic of the rhetoric of the closed fist. However, other members of the union felt those tactics would be inappropriate and make us look bad. When the ceremony began, we filed into the roped-off area and sat quietly in the audience. At that point, our action was essentially over. There were too few of us to form a visible sea of union members.

In his response to Corbett, Robert M. Browne (1970) writes, "One of the older rhetoric's chief functions has been an essentially conservative one: to keep the political system going ... The stability of the system both authorizes and is reinforced by a polite, gracious rhetoric. The speaker's very politeness testifies to his respect not only for the actual audience but also for the social structure which encloses them both" (187). This analysis helps us understand what happened at the Fordham action. Many of my colleagues wanted to maintain a polite, gracious rhetoric toward both President Tetlow and the university by not disrupting the inauguration ceremony. Their reasoning was not exclusively values based—there was also an argument that we might not have the numbers or level of support among the campus community for a more disruptive action to be tactically effective. But the value of *politeness*—accompanied by its converse, that violating situational norms of decorum is bad—reinforces and is reinforced by a conservative pressure to operate *within* existing systems, rather than to disrupt them.

The value of politeness, especially with regard to treating interlocutors respectfully, is closely tied to other rhetorical values of openness, mutuality, and respect for others' ideas, and the possibility that we might be wrong. These are important rhetorical values in many situations, especially interpersonal communication among equals and as a tactic toward power redistribution in the classroom, but these values only serve as reinforcement for our chains in situations of oppression and exploitation. Browne continues, "Established rhetorical theory tends to provide a rhetoric of continuity which will buttress the social structure ... a rhetoric honoring discussion, dialogue, flexibility, compromise ... Because they have confused the aims of rhetoric with the political aims of an existent society, modern rhetoricians are likely to regard the rhetoric of discontinuity as unacceptable rhetoric" (1970, 189).

In situations of oppression and exploitation, discussion, dialogue, flexibility, and compromise result in the exploited and oppressed making concessions to the ruling class. We should *not* be open to discussion, dialogue, flexibility, or compromise when it comes to our own suffering. Some of these activities may be tactically necessary in a given moment, but they ought not be treated as rhetorical values that it is fundamentally good to uphold. As Browne says, "To require the rhetorician of the powerless to find strategies of identification with the powerful is to ask him to run the considerable political risk of co-optation" (1970, 189). If we identify with the powerful, if we treat dialogue and compromise as values rather than tactics, then our ideas of what is "adequate" become linked to pragmatism, or what we're likely to get rather than what we deserve. We don't *have* to be happy with what we have—we can acknowledge the ways our circumstances are better than others' and even acknowledge that what we achieved might be the best we could manage given the circumstances, without viewing it as acceptable.

As Louis Althusser ([1971] 2001) discusses in his essay "Ideology and Ideological State Apparatuses," the state functions to mediate class antagonism, and it does so primarily through ideological state apparatuses (including education) rather than through repressive state apparatuses (like the police and the military). Because we live in a capitalist society, the state mediates class antagonisms in favor of the bourgeoisie, which means educational institutions are infused with bourgeois ideology—and, in fact, circulating bourgeois ideology is critical to their functioning. Even when individuals within these ideological state apparatuses try to offer counter-ideologies, the system itself is structured around these bourgeois ideologies and values. The entire idea that educators should be "unbiased" or "balanced" is one example—in a world structured by bourgeois ideology, these values result in discourse that favors the oppressor.

Browne (1970) also says that "if we see rhetoric for what it is, an instrument of politics but not politics itself, we will be more ready to see that different political options give rise to different kinds of rhetoric" (189). This point is key: that different political values and goals give rise to different rhetorical forms. In most struggles, a combination of rhetorical tactics is needed, but these decisions should be made on a *tactical* level, of what will be most *effective* in a given situation, not on a level of what rhetorical forms are *good*. Fighting against oppression and for better living and working conditions is good—and this needs to be our guiding value, not values about the best *forms* of argumentation, because as we know, the best available means of persuasion—including genre, style, and other tactics—depend on the audience, purpose, and overall rhetorical situation.

In my own primary workplace, City College of New York, we used a combination of tactics in April 2023 when trying to fight back against proposed cuts to composition (Wood 2023), which would have resulted in a pay cut for adjunct faculty and a workload increase for full-time lecturers like me. We used the rhetoric of the open hand when writing emails to administrators explaining why these cuts shouldn't happen, but we combined this with the closed fist tactic of using *mass* emails. We used the rhetoric of the closed fist when we held a sit-in in front of the dean's office, but we used the rhetoric of the open hand when creating a display board explaining to students what was happening and why we were protesting. Simultaneously, my department chair used the rhetoric of the open hand when discussing concrete alternatives with the dean.

Quite a lot of recent work in composition is concerned with issues of justice, equity, and what it means to be a socially responsible rhetorical agent. It's common for teachers to use public writing genres and other "renewable assignments" as means of showing students how writing can be used to make a difference in the world, even for school, and that saying what we think—like in a blog post or op-ed—is one form of participating in democracy. Work on language diversity and translanguaging—important work—generally doesn't dispute the value of students participating in society through engaging in written (or spoken) debates but instead argues that language differences should be recognized and celebrated. Whether or not students should use their own languages and dialects in their writing is debated, but these debates—tracing back at least to the 1960s—reinforce the value of open-handed rhetoric itself (Marback 1996, 187), containing debate to the specific forms it might take.

While many of us recognize the value of closed-fisted rhetorical techniques, we're nonetheless in the business of encouraging students to use the rhetoric of the open hand, training them in its forms, and persuading them of its value.[3] Some classes may hold more space than others for giving students opportunities to compose in closed-fisted genres, but these are the exceptions, not the rule. We're bound by curriculum and the politics of our institutions. Sometimes, closed-fisted rhetoric is antidebate, and sometimes closed-fisted rhetoric can negatively impact the classroom environment. Marback (1996) writes, "From the perspective of liberal democracy . . . the closed-fisted refusal to engage in a discussion in these terms signals all that is opposed to democratic values and civic participation" (182). Furthermore, "education in print literacy preserves and promotes the liberal humanistic values of individualism . . . Education in a particular kind of rhetoric then, a certain conception of literacy, of facility with consuming and producing written texts, stands between physical

---

3. Donald Murray specifically frames training in composition as a turn away from protest rhetorics (Marback 1996, 189).

confrontation driven by the will of the mob and the civil discourse of free persons who rationally and individually determine their own responses" (186). It's against the traditional values and stated purpose of our profession—as rhetoric and composition instructors—to encourage or engage in closed-fisted rhetoric, so it can feel unprofessional (and professionally risky) if we do so—and this is an incentive and subconscious pressure not to do it, beyond any additional, more concrete risks.

In his analysis of both the CCCC Executive Committee (EC) and the New University Caucus's (NUC's) responses to the police violence at the 1968 Democratic National Convention, Marback (1996) points out that both responses view the composition classroom as a site for possible social change to fight police violence—for the EC, composition can teach people how to handle conflict and differences without the use of "excessive" violence; for the NUC, composition can be a space to teach better values. But neither response considers how rhetoric and/or composition might be used to stop police violence in the writers' present day, how composing skills might be utilized in antiracist, antipolice movements. These movements aren't separate from our work, from our students, or from our working conditions. Our ability to enact change is framed as best used in the classroom, rather than using our Rhetoric and Composition skills in direct action in the world. Even very recent scholarship (Butts 2023) referencing the rhetoric of the closed fist argues that "we can find better ways" (46). Crucially, Nancy Welch (2011) points out that the rhetoric of the open hand versus the rhetoric of the closed fist is a false binary, and *both* types of rhetoric are necessary in organizing for adequate (or above-adequate!) pay, benefits, and social justice provisions. In order to win what we need, rhetoric and composition workers must be willing to use closed-fist rhetorics *and* apply our training in open-handed rhetorics directly to ongoing struggles.

The Legacy of Feminist Rhetorical Theory

The rhetoric of the open hand and rhetoric of the closed fist, and their attendant implications, are one way that Rhetoric and Composition professionals have theorized about mass struggle and its relationship with the profession. The other strand of rhetorical theory I want to trace, with regard to how it impacts workers' approaches to class struggle, is the legacy of feminist rhetorical theory. Curiously, the landmark articles that I will discuss here, written during roughly the same period as the debate about Corbett's ideas, don't dialogue with Corbett's initial argument or engage with the debates about protest movements of other oppressed people, despite the feminist movement using many of these same strategies.

In 1973, Karlyn Kohrs Campbell published an article in the *Quarterly Journal of Speech* arguing that feminist rhetoric is worthy of study because it has distinctive substantive and stylistic features.[4] The substantive features include how a woman taking on the role of rhetor is inherently radical due to women's subordinate position in society, and that demands for women's liberation are also inherently revolutionary. Campbell is right that traditional rhetorical styles can still be radical *if the demands are radical*. But Campbell also argues that part of what makes feminist rhetoric so innovative is that "there is no leader, rhetor, or expert" in consciousness-raising groups, there is no "message" or "party line," and "if action is suggested, no group commitment is made; each must decide whether, and if so which, action is suitable for her" (cited in 2015, 23). While this *is* stylistically innovative, and consciousness-raising conversations do have social and political value, the principle of having no shared message or group commitments has serious problems for collective action—and therefore, for making change. An important exception to the general attitude explained by Campbell is the Combahee River Collective Statement (1977), which *does* express a shared message and political line regarding Black lesbian feminism that developed *after* members "determined the need to do political work and to move beyond consciousness-raising."

In a labor organizing setting, consciousness-raising-like conversations are a common tactic, in which workers share their experiences, find common ground, and develop class consciousness about their shared working conditions and exploitation by management. But class struggle, even just within one workplace, always requires collective action. No union has full agreement on everything within its ranks (or even most things), but members must agree to *operate together* to be successful. There is lots of room for political disagreement—a union must be open to all workers, rather than just workers who already agree with a particular set of ideas—but power is always collective. While everyone ought to have a chance to voice their opinion and have it be considered, building agreement—through discussion and debate—strengthens the union, and *unity in action* is especially key. If a strike is called, each worker should not decide whether going on strike is right for them personally—if a union votes to go on strike, every worker needs to be on strike, even if they voted against it. Otherwise, the action is weakened. This is why workers who break

---

4. Campbell briefly acknowledges the protest rhetoric of "students and blacks" but doesn't engage with the scholarly discussion around these movements.

a strike, or are hired to replace striking workers, are called scabs: They're used to scab over the "wounds" the strike causes to the employer. Unity in action is vitally important for winning adequate contract provisions—the strength of a strike depends on it, and using an "every member decides for themselves" approach that Campbell praises as an innovative technique of feminist rhetoric undermines the ability to win.

Another key essay in the history of feminist rhetorical scholarship is "The Womanization of Rhetoric," by Sally Miller Gearhart (1979). Gearhart criticizes the entire notion of persuasion, arguing that the intent to persuade another person isn't just *like* violence—it *is* violence, against their right to have their own ideas. She figures persuasion as inherently patriarchal and argues for non-persuasive "communication," which creates an "atmosphere" in which entities may "persuade themselves" (57). Gearhart's description of the nonpersuasive "conflict encounter" is limited to situations in which the participants "feel equal in power to each other" and "each participant is willing on the deepest level to yield his/her position entirely to the other(s)" (57), such as a feminist classroom.

An additional limitation is Gearhart's bioessentialism, which creates significant barriers for solidarity. Her ideas about "male" communication and desire for domination, and the ideas that "in order to be authentic, we must all become more like women" (1979, 59) and that women simply *know better* and will *communicate better*, as a rule, create a very strong gender-based divide—and bioessentialism is the root of many of today's arguments in favor of the oppression of trans women. If workers of one gender are convinced that workers of other genders are *baseline worse* in their politics and communication skills, it's much harder to be collectively effective. Every movement has the potential to be stronger if it acts side by side with other movements. As the Marine Cooks and Stewards slogan went, "If you let them red-bait, they'll race-bait, and if you let them race-bait, they'll queen-bait. That's why we all have to stick together" (Bérubé 2011).

Beyond the politically reactionary ideas in Gearhart's work, her anti-persuasion stance is decimating for class struggle situations. Within a union (or among nonunionized workers in a workplace), workers must freely discuss and attempt to persuade one another about the best course of action. The alternative is to have union leaders decide what is right on behalf of everyone else, and that's undemocratic. It's not *violence* to attempt to persuade, especially in these cases, when all workers are engaged in the same struggle alongside one another. They ought to all have each other's best interests at heart, and when some segments of the workforce *don't* have each other's best interests at heart (perhaps along the lines of job title, or gender, or race, or sexuality, or disability), workers *must* persuade each other to build deeper solidarity and stand up for each other. Union decisions can be important decisions with stakes for the whole workplace—we need to take their outcomes seriously, which means arguing for what we think is best.

Within our profession, we have various values relating to professional respect: building on existing scholarship instead of tearing it down, contributing to the field instead of identifying "gaps" in the literature, and having "collegial" disagreement, often with an implication of not letting "academic" disagreements spill over into our interpersonal interactions, openness (Oleksiak 2022), and civility. These values have important merit within the professional space, but these values can spill over into other aspects of our lives where they don't belong. If we're not able or willing to openly and directly disagree with our colleagues about key issues, how can we work together to determine our collective goals and the best ways of achieving them? While Gearhart intends to apply her argument only to these particular conflict-encounter situations, the anti-persuasion tendency is common throughout the academy and beyond, such as in the other articles Timothy Oleksiak (2022) references in his overview of feminist rhetorical theories that treat openness as a prerequisite to feminist communication. Many of these authors are primarily focused on individual or small-group communication, not public rhetoric or mass rhetoric, but the ideas and values they carry still impact the readers who take them seriously, and it can be easy to fall into "openness good, closedness bad" thinking by default.

While anti-persuasion tendencies can restrict class struggle if we workers restrain ourselves from arguing when it's important to argue, the problem with anti-persuasion is even more pronounced in rhetoric facing toward the boss. Feminist rhetorical theories, correctly, often try to pay attention to the "immanent value in all human beings" (Foss and Griffin 1995, 4). This position becomes a problem when individual human beings are functioning not in their capacity as individuals but as agents of an institution—like a university—that in its capacity as an institution does not care about the immanent value in the workers as human beings. The human beings sitting across the bargaining table from me aren't speaking as Beth and Mike, nor does the institution care about whether our members can put food on the table or pay for healthcare. Success at the bargaining table is not a matter of persuading management's representatives as human beings. There is no rhetorical atmosphere we can create in which either side might be willing to change our position through seeing the other's point of view. How we relate to one another as individuals is beside the point—their job is to represent the university, and my job is to represent my coworkers, and for every issue at hand, our interests are inherently opposed to one another.

At the National Center for the Study of Collective Bargaining in Higher Education and the Professions conference in March 2023, I was shocked to hear the higher education director for a Services Employees International Union local bemoan "masculinist," fist-pounding styles of speaking at the bargaining table. But boldness and intransigence, however we choose to express them and no matter the gender of the speaker, are exactly what we need as workers to win what we need. As Rhetoric and Composition workers in (or with the potential to be in) the labor movement, we need to be willing to discover, in any situation, *all* of the available means of persuasion—and choose the best ones for the given rhetorical situation—rather than rejecting certain tactics on a philosophical level simply because they are "patriarchal." Patriarchy is about social dominance (of men over everyone else), and class struggle is about fighting back against economic *and* social dominance (of the bourgeoisie over everyone else). For all the rhetorical strategies at our disposal, their moral value and effectiveness depends on the *purpose, audience,* and *context.* When our *purpose* is to win adequate pay, benefits, and working conditions for ourselves and our colleagues, and our *audience* is the university's bargaining representatives, in the *context* of rising costs and new austerity cuts to education, feminist rhetoricians may need to embrace "non-feminist" rhetorical approaches in order to win the very feminist causes of better pay / benefits / working conditions for themselves and their colleagues.

Conclusion

For very understandable reasons, rhetoric, composition, and communication theorists like to push back against "argument = war" as a metaphor. But class struggle *is* class war—not war in the sense of military conflict (usually) but in the sense of a struggle for power and resources between the proletariat and the bourgeoisie that causes real material harm. And the rhetoric at the bargaining table is part of the diplomacy part of that war, where we try to find a resolution with words, rather than actions. At the bargaining table itself, we very often do use the rhetoric of the open hand and feign openness—we present arguments, we present testimony, we present data, and we thank the other side for their proposals, express gratitude when they express sympathy, and so on. But the bourgeoisie and its representatives, even the real human representatives we politely greet at the table, are not our allies, and they must not ever be viewed as such. While sometimes it is in our best interest to be cordial, our overall strategy must be firm, militant, and closed off to any possibility of collaboration, and we must resist the ideological pressures of the theories—no matter how important and useful they may be in other circumstances—that lead us to sympathy with the other side.

In "'We're Here, and We're Not Going Anywhere': Why Working-Class Rhetorical Traditions *Still* Matter" (emphasis in original), Welch (2011) explains that faculty at her university voted to unionize specifically because using open-handed and middle-class-professional rhetorical strategies (faculty senate resolutions, researched position papers, and appeals to professional standards) didn't work. Several years later, few tenure-track faculty marched alongside students and contingent faculty, which Welch argues was because "they hoped, against the lessons of ten years ago, that well-reasoned appeals presented to administrators in official forums or—most preferred of all—private meetings would prevail"; she argues that class *identity* and willingness to behave *as workers* fluctuate "as we learn and forget, learn and forget that our best research has little persuasive effect until we put our bodies into the argument" (228).

At the bargaining table, sometimes concessions need to be made—no side ever gets everything they want, and if they do, they weren't asking for enough. But that doesn't mean anyone needs to make ideological concessions—we adjust our proposals out of necessity, not out of agreement. We *are* class enemies. This can be a difficult concept to ingest for some academic workers, especially when many administrators, especially low-level administrators like deans, used to work as faculty themselves and may still teach occasionally. But it's not about the individual—it's about their structural position within the workplace. The dean at my school was tasked with implementing cuts to the composition program, even though many of my coworkers said she was a "friend to composition" when she was previously chair of the English department. As a person, she may well be a friend to composition—but her job, that month, was to make my coworkers and me suffer in the name of budget cuts, and it took class struggle to get her to find an alternative solution (Wood 2023).

Academic workers, in addition to their identities as teachers, researchers, students, colleagues, and so on, must also be willing to take on the subject position of "worker" and the rhetorical stance that comes with it. But the theories discussed here and their advocates aren't built for that kind of identity, which means we must be willing to discard the parts that don't work for this critical and ongoing rhetorical situation. During the time I've been drafting this chapter, West Virginia University announced it will be shuttering the entire World Languages Department—all of its graduate students and faculty will be left without positions. This is the kind of situation that requires class struggle rhetorics, and for academic workers to put their skills to immediate use.

References

Althusser, Louis. (1971) 2001. "Ideology and Ideological State Apparatuses." In *Lenin and Philosophy, and Other Essays*, translated by Ben Brewster, 85–126. New York: Monthly Review Press.

American Association of University Professors (AAUP). 2023. "The Annual Report on the Economic Status of the Profession, 2022–23." https://www.aaup.org/file/ARES-2022-23.pdf.

Applegarth, Risa. 2024. *Just Kids: Youth Activism and Rhetorical Agency*. Columbus: The Ohio State University Press.

Bérubé, Allan. 2011. *My Desire for History: Essays in Gay, Community, and Labor History*. Edited by John D'Emilio and Estelle B. Freedman. Chapel Hill: University of North Carolina Press.

Browne, Robert M. 1970. "Response to Edward P. J. Corbett, 'The Rhetoric of the Open Hand and the Rhetoric of the Closed Fist.'" *College Composition and Communication* 21 (2): 187–190. https://doi.org/10.2307/356560.

Butts, Jimmy. 2023. *Strangely Rhetorical: Composing Differently With Novelty Devices*. Logan: Utah State University Press.

Campbell, Karlyn Kohrs. (1973) 2015. "The Rhetoric of Women's Liberation: An Oxymoron." In *Landmark Essays on Rhetoric and Feminism: 1973–2000*, edited by Cheryl Glenn and Andrea A. Lunsford, 19–33. Landmark Essays Series. New York: Routledge.

Combahee River Collective. 1977. "Combahee River Collective Statement." https://www.blackpast.org/african-american-history/combahee-river-collective-statement-1977/.

Corbett, Edward P. J. 1969. "The Rhetoric of the Open Hand and the Rhetoric of the Closed Fist." *College Composition and Communication* 20 (5): 288–296. https://doi.org/10.2307/355032.

Foss, Sonja K., and Cindy L. Griffin. 1995. "Beyond Persuasion: A Proposal for an Invitational Rhetoric." *Communication Monographs* 62 (1): 2–18. https://doi.org/10.1080/03637759509376345.

Gearhart, Sally Miller. 2003. "The Womanization of Rhetoric." In *Feminism and Composition: A Critical Sourcebook*, edited by Gesa Kirsch, 53–60. Boston: Urbana, IL: Bedford / St. Martin's; published in cooperation with the National Council of Teachers of English.

Gruwell, Leigh. 2022. *Making Matters: Craft, Ethics, and New Materialist Rhetorics*. Logan: Utah State University.

Herbert, William A., Jacob Apkarian, and Joseph van der Naald. 2023. "Union Organizing and Strikes in Higher Education: The 2022–2023 Upsurge in Historical Context." National Center for the Study of Collective Bargaining in Higher Education and the Professions. https://www.hunter.cuny.edu/ncscbhep/assets/files/State%20of%20the%20Unions%202023%20Special%20Section-%20Clean%20Final.pdf.

Lee, JongHwa, and Seth Kahn, eds. 2020. *Activism and Rhetoric: Theories and Contexts for Political Engagement*, 2nd ed. New York: Routledge.

Marback, Richard. 1996. "Corbett's Hand: A Rhetorical Figure for Composition Studies." *College Composition and Communication* 47 (2): 180–198. https://doi.org/10.2307/358792.

MIT Living Wage Calculator. 2023. "Living Wage Calculation for New York County, New York." 2023. https://livingwage.mit.edu/counties/36061.

Oleksiak, Timothy. 2022. "Composing Consent as a Response to the Challenge of Openness." *College English* 84 (5): 429–446. https://doi.org/10.58680/ce202231907.

Phillips, Lisa L., Sarah Warren-Riley, and Julie Collins Bates, eds. 2024. *Grassroots Activisms: Public Rhetorics in Localized Contexts*. Intersectional Rhetorics. Columbus: The Ohio State University Press.

Welch, Nancy. 2011. "'We're Here, and We're Not Going Anywhere': Why Working-Class Rhetorical Traditions *Still* Matter." *College English* 73 (3): 221–242. https://www.jstor.org/stable/25790473.

Wood, Olivia. 2023. "Composition, the Speedup, and the Stretch-Out." *Composition Studies* (blog). May 1, 2023. https://compstudiesjournal.com/2023/05/01/composition-the-speedup-and-the-stretch-out/.

INTERLUDE 1

An Honest Job Application

KATIE MANTHEY

Note to reader: This is a piece of creative nonfiction. As someone who has applied to over 150 academic jobs during their academic career and has purposefully chosen to work at a small liberal arts college for almost a decade, the following job advertisement reflects both the conventions of academic job ads and the hidden realities behind them.

Also, there is a brief mention of suicidal ideation: Just a heads up.

***

Tenure-Track Assistant Professor of English

SMALL WOMEN'S COLLEGE, SOUTHEASTERN USA
About Us

As the oldest continuously operating women's college in the United States, we strive to provide a liberal arts education for women and gender minority students. The person in this position will be joining a contingent of about forty-five faculty who seem to be genuinely committed to the work that they do, even though almost no one here makes enough money. There are about 600 students, and they are very diverse: About 50 percent are nonwhite, 50 percent are first-generation college students, 60 percent of all students are Pell eligible;

all students are assigned female at birth or identify as female. Despite being proud of our diverse student body, we don't put a lot of time or money into academic support resources—instead we mostly rely on YOU, the professor and advisor, to help us with retention and success! That said, the students that you work with are so great that you occasionally forget that we exist in a precarious financial/enrollment position. Our college is historical, which means the outside of the buildings is beautiful, but the insides are literally falling apart. Prepare to be hot in the winter and cold in the summer and have no control over the temperature in your classroom! We also can't do any ADA updates, because we have historical buildings. At least we are a tourist destination (be ready for them to try to pop into your classes! It's so charming!).

Job Summary

Nine-month, academic faculty appointment. At this small liberal arts college, everyone on campus does everything, regardless of background or expertise. When the administration leaves you alone, you will be able to teach classes that you create in a way that you enjoy with little oversight. The college also has a very expansive definition of "scholarship" and will applaud you for work that is nontraditional that probably wouldn't count for much at an R1 or R2. While the college cares about research and publications, ultimately this is a teaching-centered school, so your course evaluations in some ways are more important than your scholarship, even though we know that student evaluations are not a good indicator of what happens in the classroom.

Responsibilities

DEPARTMENT-RELATED RESPONSIBILITIES include (a) teaching three to four undergraduate classes/semester; (b) academic advising for all major students and at least twelve new first-year students each year, regardless of intended major; (c) ongoing curriculum development and assessment; (d) internal marketing and event planning to desperately try to draw students to your program, otherwise you will become subsumed by the General Education requirements and cease to exist as a program (the darkness is closing in . . .); (e) continued engagement with academic research and publication in your subdiscipline; (f) chairing your department before tenure (stipend only available if you keep a certain number of majors, so get to it!).

COLLEGE-RELATED RESPONSIBILITIES include (a) serving on multiple college committees; (b) attending faculty meetings (we are too small for a senate, so everyone comes to everything!); (c) participating in campus strategic planning; (d) participate in ALL ADMISSIONS EVENTS THIS IS CRITICALLY IMPORTANT FOR THE LOVE OF GOD YOU NEED TO SHOW UP WE NEED STUDENTS OR WE ARE GOING TO DIE; (e) other duties as indicated by dean of the college.

ADDITIONAL RESPONSIBILITIES may include having very detailed knowledge of both the college's finances and the current student enrollment numbers; participating in casual conversations with colleagues about the looming high school population cliff; by-the-minute knowledge of our retention rate; and grant writing.

Qualifications

PhD
15–200 years teaching experience

Preferred Qualifications

White
Male
Cisgender
Straight
Able bodied
Neurotypical
Wife at home to do all the domestic labor
Christian
One of your references knows someone on the board of trustees

Benefits

- Occasional 401k match.
- Sporadic COLA increases.
- Constant existential fear of total institutional failure—never a dull moment! You'll really know you're alive.
- Health insurance that you can't afford, which also has such an outrageous deductible that every year you will wonder if it's even worth it.
- Dental insurance.
- Pretty decent mental health coverage.
- On good days, a real sense of doing something that matters.

Salary

Imagine the lowest salary you would be willing to take and subtract about $20,000. Did we mention that our campus is very pretty?

Application

To apply for this position, please answer the following short essay questions.

> QUESTION 1: What guiding ideas anchor your approach to working at a small liberal arts college? How do these ideas encourage you to grow professionally while protecting you from the unrealistic expectations we have set out in the preceding description?
>
> *As the child of academics, I know that in order to survive in academia one must do the impossible: Be simply adequate. Do not try to stand out; do not try to take on more (especially for less pay). Do not bleed for the institution, because it will never love you. Aim to do your job, go home, and get by. I also know that this is virtually impossible. With this in mind, my two personal guiding principles for this approach are there are no emergencies in Rhetoric and Composition and I care about my job at a level commensurate with my compensation. I will briefly discuss each.*
>
> 1. **THERE ARE NO EMERGENCIES IN RHETORIC AND COMPOSITION.**
>
>   Someone mentioned this to me in graduate school, and I've been desperately clinging to it since then. The idea that even in our most pressing academic moments—even when things are overwhelming and moving very quickly—the worst that will happen is most likely a grade is entered that can later be changed. We are not medical doctors—no one's lives are in our hands. If I am adequate, I am still doing my job well because even our highest stakes are not life or death. That said, I have experienced some notable exceptions:
>
>   → When a student with suicidal ideations comes into my office and tells me they need help. In this case, I will take them to the hospital myself because I know that there are limited resources at your particular small liberal arts campus (we will not be able to get a hold of anyone besides public safety, who we know would end up calling an ambulance that the student cannot afford).
>
>   → When the college is facing a financial crisis, and it's all hands on deck. At a school where everyone does everything, it's impossible not to internalize the larger existential crisis of the moment. Will enrollment bounce back? Will we stay afloat? Are the latest ideas

about directions for change from the Board of Trustees going to fundamentally change the nature of the institution in ways that are bad? How much do I internalize? Can I just be an employee? To help answer these questions, I offer my second guiding idea:

2. I CARE AT A LEVEL COMMENSURATE WITH MY COMPENSATION.

This idea helps me from internalizing the stress and existential circumstances/crises of the institution as a whole. I sometimes need to remind myself that there are people whose job is to focus only on enrollment, to focus only on marketing, to focus only on finances—my job is to focus on teaching, service, and research. I am not being paid multiple salaries, so I should not take on the emotional and existential labor of multiple jobs. There is an appropriate amount for me to care about the larger picture of the institution, and I am dedicated to doing that work. When it comes to existential crises, I am just a cog in the machine—I am not the whole machine. I will show up to admissions events, sit on committees, and offer recommendations when I can—but I will keep my focus on my students. I will do my job, but I will not try to save the college single-handedly—or maybe even at all. I will hold the line, though. I will be adequate. I will stay healthy and alive. There is only one thing that can complicate this idea:

→ If I receive an increase in pay that allows me to stop nearly all of my outside employment (which you will have previously approved, dear college, because you know just how little you pay me). While it is finally nice to get paid enough from you to pay my bills, I'll realize that my buy-in to some of the things I was able to keep at a distance before has changed. It's with respectful reluctance that I will agree to take on more, to go deeper with some of the things I've been asked to do, and to show up to events that I normally would have skipped. But hear me, college: I will still only strive to be adequate, even with this increased level of engagement/compensation. If you want more from me, pay me more. I will never give you everything, though.

QUESTION 2: Like all institutions of higher education, we expect our employees to care about the institution in a way that is unhealthy and will often use the language of "caring about students" to manipulate your boundaries. We also hope (and expect!) that you will make this job your identity and will be so driven by your loyalty to us and the idea of being a professor here that you will ignore the working conditions and low pay. If you are hired here, how will you ensure that we don't kill you?

Oh my. Well, I see the three issues raised earlier (loyalty, students, identity) as in tension with the idea that this is "just a job." I will briefly explore each tension two ways:

TENSION 1: THIS IS JUST A JOB VERSUS THIS IS A SPECIAL PLACE—AN INSTITUTION WORTH CARING ABOUT.

Your college is the oldest continuously operating women's college in America. It has been helping women and girls since before America was America. Being here on campus means being part of a tradition of social justice—a place where (white) feminism is pervasive. As a white woman myself, it feels like a comfortable space. It feels so much different from the state schools (and even other private schools) I've taught at. This is a place that feels good to be a part of.

TENSION 1: THIS IS A SPECIAL PLACE—AN INSTITUTION WORTH CARING ABOUT VERSUS THIS IS JUST A JOB.

My mentor in graduate school told me that the institution will never love me. Even one that was founded to help women—to help people who are traditionally marginalized—is still, at its heart, a business. I need to remember that if I leave this place, some people would be sad for a while, but you would replace me and the machine would keep on going—I am a cog in a larger system, and there are many cogs out there. Similarly, there are many institutions out there—this is the one I am choosing to be at right now. This is just a job, even if my cog fits well in this machine.

TENSION 2: THIS IS JUST A JOB VERSUS I REALLY CARE ABOUT MY STUDENTS.

These students are the future. They are here by choice, and they want to learn things. They are kind, curious, and vulnerable. They are predominantly cis women, nonbinary people, and trans men. Most of them don't come from wealthy backgrounds. Many of them are students of color. Many of them are neurodivergent. Many of them are queer. When I tell them I am neurodivergent and queer, they look to me for help. It's my job to help them. I really, really want them to be okay.

TENSION 2: I REALLY CARE ABOUT MY STUDENTS VERSUS THIS IS JUST A JOB.

The best way I can care for my students is to be okay myself. This means having boundaries and staying emotionally healthy. I do this by trying to keep a distance from being too sucked in to feeling things. This is just a job. Other people besides me care about these students. I need to trust the community and make sure I'm okay.

TENSION 3: THIS IS JUST A JOB VERSUS THIS IS MY IDENTITY.

I went to college for thirteen years to do this. I am inculcated in the ideas of what success and prestige and identity are for a "professor." I am a professor and I am proud. When people ask me what I do, I am happy to tell them. This identity makes me feel good about myself, for better or worse. I like being a professor—in all the different ways that statement holds meaning. This institution has opportunities for me to feel like I am valued and an important member of the intellectual community here.

TENSION 3: THIS IS MY IDENTITY VERSUS THIS IS JUST A JOB.

The idea that our identities and our work need to be connected is dangerous neoliberal bullshit. I know better. I try to tell my students this whenever I can. It still feels good to "be a professor" though. But I am so much more than my job—I am a person with hobbies, with loved ones, and with value outside of my productivity. When the day comes and I am no longer a professor (because it will happen to all of us, at some point whether termination or retirement), I will still be *me*. And that's okay.

Taken together, these tensions show that having boundaries and aiming for the middle—being adequate—will keep me alive, even if it prevents me from being the most powerful professor on campus. As an employee (and as a human), I am okay with that.

Final Thoughts

Is there anything else you would like the committee to know?

> *At every turn in my career in academia, I have hoped to make things a little less terrible (something I learned from Malea Powell)—which I see as an appropriately adequate goal. I would bring this with me to your college. Thank you for your consideration.*

Part II

Responding to Structural Inadequacy

4
A Dialogue on Un/Learning Institutional Knowledge in Bits and Doing *the Work* as Pre-Tenure Administrators

Kelin Loe, Ashanka Kumari, and Gavin P. Johnson

Standard professional advice suggests writing program, writing center, and degree program administrators be tenured faculty. Both the Conference on College Composition and Communication (CCCC) (2016) and the Council of Writing Program Administrators (CWPA) (2019) published position statements advising against untenured administrative duties; however, we know that this ideal is, often, against the norm (Dew and Horning 2007). For a range of political, economic, and bureaucratic reasons, tenure-track faculty, non-tenure-track instructors, non-tenurable staff and adjuncts, and graduate students lead complex programs. And it's a lot. Guiding programs and centers—which are often staffed by graduate students, undergraduate students, adjuncts, and staff—requires untenured administrators levying the very little cultural capital they have to keep the lights on, much less move programs forward. Although all administrators face challenges, without deep wells of institutional knowledge and cultural capital, untenured administrators perform labor rooted in precarity often drawn from the cracks in their day and the moments pivoting between classes and writing and supporting those who work in our programs and centers and . . . and . . . and.

Untenured administrative labor is so common that in "Evaluating the Intellectual Work of Writing Program Administration," the CWPA (2019) illustrates the pitfalls through the "problematic case" of Cheryl W. The narrative details a laundry list of administrative duties that are "overwhelming" despite Cheryl W.'s recent experience working in a "nationally known WAC program" and the expertise earned during her PhD. She's not only relatively new to administrative work but also new to faculty duties and her university: its unique histories, ideologies, expectations, and infrastructures. Her administrative duties limit her research productivity and impact her teaching, which do not go unnoticed. The narrative explains, "Unless there is a way to demonstrate the intellectual value of her work, Cheryl is unlikely to be rewarded for her administrative work and will be denied promotion and tenure" (CWPA 2019). Cheryl W.'s scenario rings familiar for many of us because it's a case of being more than adequate but still struggling to meet professional and personal expectations under contemporary, capitalistic logics of labor.

> KELIN: I AM CHERYL!
> Or, maybe I'm just overwhelmed lol
> I think the Department knows this is real work, but that doesn't change the six-article requirement for tenure 😳 😬 😑
> ASHANKA AND GAVIN: We will help you get to six, friend!!

Our chapter brings together the experiences of three pre-tenure faculty administrators. When we began writing this chapter, we all worked at an East Texas regional comprehensive university in the Department of Literature and Languages, which offers graduate and undergraduate degrees in literature and culture, rhetoric and writing, and applied linguistics, as well as programs in Spanish and courses in philosophy and film studies. We were hired as assistant professors of English (Ashanka in 2019, Kelin in 2021, and Gavin in 2022), but only Kelin was hired explicitly with an administrative role. Regardless, each of us received one course release per semester in return for our time and labor as pre-tenured administrators.

What brings our stories together, beyond our shared university context, is that each of us adapted to the labor of un/learning institutional knowledge in bits—stumbling over rarely discussed (but apparently very important) policies, picking up advice from colleagues in the hall, and digging through local "archives" (the stacks of papers and unorganized digital files of previous administrators) to complete mundane tasks. This un/learning is both affective and embodied, often feminized and racialized, difficult to measure, almost always invisible to others, basically unaccountable on annual evaluations and tenure and promotion documents, and easily dismissed as not real labor

(Lamos 2016). These expectations—give us more, faster, bigger—impact precarious bodies more frequently and are not a visible part of the labor calculus of the neoliberal institution.

> ASHANKA: G—I found a bunch of old student ethnography projects, want them?
>
> GAVIN: Yes, please!
>
> KELIN: The histories of our programs are looong, but our time directing them has been short. Just learning more day by day, bit by bit.

Our goal here is not to center labor as economic production but rather to theorize through story and offer paratextual commentary on our collective un/learning institutional knowledge in bits. We understand this as "learning just enough" to maintain the day-to-day duties of *the job* but performing administrative philosophies that center action-oriented social justice as *the work* (Kynard 2020). In making these distinctions, we hope to demonstrate our coalitional approach to pre-tenure administration that enables us to lead programs "without losing [our] souls" (Miller-Cochran 2018), avoid giving ourselves over to the "managerial unconscious" (Strickland 2011), and un/learn institutional knowledge in bits.

In this chapter's first draft, we told three separate stories. These reflected squarely on our individual experiences, pathways, and practices as pre-tenure administrators. We focused a lot on what Carmen Kynard (2020), invoking her mentor Suzanne Carothers, emphasizes as *the job* and *the hustle* rather than *the work* (19–20). Those narratives were very "I" focused—I did this, I did that; however, those narratives did not mirror our shared realities. Now, we rely heavily on Kynard (2020) to avoid confusing *the job*, *the hustle*, and *the work*. Kynard makes clear that *the job* is the day-to-day grind of maintaining neoliberal institutions, whereas *the work* is the deeper culture-shifting praxis of centering "Black thought and Black life in people's lives *in the academy*" (18, emphasis added). Kynard complicates these ideas further by adding *the hustle*, which "referenc[es] the ability to understand and navigate the arbitrary neoliberalist structures of the job market, publishing, tenure, and the grind of academia in a way that pushes beyond our race/class-neutralized language of 'professionalism' and 'professionalization'" (18). The three of us recognize our positionalities, and we are committed accomplices (Green 2018) to the fugitive work of Black feminism within and beyond our institutional contexts. Here, we take up Kynard's grammar of labor and consider the unaccountable labor of being pre-tenured administrators constantly *learning just enough* to be adequate alongside the coalitional potential of redefining adequacy within the neoliberal university to empower necessary anti-racist work.

> KELIN, ASHANKA, AND GAVIN (IN UNISON): We suggest that to be "adequate," we must build coalitions from the labor of un/learning in bits. Being "adequate," for us, means not centering our individual jobs, or "output," but rather relying on each other to generate a bank of knowledge that we can navigate together. It's being accountable to those who shape our daily lives and those whose lives we shape, as opposed to being accountable to the institution (Johnson 2023). It's an exercise of sideways power. It's being "in but not of" the university (Moten and Harney 2004). It's being adequate.

We are not sharing our stories because they are particularly unique or revelatory. Indeed, like the case of Cheryl W., our stories are more the norm than the exception. However, that is the point. Eileen E. Schell (1998) argues that we don't need "a list of blanket directives about power, authority, and administrative structures, but a series of local narratives and case studies that show us how writing program administrators negotiate viable models of administrative leadership" (65). We take Schell's call seriously. We aim to demonstrate a "coalitional administration" that is a process of interdependence that has helped us establish shared goals, values, and strategies, giving us tools for pursuing change centering difference, social justice, and accountability. It isn't perfect and perhaps not as radical as some may hope for, but certainly coalition, especially academic coalition, is always difficult, ongoing, and slow (Abbas et al. 2023; Chávez 2023). Our shared goal in telling these stories and engaging in this paratextual dialogue about being pre-tenured administrators calls attention to labor that does *the work*, not just *the job* or *the hustle*.

The Job, the Work, the Hustle, and Adequacy

ASHANKA

Institutions deem me adequate when I maintain a set of individual statistics that benefit them first: numbers of publications, teaching evaluation scores, grant funding I bring in, time spent serving on committees. It's a challenge wanting to remain adequate, as defined in academia, because adequacy undermines the needs of people we directly impact as teachers, scholars, and administrators. Years of both being and observing, listening to and working with students remind me for whom and why I do this. Institutions think of people as numbers first—statistics that promote the goals and values upper-level leadership and political stakeholders set often without us, much less the students that institutions supposedly serve. However, the people I work most closely with—my colleagues, collaborators, and those I am in coalition with—recognize my personhood.

> GAVIN: Like you always say, Ashanka, the institution cannot and will not love us back.
>
> KELIN: Even when they give us nice tote bags.

Coalitional adequacy involves meeting shared goals but also recognizes the individual needs—rest, time, grace, community—that can't be quantified but must be supported for us to continue *the work* and avoid burnout. To this point, adrienne maree brown (2017) emphasizes: "The idea of interdependence is that we can meet each other's needs in a variety of ways, that we can truly lean on others and they can lean on us. It means we have to decentralize our idea of where solutions and decisions happen, where ideas come from" (87). Over time, and as I try to illustrate here, it's the day-to-day people, the colleagues and collaborators I choose to be accountable to, where my definitions and understandings of adequacy shift. Careers in academia often emphasize research, specifically publication, as the most valuable and "real" work.

> ASHANKA: Gavin often reminds us in our rhetoric and composition committee meetings: Service alone will not get us tenure.
>
> GAVIN: I hate that I have to say this so often. That's definitely the job and the hustle coming into an odd conflict, innit?

I've been advised toward keeping my head down and focusing on completing the requirements for tenure—traditionally a way to garner job security and institutional power—before making waves. As a goal-oriented person, this path felt clear: Do the required research, writing, and teaching now to tenure, and I could still do administrative work I thrive in later. Un/learning this path has been difficult work.

KELIN

I hold the first tenure-track line to direct our Writing Center. It had a full-time staff director for five years, and then spent two years without leadership, just graduate students keeping the doors open while the department argued for my line and ran the search.

GAVIN: Google Sleuthing 🔍, I found an old tutor training guide and history of the WC. Lil Brannon started our Writing Center?!

KELIN: Yes! But WHEN is still up for debate—1974 or 1977—still digging in the archives for clarity!

ASHANKA: That's so cool. There's a lot of history in this Department. Something we should write about in our magical free time 🏃‍♀️ ⏰

I was hired to create a culture shift for writing on campus and build the Writing Center as an opportunity hub for graduate and undergraduate students. On paper, that should be 15 percent of my workload.

KELIN: TBH, while I'm settled in defining adequacy as coalitional accountability NOW, in the first draft, I was defining adequacy as not getting fired and maintaining healthcare for my family. Determining an adequate performance is still dizzying. 💫 😵

ASHANKA: Me too. I was thinking about adequate as clocking in and out. But then also how academia asks for EXTRA, but with the same pay. It often feels like we need to over-prove our worth by vaulting over basic requirements. My definition of adequacy was "don't burn out."

GAVIN: That's the easy definition that values isolated labor and individual survival. Linking adequacy and accountability, we get somewhere, perhaps, radical.

The job of an untenured administrator is "often untenable" (Schell 1998, 67). One way I experience that untenability is that the definition of adequate performance shifts every time I face a new audience (undergraduate tutors, deans, institutional offices). Kynard's categories of *job*, *hustle*, and *work* helped me organize how I thought about all the tasks of directing the Writing Center. As defined by a writing center director, *the job* is daily tasks that keep the Writing Center open, funded, and in compliance with university policy. *The work*, then, is the labor of creating a writing culture with a firm theoretical, practical, and reflexive understanding of how writing centers can both enact and suppress linguistic justice. Schell calls the "position," *the job*, "often untenable," not *the work*. Un/learning the desire for stability has been difficult work.

GAVIN: We can't forget the hustle, which I think can be really a gray area between the job and the work, right? The networking around campus, and promoting the Writing Center and Writing Program, and putting in award nominations and small grant funding is what Kynard is calling "hustle"—that professionalization within and of the academy—but it gets blurry when we think about how parts of the hustle can be used to support the work, like rubbing elbows to get funding to do workshops on linguistic justice or planning textbook revisions that will satisfy a grant so that grad students get a paycheck in August. Kynard (2020) is clear that "the work is not the job and it is not the hustle" (19–20), but can the grammar of the hustle ever be used ethically to further the work? Idk. 😒

ASHANKA: It's complicated. Christine Pearson Casanave's (2002) metaphor about "writing games" resonates as how I think about the strategic gameplay we navigate to survive in academia. I know all three of us seek advice and reflect regularly to move as ethically as we can so the joyful parts—the real play—of the academic game stay intact. These choices don't come down to rules so much as day-to-day movements. At the same time, it's a challenge to our identities to which we want to stay genuine and honest in our work while icky shit happens every day in academia. It's a long game, and we don't want to be injured in the pre-tenure rounds.

GAVIN

When I was interviewing for this position, future expectations of administrative work were made clear. The Rhetoric and Composition faculty, who often occupy multiple departmental administrative roles, were bringing in two new hires to make a sustainable administrative rotation possible.

ASHANKA: It's that rotation, the understanding that we are building this position with and for the next person that encourages coalitional buy-in.

KELIN: It means one person doesn't stay stuck for too long—and we don't make these roles our lives.

Considering experience and relatively recent administrative appointments for Kelin and Ashanka, we estimated that I would rotate into an administrative role (writing center director or director of writing in about three years). Having come from a previous faculty position with a heavy teaching and service load as well as a grad school experience with lots of administrative opportunities, I was excited to have more time to focus on research, learn the terrain, and establish a community beyond the university. Three years turned into three months.

GAVIN: In their feedback, Josh and Timothy asked, "Why are you doing this work?" I think they mean, since it's clear the pre-tenure administrators' position can be untenable, why are you doing more than bare minimum with these admin positions? I do it because we are in community and working together to improve our programs for students. But then I'm reminded of two conversations I've had this week that questioned if anything could improve or repair the university. Goals of improvement and repair, Brynn Fitzsimmons and Pritha Prasad (2023) explain, would suggest that there was, once upon a time, justice in the university as opposed to the university's exploitation being by design.

>ASHANKA: We do it because we want better conditions and pay, and recognize that we need to establish or find the pathways to make them realities in academia not just for ourselves and people here now, but for the next group. I would argue that we all firmly resist a replication or suffering model.

When, late in my first semester, Ashanka and I heard about shifting departmental administration, we were forced into action. Ashanka was given the opportunity to coordinate our PhD program, which has long been a career goal and personal passion, and she damn well couldn't direct the Writing Program and coordinate the PhD.

>ASHANKA: Damn right!

Over a few days of quick conversations, we decided, with the department head's approval, Ashanka would become doctoral program coordinator and I would become director of writing beginning in the spring semester (about five weeks away). Soon Ashanka was transferring program files, and we were meeting for quick-and-dirty rundowns of typical Writing Program workflows, but also continuing the anti-racist and community-conscience work Ashanka and those before her had integrated into the curriculum. Un/learning administrative expectations in a whirlwind is difficult work.

>GAVIN: There is a dissonance in my thinking. An oscillation between feeling like the work can be done in but not of the university and feeling that this job in this place can never bring transformative justice.
>
>ASHANKA: Can any job? That's "the work" we engage beyond our paychecks, but perhaps the most meaningful to each of us. The work that motivates us to continue our relationships with the academy.
>
>KELIN: It's so hard in this neolib setting to not feel like "the work" is the extra. In this revision, when we finally articulated adequate as accountability (thx, G!) and "the work" as being adequate to OUR coalition, I feel confident in doing LESS of the job, delegating the job in favor of the work. Before I'd have an anxiety spiral about whether it's appropriate to pass on this or that part of the job, and then I'd run out of time and

have to do it myself. Since the revision, for THE FIRST TIME IN THIS POSITION (!!!), I'm actually saying, "This email isn't my job" then passing it up, down, or sideways. All this to say, our coalition is giving me the confidence to do less of the job so that the work isn't extra.

GAVIN AND ASHANKA: We're so proud of you!

KELIN: 🫂 👻

Writing Program Hot Potato

ASHANKA

As Kelin accepted her position, our then-director of writing announced she'd be leaving at the end of the semester. The conversations began late in the spring 2021 semester: Who would be our next director of writing? I expressed concern that having two administrators unfamiliar with the institutional environment beginning the same semester would be rockier than the usual bumps along the new-admin environment. Given my recent work with our outgoing colleague and more recent time teaching first-year writing, I felt and was regarded as adequate to take on the role.

> GAVIN: Being adequate is no longer linked to production of/from labor but rather being accountable to each other. That is the un/learning we are doing—un/learning that our individual labor is all we are responsible for. Being in community, being accountable to community, means we get to care about changing things and not just check administrative/careerist boxes.

One afternoon after the spring semester, for about six hours, our outgoing director walked me through a document outlining her annual tasks while I furiously typed, adding notes to each section in the document. With the general tasks document as a map, I had a sense of some of the players and practices expected of my work. This document is one I revised and passed onto Gavin. Documents, Google folders, and other semi-organized materials, alongside ongoing text conversations with my former colleague, stay invaluable and key to the semi-smooth transition to the day-to-day needs at both this moment and then later to my current role as doctoral program coordinator.

GAVIN

In late December 2022, Ashanka and I were meeting for coffee to discuss my transition into the director of writing role. It became clear that while I could confidently move into the director's role, I would be learning on the job. That is, even with scholarly knowledge and experience as a hands-on associate WPA in grad school, I would step into the position with only a few bits of the institutional knowledge required to successfully lead the Writing Program. For academic administrators, institutional knowledge is essential because so much of our work is navigating the bureaucracy that we stumble into. If you are reading this and saying, "That's how it happens. No one knows what they are doing the first day," I agree, but what, then, made me think that I needed to know everything immediately? How do we define success as pre-tenure administrators when we aren't given the time or resources to acclimate as leaders and instead muddle through somehow?

By January, I was the director of writing and running the pre-semester orientation; I needed to communicate programmatic policies and outline how the shared curriculum would *likely* work for the spring semester. There were graduate students and adjuncts in the room with deep knowledge and multiple semesters of experience with the curriculum; I only knew the curriculum on paper and from teaching a truncated summer version of our first-year research class as an adjunct the summer before to bridge the pay gap between jobs.

> GAVIN: I faked it
> KELIN: You were fabulous.

Ashanka had agreed to help lead that orientation session and shared her knowledge and experience in support. She also reminded me that since everyone attending the orientation was a returning instructor, we could have a more relaxed session—a *reminder of* rather than an *orientation to* the Writing Program.

> GAVIN: What becomes possible when the "director" can step back from dictating policy and orienting instructors and rely on the knowledge and experience of those instructors when preparing for a new semester?

While the first months of this position were exhausting, as I found my stride as the director of writing with support from this coalition, I felt something more like adequate. One part of the job that has been particularly helpful, in fact, came from observing the graduate students as they teach. Sitting in on their classes and seeing different instructors interpret and deliver the curriculum gives me insight into the strengths and weaknesses of how we teach writing to center linguistic identity, literacy, and community. These bits of learning are much more satisfying than the bits of institutional knowledge gathered through the typical administrative genres of labor.

Writing Center Staff Training

KELIN

Engaging with my Rhetoric and Composition colleagues and department head daily, and the dean regularly, I feel the most accountable for making that culture shift in the Writing Center—what I'd consider *the work* in my administrative context. As I see it, a culture shift requires aligning our values with the flows of money through the Writing Center. The work can't be broken into tasks as easily as the job, so my starting point became training the staff. Investing in a consulting staff means giving them time to train, learn, and professionalize and compensating them for that time.

> GAVIN: You use the term "professionalize" but I'm not sure that's what you and the consultants actually do. Kynard (2020) calls professionalization the "white-masking discourse" of the hustle (19). But what I see you doing in the Writing Center is building a community in a space that attends to issues of linguistic justice and supporting a lot of queer and disabled students.
>
> KELIN: Oooooooo G yes. I think of tutor professionalization as what you describe—and I forget that outside of my pocket of WC colleagues that's not universally true. LITERALLY Kynard's professionalization was how things worked before I got here. Learning (and remembering) bit by bit.

To the institution, an adequate writing center is an open one. But to those who hired me to make a culture change, and to my field, I believe an adequate writing center is one where consultants are well prepared and compensated. I struggled through various options to establish a rhythm of consultant training and Writing Center expansion—but not alone. In coalition with colleagues, we built different scenarios for weeks. We drew from our different banks of institutional knowledge, from our senior colleague having the ear of the department head to one of our new colleagues, who does not yet have writing center experience, asking foundational questions that tested my acceptance of long-established writing center practices. The rotating model of administration means that my colleagues might be the next person to step into a leadership position, and that means we listen with investment and work to understand and align our programs.

When institutionalizing an undergraduate training course seemed impossible, I made one last push. I began composing a memo to the department head explaining the course as a best practice. While I don't doubt it exists, I couldn't find a source explicitly recommending the training course. I asked fellow writing center directors, and they too had no answer. I was starting to suspect that I might value this course model of staff training because it was what I knew. In meetings, the coalition grappled with the fact that at a university with a primarily first-generation-student and large commuting populations, graduation requirements make elective courses a financial burden. The course, in sum, was not logistically possible and had the nasty side effect of gatekeeping the Writing Center.

In continuing my research for the memo, I found some new thinking about the social justice potential of the staff training course. Megan Connor and Mackenzie Clinger (2023) explain how they assessed their own writing center for its actual commitments to diversity and inclusion. The training course proved problematic for two reasons. First, it requires consultants to pay for their own training. As Connor and Clinger (2023) conclude, the training course is "an exploitation," and, I realized, antithetical to the coalitional values we have about compensating training ("Weaknesses"). Second, as we feared, it severely limits who can train to work in the Writing Center—only people with room in their schedule to take an upper-division English course (Connor and Clinger 2023, "Weaknesses").

> KELIN: A—remember when I called you in a tizzy after reading that article?!
>
> ASHANKA: Yes! You relayed the article and talked through alternative ideas. Your openness to un/learning "best practices" is part of why our Writing Center is arguably the strongest it's been in years!

Instead of a training course, we implemented a paid internship. As the new paid internship began, the Texas legislature passed SB-17, a law affecting diversity, equity, and inclusion in higher education. In addition to eliminating explicitly DEI-supporting offices, the bill specifies that no employee can be required to take DEI-specific training (particularly in race, gender, and sexuality). To be in compliance with the bill, I eliminated all conversations and readings that seek to support people based on race, gender, and sexuality. Consultants can choose to research these topics, but they cannot be required to read each other's work.

Although SB-17 affects what counts as writing center training, the non-course-based, paid internship model resulted in hiring a new cohort of four interns that is more diverse in discipline and experience than any I've hired thus far—and just as intellectually invested as those in the course the previous year. While this new method of training aligns more with our mission (with *the work*), in terms of *the job* it definitely adds to the administrative workload. Knowing that I don't want to create more untenability for the next director—and because I know the coalition supports me in my fight to create the research time I need for tenure—I'm starting to draw and communicate lines in the sand for the responsibilities of the job. I am un/learning what needs to be done, what can't be done, and what shouldn't be done.

Working Through Shifts, Trauma, and Tenure

Through coalition, we aim for, as Schell says, "viability" (65) for tenability. Schell (1998) says: "Instead of being warned repeatedly about our powerlessness and exploitation (something we live with and work against daily), those of us who are untenured WPAs need strategies and tactics for managing our often untenable positions" (67). We offer our experience building a coalitional model of pre-tenure administrative labor as an emergent strategy (brown 2017). And we bring this coalition strategy to the conversation of resisting neoliberal agendas in higher education through adequacy. Why? Because an administrative coalition is predicated on a shared understanding of adequacy. For us, the foundational vocabulary for adequacy comes from Kynard's distinctions between the work, the job, and the hustle. In the myriad of administrative tasks that could easily fill a full-time job, as a coalition, we've developed a sense of shared priority and tactics for un/learning: The job tasks that allow for the institutionalization of our work are the highest priority. If our decisions align with that priority, we are accountable to one another and, by our own definition, adequate.

> ASHANKA: In my five years here, the COVID-19 pandemic and subsequent epidemics, pandemics, police violence, school shootings, violence against historically marginalized communities, an insurrection, and more, continue to weigh on us every single day. As I considered a metaphor for my shifting administrative positions and time at this institution, I recalled a bit from Hasan Minhaj's *Patriot Act* wherein he describes the compassion fatigue of endless news cycles and global issues: "It's like we have 50 tabs open in our mental browsers, and we're about to crash. Something's got to change" (*Patriot Act*, vol. 5, 2019). When working in ongoing crises where the majority of emails and conversations are filled with grief, redefining the contexts of our adequacy emphasizes how we can't close tabs when they are people.

GAVIN: This reminds me of Kaitlin Clinnin (2023) discussing the need for a "trauma-informed writing program administration [as] a community effort where all faculty and administrators are responsible for trauma-informed practices and have equal access to trauma-informed support" (117), especially her call for intentional rest and reciprocal caring relationships (128).

As our text and paratext illustrate, adequacy in this coalition is woven through with the labor required to stay in the job, the experiences of extraordinary (if all too common) environmental stressors, the managerial rhetorics of "volatility, uncertainty, complexity, and ambiguity" (VUCA) coming from upper administration that provide cover for austerity and market-driven, not coalitional, values, and, of course, the management of our unruly bodies (and unruly young humans and nonhumans). We want each other to thrive professionally and personally, so being accountable to the coalition requires supporting each other in making choices that are healthy and sustainable—in doing just enough in alignment with our shared notion of *the work*.

But Schell (1998) asks us for more than strategies alone. She warns, those who attempt decentralized administration models need to articulate the challenges they create and resist "utopian" depictions. She urges us to "write realistic case studies that address the conflicts as well as the possibilities" (77). Her own case concludes with her finding her administrative load inhibiting (76). Between Schell's case from 1998 and our narratives today, it's clear this alternative style of administration requires countless more conversations (both easy and difficult) than would be necessary in an autonomous leadership model. Those conversations, and the depth of consideration they require, certainly impede the other aspects of the job, especially research and writing time. But, then again, impeding *the job* can, in itself, be a radical act.

And the ground is always shifting. We've centered a great deal of this discussion around the concept of being "untenured" and, specifically in our cases, "pre-tenured." We have been thinking critically about how tenure (and the threat of not being granted tenure) has so often been used to stifle collaboration and coalition. What was a system designed to build academic freedom and strengthen shared governance has been eroded into a neoliberal status characterized by individual "merit." Even so, tenure has, traditionally, provided some job security to faculty administrators doing the work, but that shield is not impenetrable. While composing this chapter, the Eighty-Eighth Texas Legislature debated the future of tenure at public universities and colleges. Originally, Senate Bill 18 ("SB-18") sought to fully eliminate tenure; however, thanks to coalitional action from across the state, the final law preserved tenure under new procedures and limitations. We recognize that while our status, now, remains "pre-tenure," that system—which often demands so much more than adequate labor—is literally up for debate. Therefore, we should un/learn long-established understandings of our positions and collectively operate under different logics of labor. To us, a coalitional model of administration has meant trusting each other in imagining potentialities that center the needs of the community over our own, individual understandings of our jobs.

When we began this chapter, we were colleagues sharing a department with frequent face-to-face access to each other to meet, share ideas, grab lunch, imagine *the work* differently. Now, as it happens, things have changed. Ashanka has been tenured and taken on an associate dean position, Kelin and the Writing Center are set to physically move into a new space in the university library, and Gavin has taken a position as director of composition at a different (but nearby) university. These changes create challenges in the coalition, as we described it, but coalition is never easy nor is it static. *The work* doesn't change because our job titles and office locations have. We still rely on each other and, importantly, remind each other that un/learning is part of *the work* and adequacy can (perhaps should) be the goal as we *hustle* in our jobs.

> KELIN, ASHANKA, AND GAVIN (IN UNISON): Being adequate requires earning trust in our colleagues to carefully research, transparently share, generously respond, and ultimately <u>choose coalition</u> over institution(s). These are the conditions that make possible *the work*.

References

Abbas, Nasreen, Jameta Nicole Barlow, Wade Fletch, et al. 2023. "Dialogue and Coalition Building in a Multidisciplinary Writing Program." *Peitho* 25 (4): 134–161.

brown, adrienne maree. 2017. *Emergent Strategy: Shaping Change, Changing Worlds*. Chico, CA: AK Press.

Casanave, Christine Pearson. 2002. *Writing Games: Multicultural Case Studies of Academic Literacy Practices in Higher Education*. New York: Routledge.

Chávez, Karma R. 2023. "The Risks and Possibilities of Academic Feminist Coalition Building." *Peitho* 25 (4): 14–18.

Clinnin, Kaitlin M. 2023. "Practicing Equitable and Sustainable Trauma-Informed Writing Program Administration Through Disability Justice." *WPA: Writing Program Administration* 47 (1): 117–132.

Conference on College Composition and Communication (CCCC). 2016. *CCCC Statement of Best Practices in Faculty Hiring for Tenure-Track and Non-Tenure-Track Positions* in *Rhetoric and Composition / Writing Studies*, https://cccc.ncte.org/cccc/resources/positions/faculty-hiring.

Connor, Megan, and Mackenzie Clinger. 2023. "Beyond Numbers: Interrogating the Equity and Inclusivity of Writing Center Recruiting, Hiring, and Training Practices." *Peer Review* 7 (1). https://thepeerreview-iwca.org/issues/issue-7-1-featured-issue-reinvestigate-the-commonplaces-in-writing-centers/beyond-numbers-interrogating-the-equity-and-inclusivity-of-writing-center-recruiting-hiring-and-training-practices/.

Council of Writing Program Administrators (CWPA). 2019. "Evaluating the Intellectual Work of Writing Administration." August 27, 2023, https://wpacouncil.org/aws/CWPA/pt/sd/news_article/242849/_PARENT/layout_details/false.

Dew, Debra Frank, and Alice Horning, eds. 2007. *Untenured Faculty as Writing Program Administrators: Institutional Practices and Politics*. West Lafayette, IN: Parlor Press.

Fitzsimmons, Brynn, and Pritha Prasad. 2023. "Coalitional Refusals: Transformative Justice Beyond Repair." *Peitho* 25 (4): 58–77.

Green, Neisha-Anne. 2018. "Moving Beyond Alright: And the Emotional Toll of This, My Life Matters Too, in the Writing Center Work." *Writing Center Journal* 37 (1): 15–34.

Johnson, Gavin P. 2023. "On Being Accountable: A Queer-Feminist Pedagogies Praxis of Refusal in but Not of the Necropolitical University." Paper presented at the Feminisms and Rhetorics Conference, Spelman College, Atlanta, GA, October 3. In *The Routledge Handbook of Contemporary Feminist Rhetorics*, edited by Jacqueline Rhodes and Suban Nur Cooley, 361–370. New York: Routledge.

Kynard, Carmen. 2020. "'All I Need Is One Mic': A Black Feminist Community Meditation on the Work, the Job, and the Hustle (& Why So Many of Yall Confuse This Stuff)." *Community Literacy Journal* 14 (2): 5–24.

Lamos, Steve. 2016. "Toward Job Security for Teaching-Track Composition Faculty: Recognizing and Rewarding Affective-Labor-in-Space." *College English* 78 (4): 362–386.

Miller-Cochran, Susan. 2018. "Innovation Through Intentional Administration: Or, How to Lead a Writing Program Without Losing Your Soul." *WPA: Writing Program Administration* 42 (1): 107–122.

Moten, Fred, and Stefano Harney. 2004. "The University and the Undercommons: Seven Theses." *Social Text* 22 (2): 101–115.

Patriot Act. 2019. Vol. 5, episode 7, "How America Is Causing Global Obesity." Directed by Richard A. Preuss. Aired December 22, 2019, on Netflix.

"S.B. 17." 2024. Texas Legislature Online. Accessed November 25. https://capitol.texas.gov/tlodocs/88R/billtext/pdf/SB00171.pdf.

"S.B. 18." 2023. Texas Legislature Online. Accessed September 1. https://capitol.texas.gov/BillLookup/Text.aspx?LegSess=88R&Bill=SB18.

Schell, Eileen E. 1998. "Who's the Boss? The Possibilities and Pitfalls of Collaborative Administration for Untenured WPAs." *WPA: Writing Program Administration* 21 (2–3): 65–80.

Strickland, Donna. 2011. *The Managerial Unconscious in the History of Composition Studies*. Carbondale: Southern Illinois University Press.

5
Embodying (In)Adequacy

"Good Enough" as a Blow Against the Meritocratic Regime

CHRISTINA V. CEDILLO, VYSHALI MANIVANNAN,
ADA HUBRIG, AND BERNICE OLIVAS

COVID-19 highlighted harmful working conditions fostered by unchecked capitalism. People have lost loved ones, homes, health, and lives. Workers have had to fill in gaps created by missing staff (Jacobs 2021; Semuels 2023). Social media users have advocated for "quiet quitting," downgrading one's commitment to the job to work only regular hours, and refuse to take on additional labor for free (Morrison-Beedy 2022), while others suggest calling it "calibrated contributing" to make it clear that "a person isn't lazy, selfish, or a 'quitter' just because they've concluded that something needs to change" (Detert 2023, 1–2). Yet CEOs and pundits like *Shark Tank*'s Kevin O'Leary and Arianna Huffington have attempted to frame doing only what one is paid to do negatively, saying it justifies laziness and that workers should always strive to go above and beyond (Dill and Yang 2022; Malinsky 2022). Real estate mogul Tim Gurner went so far as to say higher rates of unemployment would adjust workers' "arrogance" (Turnbull and Sherman 2023). Their words do little to assuage the concerns of people feeling overworked and stressed and hoping for change. That said, while COVID-19 underscored these dismal conditions, it did not cause them or lead to the "mass exit" known as the Great Resignation. Research by the US Bureau of Labor Statistics shows the pandemic merely aggravated long-term

https://doi.org/10.7330/9781646428052.c005

trends already established by worker dissatisfaction and other issues (Fuller and Kerr 2022).

Writing collectively as a group of disabled academics, we contend these same conditions are reflected within the academy. The pandemic exposed academia's already harmful underpinnings. As in other workplaces, we have seen how institutions of higher learning long denied disabled faculty and students much needed accommodations only to suddenly make those available once COVID necessitated them for everyone (Al-Heeti 2020). Yet now, as people still lose loved ones, deal with long COVID, and face resurgences in infection, employers pursue their calls for a return to "normal," eliminating those same accommodations. This demand occurs, though research shows that by taking this action schools run the risk of violating ADA standards, "[reduce] their talent pool by 15% and [harm] their ability to recruit and retain diverse candidates" (Tsipursky 2023). In other words, the normal they call us back to are working conditions that were unhealthy and untenable to begin with.

We know institutions' adherence to "business as usual" comes at the expense of their employees' physical and mental well-being, even their—our—lives. Policies rely on "the proliferation of contingent positions, austerity budgeting, attacks on shared governance, and precarity grounded in bigotry and neoliberal market logic" (Kahn and Pason 2021, 110). Institutions increasingly rely on adjunct labor even as they deny adjuncts fair pay, job security, and healthcare (Kuimelis and Flannery 2023). The problem of limited mobility compounds these harms. Academics rarely have the privilege of quitting when subjected to toxic environments unless turning to employment outside the academy, though there's no guarantee conditions will improve beyond academia (Cautaerts 2023). The supposedly lucky few who can relocate must still contend with many of the same problems in other positions, given the pervasive nature of unjust conditions. We authors often ask ourselves what can we do to counter this harmful regime. We stress the option of walking away or not showing up is not always feasible to so many of us, not when we are only one paycheck away from being without health insurance, a vital need no matter how bad the one we get through our school may be.

Many disabled academics must find ways to reclaim our time, labor, and energy to protect our health and sense of self. Taking up this collection's central question—how we can reframe adequacy as an agentive position—we write reflecting on how we have individually attempted to claim "good enough" as a means of survival in a system that positions us as sources of exploitable labor. Using counter/narratives, we each explain how we have sought to endure harmful conditions despite our institutional precarity, at times still finding ourselves struggling to prioritize our well-being against ingrained beliefs that tempt us to overwork. We close by gleaning insights from the similarities and differences found across our stories.

Why We Tell Stories

Opting for "good enough" allows us to make room for our own humanity, but making peace with this decision or figuring out what "good enough" means is not easy. On the one hand, we might imagine how to best make use of our institutions' time and resources. In *The Practice of Everyday Life*, volume 1, Michel De Certeau explains how unhappy workers might disguise their own work as that of their employers, allowing them to reinscribe their jobs as places where they can make art or participate in activities that bring joy (1988, 25–26). How might we remake our classrooms, schools, and other institutional spaces to support our dreams on the system's dime? On the other hand, undoing years of internalized programming proves difficult. We often don't know how to show ourselves care and consideration, even when we easily extend such kindness toward others. Marginalized people may find this challenging, especially when having to resist stereotype threat—the risk of corroborating negative impressions about one's marginalized status—which then compels more labor to prove one's worthiness (O'Brien et al. 2021).

Thus, the stories we share are messy and still "in progress," but we share them because we want to provide others with real-world examples of the complicated processes that we experience when attempting to determine our own sense of adequate. Perhaps our stories can help those ready to navigate their own process, especially other disabled faculty. Also, we know narratives can promote solidarity among people. Faculty may find themselves unable or unwilling to speak out about adequacy and identity, or they may not have mentors with whom they can freely discuss contending with issues in their everyday praxes. We hope these stories will help provide a form of "surrogate mentorship," or mentorship found in scholarly spaces beyond one's own program (Felber et al. 2021, 236). Furthermore, as cultural rhetoricians who use narrative in our work, we believe that "constellating stories" and "challeng[ing] master narratives" allow us to connect as real people to other real people in our field (Hidalgo et al. 2021). Stories are vital to changing harmful conditions. In academia we are encouraged to remain silent or backchannel. Instead, we declare our efforts to accept "good enough" as part of the invisible labor that usually goes unacknowledged in a system that proclaims itself meritocratic but quite literally hurts us.

Christina's Narrative

I finished graduate school and moved far away from my family and friends, working a 4/4 tenure-track job that paid shit while dealing with an unexpected divorce. At first, overworking allowed me to keep my mind off those things, or at least ignore how they aggravated my already severe depression and anxiety. I told myself I was just trying to reach a point where I felt secure. I didn't dare slack off, because of things going on at that school that highlighted the specific intersection of my identities as a disabled and racialized person.

At that institution, certain administrators demonstrated blatant favoritism toward instructors who were their friends, and, despite our being a Native-serving institution, said administrators often ignored or denigrated Native faculty who won awards or published groundbreaking work while rewarding settler scholars for minimal effort because they taught "traditional" topics courses. I also heard them and their friends (white faculty) say things like courses that focused on people of color or women only filled up (while theirs didn't) because they were less rigorous and students thought they meant easy A's. So I worked harder to ensure others could see that I was a consummate teacher-scholar whose classes were just as rigorous as theirs, if not more so. Because these were just some of the microaggressions that I experienced there that pushed me to overwork, I was always worried about getting tenure.

Eventually, I worked myself sick. I ignored an ongoing medical condition, telling myself I'd see a doctor this day, then that day, so that I wouldn't miss a class or lose out on writing time or interrupt my constant grading. Meanwhile, my condition was exacerbated by not eating or sleeping due to stress. Finally, it got so unbearable that I decided to go to the ER... but only after I finished out the work week. I went to class and had one more the next day, but during class, my students kept interrupting our discussion to say I looked *bad*. And they were right. By the time I got home, I knew it was time to go. Later on, the attending doctor said had I waited that extra day, it would have been too late. I wouldn't have even made it to the ER.

Because I hadn't informed our department's administrative assistant upon being admitted, my boss scolded me for my lack of professionalism. When I told him why I hadn't reached out immediately, he offered some cursory well wishes before reiterating his point that I still needed to let the department know if I was going to be out. I wish I'd had the courage then to tell him that yes, while I'd been laid out on the ER examination table, writhing in agony, I should have asked for a phone so I could call in. Seething with rage while having to look him in the eye and pretend like everything was okay, I realized that I could work myself to death, literally, and he wouldn't give a damn.

If you died, they'd just replace you tomorrow, you know.

Your students care.

Yes, but what lesson are you teaching them if you model an utter lack of self-concern?

I'm just worried that they already see too many of their other instructors slack off. They've said as much.

It doesn't have to be a zero-sum game—working smarter, not harder?

What does that even mean?

Some students have said I'm their only POC professor and the only one who has openly admitted that they have disabilities. If I don't do well, they might wind up with no POC or disabled faculty at all.

I just don't want anyone thinking I'm unqualified, because they're already thinking "diversity hire."

People like me don't get any breaks at all. Instead, we get run into the ground.

I have a confession to make. Years later and an institution away from that place, I still find myself grappling with the issues of adequacy and inadequacy. Of feeling inadequate and trying to find when my work is adequate enough so I can let things go. Even though I know that there was a time that I almost died. No, that I almost let my dedication to overwork kill me. I'll find myself interrupting my thinking as I'm in the midst of striking bargains with myself where I say that I'll rest as long as I do X, Y, Z first. And then I'll say, *No, you go to bed right now because all you've done is good enough and you're a human being. And if shit falls apart because you didn't do this one thing, then maybe it deserves to fall apart because you sure as hell aren't getting paid as if your work is that important that it holds everything together.*

Suffice to say that deciding to focus on *good enough* isn't easy. There are some serious layers of guilt to unpack, guilt that's not even mine but got dumped on me over years and years of training and teaching. For example, I often remember how, in what was basically our "Welcome to grad school!" seminar, our professor had us read a book containing "advice" like don't sleep more than four hours a night if you expect to be competitive because that's valuable reading time you're losing out on. Rarely do we hear, "It's okay to take care of yourself," instead only ever hearing, "If you can't hack it, you should think about leaving." I just needed someone to say, "Yes, that's good enough. Just go and enjoy your day" so that I knew I could do that.

Every person needs to decide what "good enough" means for them. All I know is I try to center my own bodily needs. And I ask myself what I'd rather be doing, because then my work will just have to be good enough so I can move on to things that make me happy.

Vyshali's Narrative

போதும்—*enough*, which I've contextually conflated with *stop* since childhood—became my lodestar out of necessity when I became disabled in my MFA program in 2006. I was untreated until 2007, when I was finally diagnosed with fibromyalgia (FMS), a chronic pain disorder, and myalgic encephalomyelitis/chronic fatigue syndrome (ME/CFS), a chronic fatigue disorder. I was supposed to be attending my classes, writing my novel, teaching a class, participating in mentoring sessions for new Rhet/Comp instructors, preparing for the job market. Instead, I spent my days lying very still—an instinctive, futile ritual against changing the location or intensity of my pain—resisting hypersomnia or sleeping for up to twenty hours a day, conserving my capacities for crucial, painful, exhausting activities: eating, excreting, essential housework, (paradoxically) resting.

In spring 2007, my department chair informed me that I'd jeopardized my teaching fellowship by missing peer mentoring sessions, a contractual obligation. My mentoring group rarely used the whole allotted time, and of the five of us (four white people and me), I was still the overachiever, complying with academia's expectation that women of color engage in more intellectual and emotional labor (García Peña 2022; Zambrana 2018). My employment contracts are all predicated on an ideal employee: a professor "unencumbered" by physical, emotional, and cognitive needs, with limitless potential to extract and optimize. At twenty-three, newly encumbered, I went from being a respected model minority student/colleague to being subjected to humiliating practices designed to domesticate or eject my unruly bodymind (Campbell 2020).

No matter how much I achieved, academia would perceive and humiliate me for being a *failed* body in higher education—for *not* being enough. I'm constructed as expendable, someone who needs to constantly prove herself through overwork to compensate for her nonnormative needs (Campbell 2020). There's a great deal of Rhet/Comp scholarship about multiply marginalized scholars' precarity and labor, but in reality I'm often framed as lazy or *not doing enough*, denied accommodations, or harmfully treated like I have the capacities of a nondisabled bodymind—ironically, even in work on adequacy.

To echo Audre Lorde (1997), I don't want to theorize. To illustrate my experiences of (in)adequacy in Rhet/Comp as a multiply marginalized scholar—from an obscure country known in America more for tourism than genocide—I offer the following examples.

- When I recounted my medical situation to my Rhet/Comp department chair in 2007, I was told *in-person attendance is mandatory*. There were no workarounds. This was my first professional disclosure (Adler-Kassner et al. 2019).
- Many editors, colleagues, and peers tell me I could do more.
- I'm told by a white man rhetorician at a conference that I write extremely well, but academic audiences are more receptive to traditional scholarship. I clarify that for reasons of culture and anomalous embodiment, I adapt more easily to nonlinear, fragmented, cripqueered forms of writing. He counters that the scholarly product is more important than my need to minimize friction in the composition process. How can I be a writing studies scholar if I can't normatively write? I don't experience this question as theoretical (Chen 2023).
- Between the 2019 Easter bombings and the tenth anniversary of the Mullivaikkal massacre, a white man rhetorician says he wants me to feel emotionally supported, knowing that FMS and ME/CFS limit my energy. He asks how I am and proceeds to unburden himself: He recently discovered his ancestry, and it has left him feeling people- and state-less. I validate his feelings but tell him it's draining and painful for me to hear right now. He apologizes and continues, tacitly forcing me to counsel him. This tracks with the expectation that as a disabled woman of color, I'm expected to perform pedagogical and emotional labor for my colleagues (Gaeta 2019). I never talk to him again.
- I'm invited to contribute a narrative to this chapter amid successive health crises and cultural traumas that I hadn't planned to professionally disclose: the fortieth anniversary of Black July, increased medical expenses, imaging scans, insurance problems, medication precarity. I'm spending ten to twenty hours a week on administrative healthcare tasks alone. I'm so sick I'm approaching aphasia. My therapist says, *You have to tell yourself that whatever you accomplish is enough. It has to be. It's the*

only way through. I agree to write this piece under the impression that something shamefully rough (not well researched, not coherent) enacting my anomalous capacity would be adequate. When first-round comments are returned, the edits are vague, concerning a lack of coherence, relevance, and citation. It's more substantial than I can accommodate, but the work must be accommodated, not me.

For multiply marginalized scholars like me, (in)adequacy is a systemic problem. We might trace the problem to the internalized values academia reproduces in its subjects: ableism and racism, writing output as the metric of productivity, "always-on" work as a sign of dedication and loyalty (Campbell 2020; García Peña 2022). Overwork has made me permanently sicker. Overworking myself was—and still is—a hard habit to kick. Mostly, even when I'm dissatisfied, I produce work that's adequate to the task. Mostly, I've learned to recognize my internalized biases toward overwork, forgive myself, and do less. Sometimes, even when my bodymind shouts போதும்! at me, reminding me that I'll pay the price if I go too long, do too much, I can't comfortably refuse. I need the CV line, the money, the health insurance, the minimal contact hours to survive, even if I also know that all this exertion ends with my disappearance from public life.

Ultimately, I chose to overhaul this narrative (rather than withdraw it)—even though it hurts my body and inflames my brain—because I can't shake the radioactive dread that this refusal might be the one that "proves" my inadequacy and costs me everything I've killed myself to get. In the end, something interesting emerges: Both drafts constitute versions of adequacy. The first, produced in conditions of impossibility, is dismembered and teratogenic. The second more clearly performs academic competence, signaling direction, symmetry, coherence, and responsiveness to reviewer feedback. The first is போதும் (enough, stop): composing with my bodymind. The second is *good enough for my field*: composing against my bodymind, because my life is suddenly on the line.

For all its posturing about anti-ableism and equity, academia doesn't understand போதும் in any language. It receives *enough*, *good enough*, and *adequacy* as synonymous with mediocrity. I feel more satisfied (i.e., safer) with this second draft, but the first one more incisively enacted my point. Even in our calls for change, something needs to change.

Ada's Narrative

"Hey, can I pick your brain?"

"Got some resources I can use in my summer class? It starts tomorrow. Thx"

"I scheduled an assessment meeting..."

My phone vibrates, its pale light illuminating the sterile hospital room around me as each of these asks pour in. I do my best to ignore it, for a bit—I don't want to turn my phone off, and my partner and family cannot be here with me, but they do frequently call to check in. But these messages, emails, phone calls—some from people who know my current situation, others who don't—keep coming.

"No rest for the wicked, huh?" the kindly phlebotomist says, as she fills a third vial with my blood.

I nod and say, "Something like that," as my phone buzzes again.

"You must have been especially wicked," the phlebotomist smiles, finishing up by affixing her cotton ball and Band-Aid.

I'm recovering from another surgery. The dozenth abdominal surgery in half as many years—they should just install a zipper at this point.

As I try to heal from the latest surgery, my body feels each ask; they weigh on me even now, sitting alone in the dark. It's June, and I'm not contracted to be working at all. I especially feel the requests from those who are in precarious positions—my colleagues who are adjuncts, graduate students, or other liminal positions; my colleagues who are multiply marginalized and woefully unsupported; my disabled friends who give so much of themselves for so little reward. I don't care so much about the institutional asks I have to ignore, but the asks from my community weigh on me. I worry about those in my care networks, those people I love.

Within disability communities, there are many discussions of "internalized ableism," the ways in which living within an oppressive, ableist society has shaped our subconscious, how we often don't treat ourselves with the patience and care we deserve, how we can engage in lateral ableism or be ableist to ourselves without even realizing it.

For me, feeling *constantly and consistently* like I am a burden, like I'm not enough, like I'm inadequate is wedged so deeply into my psyche that it's sometimes hard to understand where those feelings end and where Ada begins. I'm always fighting it—trying to tell myself I matter. That I don't have to spend every waking moment of every single day being helpful to others, that I am more than my productivity.

I find myself repeating all of this all the time: *Ada, you're not a burden.*

I'm going to be painfully honest with you: I don't always believe myself. I *know* better, in an intellectual sense. But deep in my gut, my intuition is at odds with what I consciously know to be true.

And I feel this push and pull, this compulsion to help everyone, all the time, to be self-sacrificing in ways that aren't sustainable past the short term. In ways that don't honor my own needs, let alone my *wants*—I don't even know that I am ready to process my *wants*, because for so long my *wants* have been reduced to radio static being drowned out by tuning into what others around me might need.

Those around me are not villains in this story. They don't know that their ask is the forty-seventh one that afternoon. Their ask is totally reasonable—and I am grateful to be in community with them. They should be encouraged to ask. This is on me, and not having learned to set better boundaries, something wrong in my brain that—

I'm going to shut down that line of self-talk, too. It's another version of internalized ableism creeping in. A belief that's been brewing my whole life that everything about my queer, neurodivergent, disabled, Mad bodymind is wrong.

There's an ecosystem of ableism at play here, a push and pull between my own thoughts (*repeat the mantra, Ada: you are not your thoughts. You are not your thoughts*), my community, and the institutions that shape our lives—the institutions that demand so much of us, that ask us to subsist on meager handouts and are happy to reel in as much of our care work and empathy and willingness to "do good."

But I still want to "do good." I want to support and care for my community, for my colleagues, for our students. I'm perhaps naive to think there are ways I can do that while limiting the degree to which that labor contributes to the harms done by the colonial, white, capitalist institutions where we labor. Maybe it's just not wanting the feelings of guilt associated with being complicit—that's something I'm always trying to examine, the propensity to exchange one form of guilt-driven, hollowed hull of unexamined faux-benevolence for another.

And how do my compulsions to *always be working*, to always be writing, to always be doing service shape the expectations *of those around me*? How are my choices unintentionally harming the very loved ones I want to help by contributing to unrealistic labor expectations?

I'm sorting these thoughts, these feelings—I have been since I started teaching more than a decade ago as an adjunct at a community college, and my understandings have only gotten more complicated as my positionalities have shifted, as I see a wider and broader swath of how the institutional product we call "education" is packaged.

I wish I could pause time for a moment. To have the luxury to sit with the sorting. To more fully reflect and examine my reasons, my motivations, my compulsions. To tease out the internalized ableism and ways my other positionalities as a white, educated, genderqueer, disabled person from a working-class, rural family maps onto how and why I do this work. To unpack every trauma and triumph, to be more content with myself.

Writing is the closest I've been able to come to pausing time, so in my journal or on my phone or following the blinking cursor on a computer screen, I give myself a few moments. I do my best to move forward, to do this sorting, even as I feel the weight of so many things left undone, of trying to resist the internalized ableism. Of hoping that, maybe if I say, "Ada, you're enough" the right number of times, maybe I'll start to believe it.

Maybe you'll believe it for yourself, too.

Bernice's Story

I just had a full-on anxiety attack. Like chest pain, can't breathe, muscles cramping so hard it looks like an alien is trying to burst out from under my ribs. Let me tell you how broken our "walk it off, show no weakness" culture has me. I put on my headphones, toss back two shots of whiskey, and do the dishes I've been putting off because I have no energy for them. I let the music and the booze turn the anxiety into rage. I work on a combination of service work and class planning in hyperfocus for hours. I shower, coffee, run to class, and teach. I do the writing center. I make small talk with my peers and, utterly unironically, nurture a friend who works too hard. "You gotta take care of you, first. You can't drain yourself like this." When I get home, I mom. Then I work some more. When I finally settle into bed, my whole body shakes and I dry heave all the nothing I ate today. Because all that rage? I set it, I set me, on fire and burned it for fuel. I've done it for years.

Because that's what people like me do.
This is an improvement.

Ten years ago, I would have cut it out with a razor blade or beat it out of my knuckles against a wall, or walked until my feet cracked and bled, and the pain drowned out the stress hormones flooding my system. Ten years ago, I would have turned that rage inward, on myself for not being good enough, for always being behind, for failing when my family's survival depended on my wins. I would burn, bleed, and break myself until I was strong enough—to finish that paper, do that work, fix that problem, plan that class. Ten years ago, I still believed it was possible to be strong enough. This is what it looks like when life is always a battle. This is what it looks like to claw your family out of the poverty created by generations of economic disparity. This is what it looks like to never stop fighting.

I'm not strong.
I'm dysfunctional.

Academia is like that—a space built on perceptions, not reality—a place where hands that shake with exhaustion are seen as a badge of honor for many of us. It's where there is always too much work, and good work is just a reason to be given more work. It's also flexible enough to let us do it during the hours we have—the caregivers, the chronically ill, the disabled, the neurodivergent, the marginalized, the multi-marginalized. That's one gift of academia: It lets us burn ourselves out on our own schedule, doing something we love—teaching, learning, researching. There are good reasons why so many of us are drawn to the warm light of learning and teaching. And there are many reasons so many of us sizzle and fry inside that institutional fire.

We belong here.
It wasn't built for us.

So how does it get better? How did I learn "good enough"? I don't know that I did. I know that I learned to be brutally honest—with myself, my administration, my peers. I learned a variety of rhetorical moves to show/tell/inform people what my life looks like. I learned to do it hard—why am I late to this meeting? Because my seven-year-old had a meltdown in Target, the alarm went off and hit him like a sledgehammer. It ended with me sitting in blood, snot, and tears, rocking him and reminding him to breathe. Did something happen in the last seven-and-a-half minutes that was more important than comforting my child? I learned to do it softly—I'm so sorry I can't take on this service project; I'm still grieving the loss of my husband. We were married twenty years, and then he died due to an unexpected complication caused by a routine procedure. I learned to do it matter of fact—I can't take on that extra labor because I am teaching an overload. See, I need the extra money more than the "opportunity" you're offering because I am the single breadwinner for a blended-up family of seven that includes three disabled folks and an infant. I learned to do it cool, never hot—No, I won't be at that meeting, event, conference because I live with a chronic illness that has been made worse by COVID-19, and I'm in too much pain to sit on the chairs for hours at that venue.

I was lazy today because I'm exhausted. I have no regrets.

I was unproductive this summer because I prioritized not committing suicide. I have no regrets.

These are the rhetorical moves I make with my truth. I do it because I need to be able to see that what I am doing is good enough. I also do it because the people around me need to see my truth. It's the only way I have found to break the perception, the expectation that we're all effortlessly doing the work of three to five people. We're not—none of us. Some of us are trying to do it, and it's breaking us. Some of us are privileged or protected enough that they don't do it—and if they can't see us, they will be part of what breaks us. So, I put it out there. I put myself out there, alongside my work. It's not easy. Sometimes it feels dirty; it feels manipulative; it feels like I'm asking for pity. I don't think there is an easy way to shift to "good enough," because working harder, work ethic, work culture is burned into our bones.

I jokingly call myself trauma girl.

It's not really a joke. I'm okay with that. I'm doing good enough.

The Ongoing, Open-Ended Process

As we read our stories together, significant connections emerged. The most salient and troubling issue evident in each of our narratives is academia's tendency to demand so much of us that we may give to the point of debility—or worse. In Christina's story, job pressures nearly had mortal consequences; in retrospect, this fact proves a secondary narrative element, reflecting the negligible importance their health crisis had for their administrator. Vyshali relates how she dealt with untreated fibromyalgia and chronic fatigue disorder on her own. When she managed to be *over*productive despite the excruciating pain, she was still told that her efforts were not enough, revealing academia cares less about productivity and more about bodily compliance. Ada's recovery became yet another context for putting out fires, even when people were aware of their hospitalization. Their story reveals that even when dealing with critical health issues, many of us find ourselves forced to examine how guilt-driven our praxes may be. And Bernice's story shows that academia leaves us no room to mourn, for ourselves or loved ones. Instead, we are encouraged to wear depletion as a brand, proof of belonging.

Also, we note that contending with "good enough" is something we grapple with and we probably will for a long time. Just focusing on "good enough" is difficult (Christina). Overworking is "a hard habit to kick" (Vyshali). Internalized ableism makes you feel like you're never enough (Ada). You never know if you've learned to do "good enough" (Bernice). Ultimately, our stories tell us "good enough" *must* be good enough because academia's values can literally crush people.

References

Adler-Kassner, Linda, Anicca Cox, M. Melissa Elston, et al. 2019. "Building a Twenty-First-Century Feminist Ethos: Three Dialogues for WPAs." *WPA: Writing Program Administration* 42 (2): 13–36.

Al-Heeti, Abrar. 2020. "COVID-19 Exposes Hypocrisy over Lack of Disability Accommodations." *CNET*. May 21. https://www.cnet.com/health/medical/the-covid-19-crisis-highlights-how-far-accessibility-still-has-to-go/.

Campbell, F. K. 2020. The Violence of Technicism: Ableism as Humiliation and Degrading Treatment. In *Ableism in Academia: Theorising Experiences of Disabilities and Chronic Illnesses in Higher Education*, edited by N. Brown and J. Leigh, 202–224. London: UCL Press.

Cautaerts, Niels. 2023. "Leaving Academia? Think Twice Before Going into Data or Software." *Medium*. June 2023. https://medium.com/the-modern-scientist/leaving-academia-think-twice-before-going-into-data-or-software-3d48e6ae43c4.

Chen, M. 2023. "Chronic Illness, Slowness, and the Time of Writing." In *Crip Authorship: Disability as Method*, edited by M. Mills and R. Sanchez, 33–37. New York University Press.

De Certeau, Michel. 1988. *The Practice of Everyday Life*. Vol. 1. Berkeley: University of California Press.

Detert, Jim. 2023. "Let's Call Quiet Quitting What It Often Is: Calibrated Contributing." *MIT Sloan Management Review* 64 (2): 1–3. https://sloanreview.mit.edu/article/lets-call-quiet-quitting-what-it-often-is-calibrated-contributing/.

Dill, Kathryn, and Angela Yang. 2022. "The Backlash Against Quiet Quitting Is Getting Loud." *Wall Street Journal*, August 25. https://www.wsj.com/articles/the-backlash-against-quiet-quitting-is-getting-loud-11661391232.

Felber, Sarah, Jeanine Williams, and Tracy Chung. 2021. "Counter Narratives of Mentorship and Community." In "Diversity Is Not Enough: Mentorship and Community-Building as Antiracist Praxis," edited by Ersula Ore, Kim Wieser, and Christina V. Cedillo. *Rhetoric Review* 40 (3): 234–241. https://doi.org/10.1080/07350198.2021.1935157.

Fuller, Joseph, and William Kerr. 2022. "The Great Resignation Didn't Start with the Pandemic." *Harvard Business Review*, March 23. https://hbr.org/2022/03/the-great-resignation-didnt-start-with-the-pandemic.

Gaeta, A. 2019. "Cripping Emotional Labor: A Field Guide." *Disability Visibility*. June 3. https://disabilityvisibilityproject.com/2019/06/03/cripping-emotional-labor-a-field-guide/.

García Peña, L. 2022. *Community as Rebellion: A Syllabus for Surviving Academia as a Woman of Color*. Chicago: Haymarket Books.

Hidalgo, Alexandra, Catheryn Jennings, Ana Milena Ribero, and Kimberly Wieser. 2021. "Constellating Stories and Counterstories: Cultural Rhetorics Scholarship Principles." *constellations: a cultural rhetorics publishing space*, no. 4 (May 11). https://constell8cr.com/conversations/cultural-rhetorics-scholarship/.

Jacobs, Andrew. 2021. "A Parallel Pandemic Hits Health Care Workers: Trauma and Exhaustion." *New York Times*, February 4. https://www.nytimes.com/2021/02/04/health/health-care-workers-burned-out-quitting.html.

Kahn, Seth, and Amy Pason. 2021. "What Do We Mean by Academic Labor (in Rhetorical Studies)?" *Rhetoric and Public Affairs* 24 (1–2): 109–128. https://doi.org/10.14321/rhetpublaffa.24.1-2.0109.

Kuimelis, Carolyn, and Mary Ellen Flannery. 2023. "Life as a Contingent Faculty Member." *NEA Today*, May 23. https://www.nea.org/nea-today/all-news-articles/life-contingent-faculty-member#:~:text=becoming%20more%20urgent.-,With%20low%20pay%20and%20little%20access%20to%20employer%2Dprovided%20benefits,like%20laptops%20and%20office%20space.

Lorde, Audre. 1997. "The Uses of Anger." *Women's Studies Quarterly* 25 (1/2): 278–285.

Malinsky, Gili. 2022. "Don't Try Quiet Quitting, Says Kevin O'Leary: It's 'a Really Bad Idea.'" *CNBC*. August 20. https://www.cnbc.com/2022/08/20/kevin-oleary-quiet-quitting-is-a-really-bad-idea.html.

Morrison-Beedy, Dianne. 2022. "Are We Addressing 'Quiet Quitting' in Faculty, Staff, and Students in Academic Settings?" *Building Healthy Academic Communities Journal* 6 (2): 7–8. https://doi.org/10.18061/bhac.v6i2.9309.

O'Brien, M., Cynthia Pengilly, and Brittney Poston (Sound Editor). 2021. "The Cultural Tax Refund: Reconsidering Invisible Labor and Cultural Taxation for Early-Career Researchers of Color." *Journal of Multimodal Rhetorics* 4 (2). http://journalofmultimodalrhetorics.com/4-2-issue-0-brien-and-pengilly.

Semuels, Alana. 2023. "No More Mr. Nice Boss: Flexible Employers Were a Pandemic Blip." *Time*. February 21. https://time.com/6256070/no-more-mr-nice-boss/.

Tsipursky, Gleb. 2023. "Disabled People Have Been Demanding Remote Work for Decades. Here's What Happened When the Pandemic Made it Possible." *Fortune*. January 23, 2023. https://fortune.com/well/2023/01/03/disabled-people-remote-work-jobs-pandemic-covid-careers-health-gleb-tsipursky/.

Turnbull, Tiffanie, and Natalie Sherman, 2023. "Tim Gurner Apologises over Call for More Unemployment to Fix Worker Attitudes." *BBC*. September 14, 2023. https://www.bbc.com/news/business-66803279.

Zambrana, R. 2018. *Toxic Ivory Towers: The Consequences of Work Stress on Underrepresented Minority Faculty*. New Brunswick: Rutgers University Press.

6

Temporarily Adequate

Learning to Be Enough at the Writing Center

LAUREN SILBER, MALAIKA FERNANDES, TENZIN JAMDOL,
AUDREY AUERBACH NELSON, XIRAN TAN, AND SHAOXUAN TIAN

In late spring 2023, we met in person for the first time since beginning this project two months earlier. We'd been independently building a bibliography, reading based on our interests, and responding to journaling prompts while considering our respective relationships with education, the institution of Wesleyan, and writing.

The meeting started with updates: It was finals week, and no one had gotten much done. As if all programmed the same, we each responded to our "I didn't do a lot" with a resounding "It's okay!" and "You're doing good."

After a go-around of sorries, the room fell silent.

"Honestly, I've mostly self-reconciled . . . accepting myself for as little and as much as I can accomplish." Shaoxuan said, breaking the silence. "What's more difficult is whether and how to bring about these options when my mentees panic about their papers; people sometimes directly ask 'do you think this is good enough?'"

Audrey agreed: "Yeah, I like the part of adequacy where I can tell *myself*, 'This is good enough; stop and go to bed.' But I'm insecure saying that to people in a session. Because—how do I know? I'm not going to bear the consequences, and I'm not grading their papers, either. And if I do say it, even if it's not true,

https://doi.org/10.7330/9781646428052.c006

then what *are* we doing at the writing center? How can we really be of help to people?" Audrey and Shaoxuan's confusion prompted more.

"As a First Generation Low-Income (FGLI) student, I really want to celebrate whatever works my mentees with similar backgrounds produced, but often feel uneasy as if oblivious to the class, race, and cultural inequalities that color their upbringing and life ongoing," Tenzin added. She had been writing substantially about her navigation of Wesleyan, having come from an underfunded public school. "I appreciate the writing center work for being so healing and supportive, but 'enough' does not land equally on different people."

"And English-as-second-language students as well," Xiran said, complicating the story. "I find both myself and my ESL mentees forever subject to language insecurity. Sometimes people were referred to the writing center by professors with very strict writing standards. Sometimes people want to assimilate into dominant language norms. What's a writing center staff's position in saying their works were good enough then?"

Malaika chimed in: "My mentee and I once joked saying when your professor says, 'it's okay,' it means the paper's not good enough; when the feedback says, 'awesome!' we're good."

Everyone laughed. Shaoxuan finally asked, "So if we can never be *really* good enough or just okay, what's the whole point of us writing for this adequacy project?"

From this eruption of questions, considerations, and confusions, we—a non-tenure-track writing center director and five undergraduate student staff at Wesleyan University's writing center—present a collaborative reflection on how we flounder to meet institutional expectations as writers, learners, and educators. We intend to show the power of mutual recognition and confirmation burgeoning from daily interactions, despite our positionalities' limitations. We ask: What does it mean to be (in)adequate employees at a liberal arts college and support "good enough academic work" at an undergraduate writing center? How might personal and structural factors complicate and inspire our efforts to affirm and challenge each other as colleagues and mentees/mentors? More broadly, how might we work within and against institutional constraints to produce meaningful change for communities?

We begin by grounding our argumentation in our personal backgrounds and our writing center's structural conditions, before introducing our methodological choices. Then we review scholarly discourses on writing center history, failure pedagogy, capitalist time, and code-meshing—all of which inform our thinking on (in)adequacy. Our theoretical investigation gradually disintegrates into a multivoiced mapping of writing center work at Wesleyan. We reserve the latter part of this chapter for autoethnographic narratives of real-life mentoring experiences that strategically navigate what it means to "be good enough." We don't believe in a cure-all; instead, we continue to hold complexities, self-question, and make more informed decisions together, recognizing that discomfort is part of our theorization.

Who, Where, and How

Our collective thinking around adequacy and writing center work is shaped by our different positionalities, relationships to English academic writing, and institutions of learning more generally.

Xiran is a rising senior and writing mentor from Guangdong, China. They grew up in a Cantonese household but were required to learn Mandarin in school—the "proper, common" Chinese—so they think a lot about standardized language and power structure and translanguaging.

A rising junior and second-year writing mentor, Tenzin clings to her privilege as an American-born-and-educated student that's made reading, writing, and speaking in English much easier for her than for her parents. With this, she struggles with whether to standardize, adjust, or unlearn her definition of adequacy, but as an FGLI student of color, she also questions whether the effort will really matter beyond this chapter.

A former writing mentor, workshop tutor, and thesis mentor, Shaoxuan attended Chinese public schools before Wesleyan. Picking up an interest in writing during college, she constantly struggles to home it. She's also the center's 2023–2024 hourly waged post-baccalaureate fellow assistant director.

Malaika was a writing mentor, thesis mentor, and workshop tutor for two years before graduation. She grew up around many languages and a regard for British English, having attended a US public school and then a predominantly English-speaking private international school in India.

Lauren is our faculty director. She is a non-tenure-track professor tired of the grind culture of excellence. She is also white, monolingual (English), and carries an American passport, which greatly shapes her relationship to and experiences with success.

Audrey works as an undergraduate workshop tutor and writing mentor. Until Wesleyan, she attended predominantly white and homogenous public schools, which reproduced narrow definitions of what it means to write. This year, she's tried to unwind these understandings and confront the origins of her own perfectionism.

Resonating with our collective desire to narrate the workshop's day-to-day life and theorize adequacy, we embraced the chaos of six people co-writing. Together, we've decided not to perfect our ideas for a singular argumentation but instead to purposefully cobble together vignettes, thought trinkets, and impactful scholarship. We consider this approach a reflection of values promoted by our writing center: Writing is a process and does not have to be done in isolation.

Peers at the Indiana University–Purdue University Indianapolis' University Writing Center inspired how we collaborate in their article "Listening Across," which features four experiences of the same conflict to make visible colonial ways of knowing and the institutional power's productive nature from within. Like them, we also "bounce up and against" colliding affects, thoughts, backgrounds, and experiences to conceptualize Wesleyan's writing center space (Brooks-Gillies et al. 2022).

You're invited to sit with this curation: What ideologies, experiences, and discourses shape your impressions of this jumpy choreograph of writing center staff at work? Where could these incongruent reflective articulations lead Wesleyan's writing center—and you?

Good Enough Writing, Good Enough Tutoring

While we try to affirm each other as always-already-adequate peers, the writing center is never an escape from extractive institutional expectations, as evidenced by our opening vignette. Indeed, our theorization of adequacy revolves around the intersectional dilemmas that we face as writing center workers.

WRITING COMPETENCY EDUCATION AT AMERICAN UNIVERSITIES

University writing centers have long been tied to concerns around adequacy. As Sharon Crowley details in *Composition in the University*, when writing instruction became a requirement for students entering American higher education institutions during the late nineteenth century, writing was used to measure "student *inadequacy*" (1998, 7; italics added). These writing curricula not only shifted the responsibility of success and failure onto individual students but also created an "internal boundary" to "stratify diverse" populations who were not considered "legitimate" university members, such as immigrants, people of color, working-class folks, and women (12).

Writing labs and clinics emerged alongside such ideologies and performance-based educational policies. As Hidy Basta and Alexandra Smith explain, American writing centers consolidated "a deficit model—one that locates the wrongness (i.e., deviation from the acceptable limits of standardized academic discourse) in either the student or their writing" (2022, 1). Today, more focus is placed on how writing centers can be transformative spaces recentering student agency and social change, usually through peer-to-peer interactions (Boquet 1999, 477). For many, the peer-tutor model was the best way to both challenge what Paulo Freire called the banking model of education and the power dynamics of teacher-student (1986). Particularly when extra- or co-curricular in nature, peer tutoring enables writing center workers to "wrest authority out of the hands of the institution and place it in the hands of the students" (466). Moreover, because writing is inherently tied to one's personal existence, writing centers have increasingly prioritized supporting writing true to students' identities.

It is undeniable that the field promotes student-centered learning, racial and linguistic justice, neurodivergent writing practices, and investigating decolonial and anticapitalist pedagogy. However, given the institutional context of writing centers, normative expectations are never far away. Liberatory approaches to writing center work are always complicated, as Laura Greenfield points out in *Radical Writing Center Praxis*, and no one feels tensions between radical and normative successes quite like the writing center worker. Though empowered by radical educational possibilities, peer staff are nevertheless employed by the university to "mend" writing inadequacy and thus erase the sociopolitical entanglement of academic success norms, which universities incessantly reproduce.

> AUDREY: I'm wondering about the agency involved in saying, "That's good enough." How the connotations change depending on who says it.
> Today I felt paralyzed because a tutee kept asking me, "Do you think . . . ? . . . this is right? . . . this is okay? . . . this is good?"
>
> MALAIKA: A tutee asks me to look at her English translation of a short story from another language. The words are beautiful, and the borrowed idioms make new meaning in English. But almost like punctuation, every few lines, she's added in parentheses in her draft, *does this make sense?* I don't know what to tell her. I don't understand everything she's written; sometimes, I don't understand my own writing. *Does this make sense?*

WESLEYAN'S WRITING CENTER AND (IN)ADEQUACY

Though Wesleyan's writing center shares the historically common dilemmas of American writing centers, it also has some particularities that shape our relationship with adequacy as writing center workers. Wesleyan's open curriculum is one such characteristic. Without required general education requirements, Wesleyan expects students to craft their own educational trajectories by dabbling in different disciplines and acquiring key academic skills—writing included—to achieve what Wesleyan's president, Michael Roth, calls a "liberal education" (2014).

Yet Wesleyan's curriculum is unusually configured to teach writing. Though writing-intensive "first-year seminars" are designed to prepare first-year students for Wesleyan's academic expectations, these courses are not mandatory and do not share learning objectives. Consequently, students more often learn "college writing" through osmosis in their majors, during office hours, and at the writing center. Without a writing program or writing courses, our writing center functions as a crucial co-curricular component of the school's educational mission and writing education. And undergraduate staff are keenly aware of the responsibility they have in teaching writing at Wesleyan. Sometimes, this responsibility is a burden.

As an elite, small liberal arts college, Wesleyan has a devoted alumni network regularly making financial contributions to university programs. Unlike most of our peer institutions, our writing center runs on one such donation restricted for paying undergraduate peer writing tutors and currently not contingent on assessments of the center's efficacy. Without funding pressures, tutors are able to rethink their writing center meetings' products in unique ways. A session's "product" may be confidence or a brief reprieve from stress as often as clearer sentences or an understanding of APA citation guidelines.

At present, with around thirty undergraduate student staff from various disciplines, we primarily offer "workshop tutoring" (forty-five-minute one-on-one, by-appointment tutoring sessions), "writing mentoring" (semester-long and weekly one-on-one quarter-credit tutorials), and smaller-scale initiatives, including class visits to introduce students to the writing center, in-class writing workshops, peer mentoring for thesis writers, writing retreats for thesis writers, co-writing sessions for interested students, multilingual writing specialist training for writing center staff, and various online resource repositories for different student groups.

Given our particular context—the writing center's co-curricular nature, temporary relief from constantly proving our value, our positions in an elite school—we regularly occupy and flow between various roles. We are teachers and students. We pay the university tuition and are paid by the institution. We reproduce academic genres for classes, and we push other students to challenge dominant language ideologies and hardened genres. While unable to escape from the capitalist drive to be productive and successful, we find that the conflictual, compelling expectations we shoulder while occupying intersectional institutional positions push us to challenge the perfectionist expectations from one role, as it intrudes our commitments to others. In one way or the other, we will always fail.

> XIRAN: To be adequate in the dominance/colonialism of "standard English" (and also to be different from the stereotype of international students who can't command "good" English) is part of the reason I insisted on majoring in English and working in the writing center. It's the wows people offer when they learn my major and position as a mentor that make me legible and legit in this institution. And I in turn reinforce it.
>
> LAUREN: It's not lost on me how many tissues I go through a semester. Nor how many times a writing tutor asks to meet, hoping to release the confusion, desperation, and burnout they've been holding behind their eyelids all semester, all year, all of their years long. Too often it's a senior who wants me to explain why their adherence to academic expectations of success feels disastrously anticlimactic in May. People graduate with jobs because of connections more than GPAs. There is no place on my CV to list these moments of disillusionment with the very institution that has validated their excellence. But there is a reason my office is always full and my tissue box always empty.
>
> SHAOXUAN: I realize I'd never seriously examined "adequacy" despite thinking around it since May. The dictionary says it means a conditional quality of "being equal." If an institutional writing pedagogy isn't intended to make works and writers "equal" (and thus equally sufficient) and we as workers/mentors can never transcend the sociopolitical conditions of inequality, how can we unconditionally affirm each other's legitimate membership, claim moments of "good enough" for ourselves and each other without indulging in just-feeling-good-about-ourselves?

We propose "good-enoughness" or "adequacy" as an alternative to success in higher education. Here, we work alongside Jack Halberstam, who, in *The Queer Art of Failure*, insists that failure allows us to "think about ways of being and knowing that stand outside of conventional understandings of success" precisely because success is constructed to uphold our cis-heteropatriarchal, white-supremacist, "capitalist society" (2011, 2). For Halberstam, failure (success's presumed opposite) might lead us towards liberation, or at least counterhegemonic, anticapitalist, and nonnormative ways of being in the world.

Situating failure in the context of doctoral students, James Burford suggests that *"not writing may be an investment in an alternative strategy"* for writing—to "estrange ourselves from normative routes of thinking... which would ordinarily cast... not writing as a problem of pedagogy, ability, or attitude" (2017, 482; emphasis added). Disillusioned with the toxic institutional promise of "success," we follow Halberstam and Burford to ask, *"How do you want to fail"* and *"what does that failure/nonproductive time do for you?"* In doing so, we affirm the invisible labor of decision making and celebrate writers and workers for trying their best in each scenario.

> LAUREN: I often want to tell people to stop. Let it go. It surprises my students. They feel relief. But mostly tension. If they don't push themselves beyond good enough, they know I might not give them an A. A's are, after all, reserved for above-average work. It's my job to "accurately" assess their writing given Wesleyan's academic English standards. But if their job as students is to listen to the boss—I mean the professor—then not following my directions (advice) is also a failure. What a terrible position I put them in.

Trying your best, however, is often not enough in the contact zone of university writing centers. If we cannot tell students to fail a paper or class, perhaps we can soften what it means to succeed or create space for "fail in your own way," helping students carve out space to temporarily be enough and rehearse constructing those "enoughness" for themselves beyond a mentoring session. As Allison Carr writes, "Failure causes notice," forcing us to think more deeply about how we got to where we are and where we're going (2013). Failure presents an opportunity for students to consider the systems that *make* them and their writing successful or inadequate, particularly by exposing, as Souradeep Roy and Senjuti Chakraborti note, "the contradictions in the classroom" (2020). A "good-enough" writing mentoring session illuminates the very unequal conditions at play in the university and centers the "how" and "why (not)" of being adequate for learners and workers *themselves*. A writing session spent making origami and eating Doritos to cope with stress is good enough; a session wherein the writer decides they need more sleep and leaves early is good enough; a session where the writing center worker left thinking they could have used a teaching tool is also good enough. We'll always be hosting "wrong" sessions, but each session is also adequate when we've tried our best as workers, learners, writers, educators.

> MALAIKA: Maybe telling a tutee "this is good enough" means: "This is the point where you make a choice about your priorities. What do you need right now? You could choose to set this draft aside, submit it, or spend the next several days rewriting. You could choose to move on to your next assignment. You could choose to get a good night's sleep. Or, go eat something, go hang out with your friends. Or, stick around and talk about split infinitives, if that's really what you need."

We cannot imagine a world of "enough" without also considering our identities, language ideologies and standards, and how time, labor, and power shape our daily lives (cf. Feigenbaum 2021; Sherwood 2021; Welch 1999; Williams 2021). Because the university functions within capitalism's ever-increasing demand for workers' labor-time, students shoulder the responsibility and anxiety of securing their futures in the precarious job market by spending additional time and labor on their classwork. Refusing to give more time while remaining in the system is declaring oneself to be enough—as a form of "resistance in place"—but it is also risking being left behind (Odell 2022, 2023). Time is not the only measurement of such resistance. Students can expend extensive time and labor to create "code-meshed" writing that authentically "blend[s] rhetorical styles of various ethnic and cultural groups in both formal *and* informal speech acts," while still failing to meet "the one set of rules that people be applyin to everybody's dialects" (Young 2010, 112, 114). These students' choice of language and style forges another space of good-enough-ness and risk. These are all choices that we affirm and celebrate even as we end with lingering confusion and feelings of insecurity as writing center workers. We also claim these uneasy affects as what feeds the vitality of our work and the possibilities for new forms of community and belonging to emerge.

> AUDREY: Adequacy, for us, lives between the fragile binary of failing and succeeding. It's a third, more challenging space we want to occupy: the option to know what the system wants, to maneuver our way through it, and to claim the choice to be enough.
>
> SHAOXUAN: We often talked about feeling uneasy/embarrassed/insecure when saying "enough/adequate" to others. I think we've every reason to feel so because that's how our work is conditioned. Those moments wherein we find each other "sufficient" as workers/mentors/writers are just as precarious as how this adequacy research disturbs us.

TENZIN: How revolutionary can permitting adequacy really be for FGLI/ POC? Is it so progressive that it's almost backward? Does it permit a mediocrity that traps already restricted groups? If I am not reminded every week and every time I face someone from the writing center that doing just okay can be forgivable, forget I'm writing this, would I have even given adequacy a second thought?

WRITINGS THAT BLUNDER AND STORIES THAT RUPTURE

Imagine the novel possibilities for thought and action that might come with a deferral of critical distance, in pursuit of a less guarded, even reckless contamination by circumstance. Imagine ways of writing that might put ourselves more deeply at risk than what we have tried till now. What could such experiments look like, and what, if anything, might they achieve?
—*Anand McLean and Stuart Pandian, Crumpled Paper Boat: Experiments in Ethnographic Writing* (2017, 3)

Conversation rather than mastery seems to offer one very concrete way of being in relation to another form of being and knowing without seeking to measure that life modality by the standards that are external to it . . . The desire to be taken seriously is precisely what compels people to follow the tried and true paths of knowledge production around which I would map a few detours.
—*Jack Halberstam, The Queer Art of Failure* (2011, 12)

Playing with expectations of success, we risk our academic labor on something that might fail to be taken seriously. We "recklessly contaminate" the urge for rigor, unwrapping ourselves for "visionary insights" and "flights of fancy" (Halberstam 2011, 7; McLean and Pandian 2017, 3). Turning to the practical, we seek to understand how we each deal with adequacy in session: where it crops up, where it nags at us, and how we pin it down. It is these unplanned moments wherein we survive, and it is by sharing these sparkles with each other that we cultivate supportive communities. In fact, this decision to bring unscalable,[1] daily mentoring interactions into scholarly publication is an embrace of failure and a choice to claim that we are always already enough.

LAUREN: There is something importantly ephemeral about writing center work. In forty-five minutes, two people sit together and try to understand one another. Inevitably time runs out—the appointment ends without a guarantee that writing will "improve" or "get better." What's guaranteed is that two people will try to connect with one another. Can we value these passing connective attempts just as much as we value

---
1. In *The Mushroom at the End of the World*, Anna Tsing explains how her ethnographic practice is not committed to scalability, a mainstay of scientific studies *and* racial capitalism (37). We, like Tsing, push against drives to produce scalable research in order to maintain "meaningful diversity . . . that might change things" (38).

better grades, metacognitive awareness, and more developed writing? Better yet—should we?

XIRAN: When my writing mentor suggested to revise an essay together, I almost felt insulted: A revisit is to declare what I did before wasn't good enough; it's to pour in unproductive labor for something already judged by the ultimate authority; it's to go against the current of linear time that is so scarce in college. But as I became a mentor, I wonder how we can imagine scarcity as abundance. Is it possible to carve out forty-five minutes in the forever forward-running race to breathe between lines that have been packed so tightly into tiny calendar boxes and evaluative criteria?

AUDREY: It's the last day before theses are due. Tomorrow the steps outside of Olin Library will be sticky with champagne. One of my fellow tutors sits across from me, a senior with a creative thesis underway. She tells me she stayed up way too late last night, rewriting parts of her novella until she couldn't tell what was better—the old stuff or the new. "I just need you to read it and tell me, 'It's fine,'" she says. So we go through the bookmarks one by one.

"This is fine," I say. "Are you sure?" she asks, and then answers herself, "Yes, no, I see now." She's smiling as she deletes the bookmark.

Then we come to a section that I stumble over. I carefully point out the question I had, the characterization that seems to be missing. And she says, "Yes, I see, what if I just—"

She pulls and tucks the writing in a new way. The sag in the paragraph yanks taut, and it's fine, now, and she says so before I do, beaming.

Then there's another lag, another piece that doesn't fit.

"This is a plot advancement paragraph and it reads like one. But what if—"

Buoyed by our previous teamwork, her quick rearrangement of words on the page, we play with the section for almost an entire session. Nothing clicks. I'm proposing, suggesting, asking questions—but she counters every point. The intricacies of her characters loop her deeper until we're both turning blindly, struggling to find a way out.

"You know," I say finally. "This is fine as it is."

She turns her face up toward me. I can picture her relief between us, picture it carrying her into tomorrow, picture it there even when she's on the steps of the library with a bottle of champagne. "Do you?"

"It's okay if the wheels of the plot show a little. You need to get them from point A to point B, and you get them there. That's fine. That's awesome."

She stares at her computer for a second more, then heaves a huge breath and looks back at me. "You're right," she says. "I'm going to leave it."

MALAIKA: It was around the time that I joined the Writing Workshop that I stopped writing. I don't know if the two events were related. Like many during the pandemic, I struggled with an increasing workload, a new in-person world after two years in isolation, the pressure of making up lost time, and the grief of losing a loved one.

But there was also the creeping shame that accompanied every workshop session, in which I hypocritically advised my tutees on *outlines* and *to-do lists*. Outside of mandatory in-person meetings, I was barely working. When I returned to my apartment, I'd spend my few private moments lying on unwashed sheets until my next commitment sucked me back into the world. Despite the burnout, I'd approach my tutoring with as much chirpiness as I could muster, saying brightly: *Have you tried making a to-do list?*

That semester, my mentee's grades started slipping. They stopped bringing writing into our weekly meetings, and then stopped attending them altogether; later, they informed me that they'd taken a leave of absence. I didn't tell them that I was also struggling to work, that I was considering a leave of absence. I was too caught up in the endless waves of passing deadlines and unfinished writing to recognize the pattern of overwork that had seized us both.

Two years later, I've completed my time at Wesleyan; I'll never have the chance to reach out to this mentee, or any other, to tell them that maybe I was wrong about the productivity tools. Maybe the answer wasn't always to do more. I can only remind myself that my ultimate goal isn't to be the most prolific writer or the best worker. When I'm struggling to write, sometimes I just shouldn't. I wish someone had told me that earlier.

XIRAN: There were moments when I was unable to respond to my mentees. One of them told me that he had been confident of his writing and hastily added, "Well, but you are an English major. You must know better than me." I stared at him, the first native-English-speaker, white-American mentee I had been paired with, and all of a sudden, I found myself unable to reject his comment, which I knew to be untrue. I had to cling onto this label to show I've mastered the master's language and am good enough to be here (in the mentor's chair, at this school, and in this country). So I chose silence.

I was again at a loss for words when my other mentee apologized for taking longer to translate the word that popped up in her head into English. I waved my hands, unable to express myself: How do I tell her this is also my everyday, dancing among languages without living in one, floating in the in-between spaces of words and meaning. So when we were choosing a particular verb, instead of saying anything definitive, we looked up customary English expressions together. Then, I was no longer an English major, writing mentor, or an international student. We were just two travelers going through forests of languages picking the fruits we vibed with—we felt their weight, color, and scent with our histories of reading and languaging. When she put the verb into the essay, it wasn't the jewel of the whole piece, but it fit just enough.

AUDREY: Is it radical to say, "Yes, this is good enough"? I'd like to think this only affirms what the student already knows. But I fear instead that my confirmation enforces previous power structures. If I say, "Good enough," doesn't that carry the same weight as, "*Not* good enough"? Either way, the student's peace of mind depends on *my* answer, *my* permission, *my* power.

Today I was lucky. Every time my tutee asked, "Is this okay?," he'd answer his own question. And maybe this was a window into a solid answer to my dilemma of permission and power. But so many other times I hem and haw, and my tutee looks at me with disappointment until I cave: "Yup, looks great to me!" It feels like an out, like letting them and myself off the hook. Certainly not like something radical.

SHAOXUAN: G had a stable pattern of saying sorry: every two sentences. The first time we met, she alerted me of her "unproficiency in English" as a second-generation immigrant, although she grew up speaking English while I arrived as an ESL student.

I used to apologize for unclear sentences/typos myself, but somehow listening to her repeated sorries as "mentor in the room" was simply utterly intolerable. In week three, I couldn't stand it anymore: "Hey can we make a rule: no sorry in this room?"

"... yes. AH YES!"

I heard myself continuing: "If you care so much about how undocumented Asian immigrant youth develop critical consciousness about injustice (her thesis topic), I think it's incoherent that you call your own writing 'terrible English' all the time. To confidently cultivate a multilingual writerly voice is a political action aligning with your thesis and career ambition..."

Sometimes there are words I can't imagine saying to myself but have only brimming eagerness to have my mentees hear.

I guess to some extent we both have, as her end-of-semester feedback suggests, "learned to become unapologetic about [our] process of writing."

We bumped into each other a few weeks after and simultaneously sorry-sorry-sorried right away and paused and both laughed.

Get Lost Too

We offer you our stories and thoughts not to better your own writing center. Like Elizabeth Boquet said in 1999, writing center workers might focus less on "what a Writing Center should ideally be" and more on how our work has a "tendency to go off-task," "to wander, circle, and return again" (478, 479). Arriving at this chapter's end without a singular conclusion, you may leave wondering: What *is* adequacy? How can adequacy shape the way I hire, train, and mentor writing center workers? How might adequacy inform in-session work?

Instead of seeking generalizable answers, we hope that you ask questions. That you try holding space for your workers to think through the complexities working as contingent teachers within a higher education institution that is constantly bettering itself, in an economy that profits off of our feelings of not being good enough or wanting a life of *more more more*.

For those seeking "something more concrete," a try-to-be-enough checklist:

- Co-write a chapter with undergraduate staff at the writing center you've been hired to run. Struggle to stay focused (it's summer after all). Continue to miss deadlines (as you regularly do). Be honest. Let your co-writers *see you*. Write when you can. Share what you did. Read what they write. Feel inspired and also like the least helpful, interesting, or insightful co-writer.
- Pay your staff no matter what. Resist the urge to quantify all work under rubrics derived from models that hold efficiency and efficacy as the markers of a job well done.
- Hire students who have failed assignments. Hire students with low GPAs. Hire students who struggle to find faculty recommenders. Better yet, stop asking for transcripts, writing samples, and faculty references and start asking: "What does good writing look like, where did you learn this, and do you agree?"
- Have your staff share why they almost didn't apply. Post those responses on your website and social media. Flier campus with your staff's doubts. Normalize being a writing tutor who doesn't know everything and is uncertain about their writing. Hire people who connect with this framework.

- Tell the student you're mentoring: "I don't know." Let them watch you Google whatever grammar rule they asked about. Let them watch you shrug. "I still don't know. Should we take our best guess?"
- Say good writing looks many different ways, but also say it's okay to want good grades. No one easily shifts from one motivational ideology to another—our pasts and the neural pathways they've created cannot simply be erased. Make room for the inevitable fact that they may initially behave with greater loyalty to systems they know.
- Remember: Give time, hold space, trust fully. Undergraduates can tell how they best learn if you let them. Trust students in overcoming their own conditionings—even if it takes longer than one semester. Also trust once they accept their limitations, what they eventually produce can be way more ambitious.
- Add to this list.

References

Basta, Hidy, and Alexandra Smith. 2022. "(Re)envisioning the Writing Center: Pragmatic Steps for Dismantling White Language Supremacy." *Praxis: A Writing Center Journal* 19(1).

Boquet, Elizabeth H. 1999. "'Our Little Secret': A History of Writing Centers, Pre- to Post-Open Admissions." *College Composition and Communication* 50(3): 463–482.

Brooks-Gillies, Marlee, Varshini Balaji, KC Chan-Brose, and Kelin Hull. 2022. "Listening Across: A Cultural Rhetorics Approach to Understanding Power Dynamics Within A University Writing Center." *Praxis: A Writing Center Journal* 19(1).

Burford, James. 2017. "Not Writing, and Giving 'Zero-F**ks' About It: Queer(y)ing Doctoral 'Failure.'" *Discourse* (Abingdon, England) 38(4): 473–484.

Carr, Allison. 2013. "In Support of Failure." *Forum—Conference on College Composition and Communication* 27 (Spring).

Crowley, Sharon. 1998. *Composition in the University: Historical and Polemical Essays.* Pittsburgh: University of Pittsburgh Press.

Feigenbaum, Paul. 2021. "Welcome to 'Failure Club': Supporting Intrinsic Motivation, Sort of, in College Writing." *Pedagogy: Critical Approaches to Teaching Literature, Language, Culture, and Composition* 21(3): 403–426.

Freire, Paulo. 1986. *Pedagogy of the Oppressed.* New York: Continuum.

Greenfield, Laura. 2019. *Radical Writing Center Praxis.* Logan: Utah State University Press.

Halberstam, Jack. 2011. *The Queer Art of Failure.* Durham, NC: Duke University Press.

Odell, Jenny. 2022. *How to Do Nothing: Resisting the Attention Economy.* Brooklyn, NY: Melville House.

Odell, Jenny. 2023. *Saving Time: Discovering a Life Beyond the Clock.* New York: Random House Publishing Group.

Pandian, Anand, and Stuart McLean. 2017. *Crumpled Paper Boat: Experiments in Ethnographic Writing*. Edited by Anand Pandian and Stuart (Stuart John) McLean. Durham, NC: Duke University Press.

Roth, Michael S. 2014. *Beyond the University: Why Liberal Education Matters*. New Haven, CT: Yale University Press.

Roy, Souradeep, and Senjuti Chakraborti. 2020. "Introduction: A Writing Pedagogy of Failure." *Sanglap: Journal of Literary and Cultural Inquiry* 7(1).

Sherwood, Steve. 2021. "Building Networks of Enterprise: Sustained Learning in the Writing Center." *Writing Center Journal* 39(1–2): 381–398.

Tsing, Anna Lowenhaupt. 2015. *The Mushroom at the End of the World: On the Possibility of Life in Capitalist Ruins*. Princeton, NJ: Princeton University Press.

Welch, Nancy. 1999. "Playing with Reality: Writing Centers After the Mirror Stage." *College Composition and Communication* 51(1): 51–69.

Williams, Amy D. 2021. "Welling Desire and Affective Rupture: Helping Students Become Hopeful Writers." *Forum—Conference on College Composition and Communication* 47 (Fall).

Young, Vershawn Ashanti. 2010. "Should Writers Use They Own English?" *Iowa Journal of Cultural Studies* 12(1): 110–117.

7
A Labor of Love

A Generational Conversation About Success, Living Well, and All That

JEN WINGARD AND RACHELLE A. C. JOPLIN

Meritocracy: The Big Myth of Academe

Although many of us teach our students that meritocracy is a myth that disguises privilege, those of us who are successful in the academy often forget to interrogate our own complicity in that myth. Rachelle and I are not strangers to the underlying belief that if you work hard enough, do the "right" things, and go above and beyond, you will be rewarded. There is something about the work ethic of the boomers, passed down to Generation X, and then retranslated to millennials here, but that is for a different article.

Instead, this chapter asks, What happens when someone does "all the right things" and ends up jobless? How do our expectations and implicit beliefs allow this narrative to fall into arguments of kairos, individual presentation, or failure of mentorship? What happens if we take seriously the conversations and embedded beliefs that propel a student through graduate school and guides how faculty mentor graduate students?

My faculty cohort has done a good job mentoring students who have varied goals after receiving their PhD in Rhetoric, Composition, and Pedagogy (RCP) from the University of Houston. In fact, our entire concentration has successfully placed students in a variety of full-time jobs. We have graduates who work in public and private high schools across Texas, work in two-year colleges across the US, and are tenure-track faculty running writing programs and writing centers in research-intensive universities across the country. For a relatively young PhD, the RCP faculty has mentored students well and have increased the placement rate for our graduate programs overall.

For me, it has been about following a student's lead, and discovering what they want to do once they have completed their degree. I have had success placing students in a variety of positions, so I do not adhere to the notion that an R1 or R2 job is the best. But instead, I attempt to help students get to where they want to go. And this chapter is about a student who wanted to "go big" and get a job in a research university. And I wanted to help Rachelle get there. After all, she had the training, the initiative, and the curiosity often needed, so I wasn't concerned about her goals.

Rachelle's specific desires centered on being the type of "academic rockstar" she had seen in her work thus far. She wanted to be the next Jan Swearingen, to have a legacy of loving and successful mentorship, to publish copious amounts of scholarship that was groundbreaking and cited for generations to come. In short, her goals were shaped by an understanding of the type of success she had already seen in the academy, one built upon an ethic of hard work with something to say. She trusted in the meritocracy, and wanted to pursue the traditionally scaffolded method of success.

Both Rachelle's and Jen's understanding about mentoring and student placement assumed a certain unspoken stability, predictability, and meritocracy to the job market and academic life in general. And even though Jen is a first-generation college student and professor, she allowed her own academic trajectory, especially in connection with Rachelle, who reminded her a lot of her graduate student self, to shape how she advised Rachelle about R1/R2 job placement in the academy without focusing on the very barriers present in the academy for students and faculty that she writes about in her scholarship.

Kelly Ritter just published an article in *Slate* (2023) addressing the challenges presented by the academy due to the linking of faculty mobility and success. She discussed how her academic trajectory had her move to several universities throughout her career, limiting her family in building community roots. This is not uncommon as faculty seek pay and prestige increases. And Jen is an anomaly remaining at her first university, getting promoted and tenured, and allowing her son to live in one place throughout his schooling.

The ability to succeed and grow a reputation in the academy without moving institutions is rare, as Ritter reminds us. But as Rachelle continued her work in graduate school, she began to want that type of permanence. In other words, she didn't want to allow the job market to dictate where she lived and for how long. And that was just one of the many conflicts she found surrounding the job market. How does one become successful without being mobile?

In addition to shifting ideas about job location and mobility, there are other questions Rachelle began asking that I think speak to the need for us all to reflect on our ideas of work, success, and job placement in the academy. And it is those of us mentoring graduate students, even those of us who do it well, who need to reflect on how we promote an adherence to (over?)work not only through our conversations but through our own actions. Some questions we hope to raise in this chapter:

- What does it mean to mentor students when they most likely won't ever hold a position like ours?
- How do we responsibly build PhD programs when the job market is still recovering from 2020 *and* there are fewer tenure-line jobs available?
- How do we help graduate students create meaningful lives when the larger push at the university is to do more, because that is what "good workers" do?

These are the questions that the authors have grappled with, Jen as a mentor and graduate studies director over the past several years, and Rachelle as a graduate student in a time of flux in the university. Neither of us really have solid answers, but a mentoring relationship that acknowledges this context and focuses on radical honesty has proved fruitful.

Love: Feminist Mentorship and Radical Honesty

Feminist Mentorship is something both Rachelle and I know well from our studies and working together as editorial staff of *Peitho*. Kathryn Gindlesparger and Holly Ryan's article "Feminist Fissures: Navigating Conflict in Mentoring Relationships" (2016) builds on the work of Michelle Bailiff, D. Diane Davis, and Roxanne Mountford's book *Women's Ways of Making It in Rhetoric and Composition*. Gindlesparger and Ryan discuss how moving from graduate students in a dissertation mentorship group to junior professor colleagues at two small liberal arts institutions created conflict because they did not understand that mentorship could move past the page.

Steph Ceraso and Pamela VanHaitsma continue the discussion in "'Making It' in the Academy Through Horizontal Mentorship" (2017). In their article, they demonstrate what Gindlesparger and Ryan work toward—a feminist mentoring relationship with scholars in the same rank and with roughly the same job type and life goals. Having regular meetings gave them the support of another scholar in a similar place in their career to help navigate situations that are often seen as invisible by those at different points in their career or with different identities (211–212), thus making their mentoring relationship extremely valuable as they began new careers.

Rachelle and I were very interested in the horizontal mentorship model. How might the work of Gindlesparger and Ryan or VanHaitsma and Ceraso be shifted to a vertical mentorship relationship? This is what Rachelle and I attempted during her time at University of Houston. We worked together not only as faculty mentor and student but also as editorial staff on *Peitho*. Because of the varied ways we interacted, we could adjust our mentoring relationship from a traditional vertical model to one that drew on the tenets of horizontal mentorship. By working to acknowledge that we were both humans, with limits, and not just feminist rockstars heeding a higher call, we were able to focus on a more holistic model of mentorship, not one based only on achievement.

We wanted to tell our stories from a place of radical honesty, something we both understand as vital to the movement of mentorship and how to be "adequate" in the academy. Jessica Restaino notes powerfully in her memoir *Surrender: Feminist Rhetoric and Ethics in Love and Illness* (2019) that we should be more open and willing to encounter and examine "data that moves us, that overwhelms us" (6)—and the experience of going through a graduate degree from 2017 to 2022 was certainly overwhelming.

Additionally, we take the call from Malea Powell et al. (2017) in their performance from *enculturation* to heart, heeding the need for stories to be told in ways that address all parties as participants and all elements as necessary. We wanted to "constellate" our experience, as mentor and mentee, and draw together both our cerebral knowledge—that of the institution, that of the field—and our emotional sensations—which included exhaustion, pressure, performance, and also never being "enough." Powell reminds us that "all meaning-making matters," so both our lived experiences in the moment, as well as our incisive hindsight, reverberate in this piece.

Part of what we want to draw out is that mentorship is not a perfect system. Approaching our past selves with understanding and empathy informed our framing of this chapter. We wanted to discuss our journey as an interaction between us and between who we actually were along the way. We take the call of empathy and accountability from works such as Aja Martinez's "counterstory";

there is a responsibility to utilize both our privilege and our lived experiences to invite critical response. We also take deep inspiration from Sara Ahmed's *Living a Feminist Life*, and the practice of the "feminist killjoy." (2010a). For Ahmed, being a feminist means that we must attend to the difficult questions that create conflict no matter how much discomfort and resistance we face. We must be willing to engage with the "ugly emotions" of ourselves and others. In this chapter, we draw on our willingness to be angry, to be hurt and feel hopeless, and to *take up space*. After all, there is healing in sharing the pain. There is opportunity in the failure and the adequacy of radical honesty through hindsight.

Practice: Sharing Our Lettered Selves

We wrote these not-quite-fictional letters to each other for this chapter as representations, simulacra, of who we were in those moments. We also wrote letters to the letters, alongside, telling each other and ourselves what we REALLY were, where the radical honesty needs to bleed through a bit more beyond the realism. Our mentorship was, is, beautiful and exceedingly helpful, loving—and we want to challenge the notion of holistic wellness and mentorship by exposing our broken bits and anger in these letters.

The two-column format is a way for us to reflect and demonstrate how even in the best moments of mentorship, the honesty needed to fully understand the opportunities available in our current economic moment was often obfuscated. Whether because of hope, cheerleading, or parroting conventional wisdom, the first column represents how sometimes what is said in kindness falls short. The second column is inflected with radical honesty. Yes, we grant that hindsight plays a part in it, but inasmuch as those letters are reflective, they are aspirational too. What would it have meant if we spoke the quiet part out loud? How different would Rachelle's and my own experience around graduate school and mentorship been?

But mostly what these letters show is that while working together, we found that the mentorship was able to sustain difficulties and disappointments. We were able to discuss these things with kindness and purpose, so that we could move forward with our relationship intact. Jen was very conscious of the weight a mentor's words have on a mentee, and Rachelle was beginning to understand what she needed from a mentor as the requirements on her became weightier.

For us, it is within failure that change and growth are most able to flourish, if that failure is recognized and honored. In their book *The Queer Art of Failure*, Jack Halberstam discusses how failure can provide opportunity not only to change your personal perspective, but to also reveal how institutions fail all the time. Halberstam is adamant that failure, in and of itself, is a freeing act. It's a rebellious act, it's a queer, artistic *opportunity* that can create fissures for making meaning. And is that not what rhetoric ultimately is?

The idea of failure as transformative has become important for framing this mentorship story and connecting it to the idea of adequacy. For so long, we have both subscribed to the idea that hard work leads to success. Although we may teach our students about the myth of meritocracy, that myth has saturated both our understanding of the academy and the opportunities therein. And by taking the time to really honor this particular failure, we hope to reframe that idea of hard work, fairness, and exhaustion as key features of academic success. Instead, we hope to begin a conversation wherein we can all find joy in being adequate.

BOX 7.1. THE LETTERS

Fall 2017, Year 1, Semester 1

THE PRESENT-PAST REALITY

Dr. Wingard,

I've never lived through a major natural disaster before, and I was a newly-wed, too. But I was singularly focused on being sure I was good at school. Then I could achieve success, which would make the rest of life fall into place. Predictable excellence.

I've been reading all these manuals for grad school and how to get a PhD, your Semenza and your Kelsky. It's funny, I always feel satisfied when I read these books and I'm already doing the things they say to do. "Have a 5- and 10-year plan," "go to conferences and network with people in your field," "submit for publication often and use your seminar papers as drafting opportunities." I feel like I'm *good* at grad school. It's the thing I've been trained to do for the first five years of my scholarly career.

Our meeting in late fall of 2017 is burned into my mind. You told me it would take hard work. That if I wanted that sexy, R1 tenure-track job, we had to start that preparation and groundwork *now*. Well, I get to network with people because of our journal. I'll be utilizing two of my courses this year to draft two publications I have in the pipeline. I have a graduation plan, a 10-year plan.

The thing is, I've always worked hard, and I've always gotten what I wanted, in the end. I don't see why that would change now that I'm finally at the place I always wanted to get—earning a PhD in "wordsmithing," as some of my nonacademic friends like to say.

I feel like I have all the answers. Now it's just a matter of getting through the semesters, in a neat row, doing the things on my plan, and getting to that finish line on time.

I'm excited.

With high spirits,
Rachelle

HINDSIGHT GRANTS RADICAL HONESTY

Jen,

School is the thing I know how to do. It is predictable, it is easy, it is knowable and manageable. I want, and need, to know the exact steps towards achieving the highest form of success accessible to me from this juncture.

I am willing to do anything you tell me to do in order to achieve this success, because my assumption is that once I actually get to the "end"—get a job—I will achieve full actualization as a person, and will feel the weight and satisfaction of meaning in my work.

I don't want to actually know how to become a holistic person. I just want to know how to be good at this thing so that I can check it off my life-list.

Fall 2017, Year 1, Semester 1

THE PRESENT-PAST REALITY

Hello Rachelle,

I am so pleased that you will be the editorial assistant of *Peitho*. *Peitho* has been a one-woman show since I became editor, and I have some big goals for the journal. Having someone work with the submission system, contact authors and reviewers, and keep track of essays in the pipeline will be a huge help to me.

Additionally, working with the journal can help you network within the field of feminist rhetoric and historiography. You will be able to contact like-minded graduate students, as well as senior faculty who are doing work that aligns with your interests. And it will allow you to hone your own writing skills through participation in the editing process. I have found that to become a good writer, you first and foremost must be a good reader. And this position will allow you to do just that.

On a personal note: My mentor Eileen Schell once told me how exciting it is to work with students who *get* your work. And meeting you allows me to see that firsthand. So thank you for choosing UH. I look forward to working with you.

Welcome, Dr. Wingard (aka Jen)

HINDSIGHT GRANTS RADICAL HONESTY

Rachelle,

I have a question, and it is one that might be a little presumptuous because we just met and began working together, but aren't you tired?

You have been in school almost all of your life, and you are seeking a profession that will keep you in school for years to come. Don't you want a break?

I like this job. But I also don't know if I would like it as much if I hadn't had a ton of other jobs before this one. Maybe I would, but I always worry about the students who push through to an end goal without taking a breath . . . a beat . . . to think about what this life really looks like.

But I have to take you at your word. You want this life, so I will help you get it to the best of my ability. I do know that the job market is changing, but I think we have some time before that shift comes.

So in the meantime I recommend you work your a$$ off. Graduate school will try to break you, but if you keep your goals in mind, you can make it through (relatively) unscathed. Just don't be afraid when you feel like your thinking, words, and life are out of control or breaking down.

I wish there was a more humane way to do all of this. I am trying to figure that out.

Yours in the struggle, Jen

Spring 2020, Year 3, Semester 2

THE PRESENT-PAST REALITY

Dear Dr. Wingard,

Everything happened so fast. You told me, lovingly and sternly, to rest. And then all of my disassociating, all of my micromanaging of my relationships, all of the toxicity in my loved ones, it all overflowed right as 2020 began.

And then, COVID.

I haven't been able to think about anything since comprehensive exams. Certainly not academically. I half-jokingly told you that, if nothing else, I'd probably start going to therapy when I was on the job market. As a preventative measure from the pressure.

Well, instead, I'm in therapy now. And it was reactionary.

My brain feels like it's on fire. All the time. I don't know where my body ends and begins. I can drag myself into a functional enough state to conduct my online class, to do *Peitho*, and that's about it. The things I'm getting paid to do. I feel . . . inadequate. I feel like I'm running out of time. But I also feel like time has, essentially, stopped. In the world. In my head.

Fuck, I have no idea what to write my dissertation about. I know what would be attractive for the market, but, I'm not sure I have a "there" there. You always taught me to find something that pissed me off enough, that interested me enough, to define me academically. And right now, all I know for sure is that I am tired, and anxious, and intentionally isolated.

Have you ever thought about video games and memory? I kinda can't stop thinking about it. Video games are the only thing sparking any kind of joy in me, lately. That and my students, who are so freaked out by this pandemic that being there for them is, oddly, a panacea for my desperation for control over anything in my life.

I miss you. I miss feeling like I knew what I was doing.

Exhaustedly,
Rachelle

HINDSIGHT GRANTS RADICAL HONESTY

Jen,

Honestly, I want to quit. I want to just stop doing this and do something that gives me meaning and makes me feel worthy of the praise I so desperately want.

I'm trying to do everything everyone tells me I should do, even the holistic things, but nothing seems to help or make me feel like I'm actually accomplishing something. Everything is hard and nothing gets "done."

I'm angry because this was supposed to be easy, and I want it to go back to being easy instead of having to do the hard work of reconciling my humanity with my success.

Spring 2020, Year 3, Semester 2

THE PRESENT-PAST REALITY

Oh Rachelle,

I feel this acutely. I have been working as graduate director during COVID, and although UH has been fortunate because our student population is primarily commuter, the shift to online learning exclusively has been a challenge for graduate students and undergraduates too. And the halt to research caused by the pivot in teaching mode, illness, and stress is being felt across the academy.

And then there's the overwhelming hate we hear each day from our government, president, and the media. It is exhausting to live in Texas, but the US is catching up with that exhaustion it seems. I don't mean to cheapen your personal struggles, but as you know, I do like to contextualize individual responses within global contexts. I just keep thinking we are in the darkest timeline.

I am glad that you are working toward making yourself feel whole again. I have to say that I may need to do the same at some point, but I have not taken that seriously enough for far too long. I am beginning to figure out that I am an overworker to manage my own anxiety. But I don't quite know how to be any other way. I look forward to hearing about your journey as it could teach me some things, I am sure!

As far as video games and memory, I have read around and my work has dabbled in memory studies, but I have to say, I am not a video gamer. Other than story/puzzle games I have done with my kiddo since they were little, I am not familiar with videogames. That's not to say that I wouldn't be willing to work with you if this is what you want to explore. Dissertations are a time for you to become the expert on something, and I am here to support and guide you. In other words, this is the chance for you to teach me about something important to you. I can help you shape it. It's a role reversal, and it is exactly where you should be right now.

I know you are tired, but you can do this. And I bet you can even do it in more healthy ways than you thought.

Sending you lots of love, and I miss you too!

Jen

HINDSIGHT GRANTS RADICAL HONESTY

Rachelle,

Remember when I asked you if you were tired?

Sorry, I shouldn't be snarky about this because what you are feeling is real. All the work you have done, the time you have invested, and the choices you have made seem like the easy road for someone who is "good at school." I know this narrative well because I am also "good at school."

I had a similar breakdown post exams. What I had been taught—how to research, how to write, how to think—wasn't translating to the work I needed to do for a dissertation. I remember crying at my first meeting with my directors. And as you probably know, I am not big on emotional displays.

But I felt like I couldn't do it. I didn't know how, and furthermore the work I needed to do seemed so intense that I wasn't sure I wanted to do it anymore. At that point, I too contemplated quitting.

I wish I could tell you that everything resolved itself easily after that moment, and I was able to find the magic set of skills to make the work of a sustained research writing project easy. But alas, I did not.

What I did find was that engaging with the "stuff" I was researching gave me focus and energy to complete the project. When I was working at the level of abstraction, it didn't work. But actually looking at material that represented reality helped.

I don't know how helpful this is for you right now. But I wanted to try to give you a way out of the mire. But even if it doesn't move you forward, it is okay.

I want to write that again:

It is okay—if you want to quit.

It is okay—if you need to prioritize your own sanity.

It is okay—if you need to rethink things.

It is okay.

The academy is really good at making those in it feel that what we are doing is all encompassing, all the time. But it is just a job. A really good job sometimes. An exhausting one at other times. So anytime you need to step back and reflect, recharge, retreat . . . **It is okay**.

And *you* will be okay.

Jen

Summer 2022, Post-Year 5, Graduation

THE PRESENT-PAST REALITY

Dear Jen,

Why is everything happening so damn slow? I understand that COVID has done a number on . . . well, everything, but I thought I would be a shoo-in for a job. I've applied for jobs that read like they were written *for me*. I've barely gotten any responses. The responses I've gotten, one of them literally told me I should be thankful they even contacted me.

I thought I was successful.

I finished my degree, on time. In fact, I did a run from BA to PhD in 10 flat years—I'm a doctor before I'm 30. I worked my ass off for 10. Years.

I wrote a dissertation that burned me out so thoroughly on something I loved, I had to generate an entirely new hyperfixation. I haven't played a video game for fun in months, because I can't remember what that feels like. The analysis and the fandom interactions and the memory, the memories, the memento mori . . . it's all this drama, it's all this exhaustion, and I don't want anything to do with it anymore.

I've been in therapy for two years . . . which has taught me that grad school pretty thoroughly fucked me up. It isn't the *only* thing that fucked me up, sure. But what is the definition of success but how warm the flames from the wreckage of your mental health burn as you walk across that felt-carpet stage?

Why don't I have a job, Jen? Did we not start early enough? Should I have known better, somehow, 2 years ago, 5 years ago, 8 years ago? Did I do something wrong?

Or is it just the fact that I want the same jobs as everyone else does right now? That everyone wants the jobs above the Mason-Dixon line, doing fancy, cutting-edge rhetoric and composition work, with governments that don't actively hate them. And somehow, someway, I am less qualified than them.

Because I'm young. Because I only have four publications, over a dozen conference presentations, multiple certifications and awards. I don't have "real-world" experience like some other people do. I'm burdened with the stopped watch of a pandemic, of brain-drain, of excellence that isn't excellent enough.

I worked hard. I did what you said. I did what everyone said. I was supposed to be a rockstar. Everyone is confused as to why I don't have a job. But they also won't give me one either. It's fascinating.

I don't think I want to do this anymore. Not that I know what I want, I'm 28 and I've never worked towards anything else. But I know I never want to feel this disappointment again.

I'm sorry if I failed you. I'll try to learn to forgive myself.

Hoping for the best,
Rachelle

HINDSIGHT GRANTS RADICAL HONESTY

Jen,
This is actually pretty honest. I'd be even more blunt that I want to quit. I want to take my ball and go home, because clearly if academia isn't going to appreciate my presence, then maybe they'll miss my absence—but they won't.

I'm angry because I worked my ass off and no one cared. It resulted in nothing, it feels. I couldn't cross the final thing off the to-do list in a neat, pretty way.

And now I have to actually confront the gnawing hole inside my chest that is the existential dread I've avoided for so long by staying in school.

I should not have ever trusted academia to define me or tell me what was important in life.

Summer 2022, Post-Year 5, Graduation

THE PRESENT-PAST REALITY

Rachelle,
First of all, you have not disappointed me at all.

I feel that I owe you an apology. Early on, I told you I was excited that you were coming to UH because I saw myself in you. It wasn't just your scholarly interests, but it was also your drive, your work ethic, your commitment to doing your best even in times of adversity. I know that way of being in the world, and instead of mentoring you to perhaps ease up on yourself, I leaned in and taught you how to be me.

Did I ever share with you the Joan Didion essay "Goodbye to All That"? In it she has a quote that I think will resonate with you: "That was the year, my twenty-eighth, when I was discovering that not all of the promises would be kept, that some things are in fact irrevocable and that it had counted after all, every evasion and every procrastination, every mistake, every word, all of it" (233).

When I was 28, I quit my job as a HS teacher, got married a second time, and moved 3,500 miles to the other side of the country to begin my PhD. There is something about 28 that is meaningful in all of our development. I think it is important to note the need for change and the reflection on disappointment is something that can be shared across generations.

If it's any consolation, I am proud of you. Not only because of the work you are doing and have done as a scholar but also the work you are doing to be a more whole person. That is the work that's most important.

Well done, Jen

HINDSIGHT GRANTS RADICAL HONESTY

Rachelle,

I am sorry. You don't need to be sorry. You did all the things, and here we are.

I still don't quite understand it myself. I know that the job market was shifting, and I know the COVID accelerated those changes. But what I never expected was that you would be here at the end of grad school with no job offer.

I am heartbroken too. Even though I am critical of the academy, there is a part of me that holds on to the idea that the academy is fair. (Wow, my white passing privilege is showing.)

But this isn't fair. And it is not how things are supposed to go. But there are lots of things happening in the academy right now where excellent work and research are falling flat.

The longer I do this, I find that my value is that I do the work, do it well, and rarely complain. It is when I begin to discuss things others don't want to consider that I am met with resistance. The academy doesn't want thoughtful workers, only pliable ones.

So perhaps you are ahead of the curve in realizing this about this career path. All the talk of academic freedom is important, but it really doesn't apply to the day-to-day. That work is suffering from the same changes as work across all sectors—mission creep, job acceleration, more responsibility for stagnant wages.

What a myth we have invested in—with our time, our labor, and our whole selves. Again, I am sorry I didn't warn you about this sooner. I am sorry that I was operating from the same misinformation you were.

But now we both see more clearly, and the question is what do we do now?

Love, Jen

Labor and Love: A Work In Progress

As the letters discuss, our mentoring relationship was marked by not only personal revelations but also global and local crises. Houston suffered significant weather events (Hurricane Harvey, winter freezes that downed the power grid) and an increasingly conservative political climate (legislation targeting women and the LGBTQ community). As Raj Mankad states: "Houston is a cheap place to live if you don't count the trauma tax" (2021). Both Rachelle and Jen felt this trauma and were living with the precarity that Houston and Texas provided daily.

And in the middle of all these macro-traumas, COVID happened. And universities shut down, downsized, and waited until they could return to some semblance of what worked before. We are not saying that COVID created the "new" normal of labor in the university. But we do think it "sped up" changes that were already coming. Just like the ubiquity of self-checkout lines and the timing screens at drive-thrus, labor requirements in the academy are being redefined through corporate terms such as "efficiencies," "redundancies," and "workflows." And now what is being framed as a "new normal"[1] has been a relationship between corporate monies and practice since the instantiation of public universities. It is just the methods and foci of corporate practice have changed. And thus, the university's understanding of its place in the school-to-work pipeline has changed too.

And this is where we found ourselves when Rachelle went out on the job market. She had done all the things. She had published, networked, taught at all levels, finished the dissertation on time, and graduated without a job offer. Which led to some soul searching for both of us. And it is there that failure created an opportunity.

This all begs the question: If Rachelle had gotten an R1 job, would we even be having this critical reflection? And the answer is, probably not. She would have been shuffled along the traditional academic success pipeline with no reason to question whether it was what she wanted, what was best for her, or what was right—or adequate—for the academy as a whole.

The meritocracy of academia is upheld by the success of those who benefit from it, and the lack of influence from those it harms. Rachelle's "failure" of the system allows us a unique opportunity to confront the realities of the meritocratic system in academia, one that many scholars of color, queer scholars,

---

1. The University of Houston set up a "New Normal Committee" to address returning to campus post-COVID shutdown.

and women/nonbinary/trans scholars have discussed copiously.[2] Academic meritocracy speaks to people who seek a sense of clear trajectory toward success, for whom the statement of "work hard, do the right things, and you'll get the job" is grounded and true.

How, then, can we adjust the conversation to combat this meritocracy? To inform our mentors and mentees from a scaffolding of adequacy rather than success and failure? We believe it begins with acknowledging the system at the outset: that academia is built, fundamentally, on a particular trajectory of success. Even as scores of people seek non-R1 jobs, it is the case that graduate school programs, conference experiences, and mentor relationships on every scale are built to accommodate for this traditional success goal subliminally via pushes for publications, conference participation, and certain opinions or networks to engage in or avoid. To change academic meritocracy, we must see it, first.

We also believe that we must incorporate ideals of feminist holistic care in our mentorship. Combating the academic meritocracy framework requires a deep self-knowledge: one that is informed by personal drive and desires rather than by "what it looks like to be successful." Mentors and mentees alike navigate this sticky situation:[3] Jen brought her many years of careful mentorship and acute knowledge of the potential for success, and Rachelle brought her uncritical lens of academic success and checkbox mentality, to the table. What would it look like for mentorship relationships to first address where the partners are in their ideas of success, of adequacy, and to then build a framework from that foundation?

Adequacy is a rebellion against the concept of a rigid definition of success, of what makes a meritocracy thrive. A definition offered with no space for ability, for stage of life, for holistic wellness and vibrancy. We have reflected on our definitions of excellence and success in these letters with kind eyes, with critical eyes, in the hopes that our honesty will encourage mentorship to be more radically loving. We desire a mentorship model that builds toward healthy, responsible mentors, creating opportunities for vibrant, healthy mentees, in the face of shifting and violent upheavals in the market. We hope by sharing

---

2. See Martinez in *Counterstory* (2020), Ahmed in *On Being Included* (2012), Malea Powell et al. in *enculturation* (2014), among many, many others.
3. I derive my understanding of "sticky" from Ahmed's discussion of stickiness and haps throughout her work, most notably in *The Promise of Happiness* (2010b). While this topic is beyond the scope of this chapter, it is imperative to note how the influence of desiring a meritocratic outcome from the job market created a particular "sticky affect" that bore out in this work itself.

our experiences with success and failure under a veil of meritocracy, we can interrogate the very structure that seemed to call for this critical reflection in the first place. We seek to address the marketplace by navigating it with an air of communal responsibility to ourselves and to each other, rather than to the jobs—which, let's be honest, are dwindling in quality and in number.

Adequacy is loving, and it is relational, and we're slowly starting to learn that it is enough. It is enough to quit. It is enough to "just finish." And it is more than enough to dismantle a meritocracy by loving through the mentorship process.

References

Ahmed, Sara. 2010a. "Feminist Killjoys (And Other Willful Subjects)." *Scholar and Feminist Online.* "Polyphonic Feminisms: Acting in Concert" 8 (3). http://sfonline.barnard.edu/polyphonic/print_ahmed.htm.

Ahmed, Sara. 2010b. *The Promise of Happiness.* Durham, NC: Duke University Press.

Ahmed, Sara. 2012. *On Being Included: Racism and Diversity in Institutional Life.* Durham, NC: Duke University Press.

Ahmed, Sara. 2017. *Living a Feminist Life.* Durham, NC: Duke University Press.

Didion, Joan. 1968. "Goodbye to All That." In *Slouching Toward Bethlehem,* by Joan Didion, 223–238. New York: Farrar, Straus, and Giroux.

Gindlesparger, Kathryn, and Holly Ryan. 2016. "Feminist Fissures: Navigating Conflict in Mentoring Relationships." *Peitho* 19, no. 1. https://cfshrc.org/wp-content/uploads/2017/01/19.1_Gindlesparger-and-Ryan_FINAL.pdf.

Halberstam, J. Jack. 2011. *The Queer Art of Failure.* Dunham, NC: Duke University Press.

Mankad, Raj. 2021. "Houston Is a Cheap Place to Live—If You Don't Count the Trauma Tax." *Houston Chronicle.* February 21. https://www.houstonchronicle.com/opinion/outlook/article/Essay-Houston-is-a-cheap-place-to-live-if-15966458.php.

Martinez, Aja. 2020. "Counterstory: The Rhetoric and Writing of Critical Race Theory." National Council for the Teaching of English Series in Rhetoric and Writing.

Powell, Malea, Daisy Levy, Riley-Mukavetz, et al. 2014. "Our Story Begins Here: Constellating Cultural Rhetorics." *enculturation* October 25. https://enculturation.net/our-story-begins-here.

Restaino, Jessica. 2019. *Surrender: Feminist Rhetoric and Ethics in Love and Illness.* Carbondale: Southern Illinois University Press.

Ritter, Kelly. 2023. "Want to Be a College Professor? Get Ready to Move." *Slate* October 30. https://slate.com/human-interest/2023/10/faculty-mobility-academic-job-market.html.

VanHaitsma, Pamala, and Steph Ceraso. 2017. "'Making It' in the Academy Through Horizontal Mentoring." *Peitho* 19, no. 2. https://cfshrc.org/wp-content/uploads/2017/03/VanHaitsma-and-Cesaro_Making-It-in-the-Acadamy_Final.pdf.

INTERLUDE 2

Overachieving to Leave

Reflections on an Early Career in Transition

SARA DOAN

November 27, 2024

Trigger Warning: Sexual harassment; suicidal thoughts

When you're (allegedly) groped by your grad professor at a conference.

Any tenure-track job feels adequate (as long as it's a 3-3).

You conferenced and published and carved a whole year off your PhD program (with very little help from your advisor and two Title IX reports).

Your best campus visit, the search chair didn't have a place picked out for dinner (which you should have taken as a red flag).

You drop your chopsticks on the floor. Twice.

Yellow flag behavior becomes b* eating crackers[1] (annoyance is not sustainable).

You publish a third of your department's research (realistically, probably half).

In the first year, you go to your chair for help with the workload (you're suicidal; don't take Singulair).

---

1. https://en.wiktionary.org/wiki/bitch_eating_crackers. Last accessed July 28, 2025.

She cocks an eyebrow, shrugs. "You'll get through it." (You did, but yikes.)

There's a plague. You study it. (Lockdown was a relief.)
"You're not an expert in that," says your mother, the tradwife
 (overachieving to leave isn't new).
A purple-haired professor—your parents' biggest disappointment
 (not homeschooling eight babies).
Your charts article had something like 6,000 downloads.

Admin makes you teach in-person before vaccines
 ("I'm not asking you to do anything I'm not willing to do." says your
 interim dean that summer).
A grown man tries to pass his motorcycle helmet as a face covering
 (and sexually harasses you. yay).
Next semester, masks are gone (cue the panic attacks);
 your coworkers take theirs off to speak.
It's still 2021.

You teach eight preps in eight semesters
 (with some of the best evals in the department).
Submit your book proposal on charts; the next week
 (despite applause at the faculty meeting),
  your department gives the charts class (you taught three times) to a
  lecturer.
"You're easier to schedule."

You write (overcompensate from spite).
You apply for jobs (because you care too much to stay).
You change jobs (still burned out but better paid).
Overachieving lets you leave.
But how do you do the work to stay?

Part III

Adequacy as a Path Toward Change

8
Confrontations with Adequacy in Pandemic Teacher Training

CRYSTAL BROCH COLOMBINI, STEPHANIE L. KERSCHBAUM,
AND SARA WEBB-SUNDERHAUS

Writing program administrators (WPAs) often navigate a perpetual gap between idealistic aims and realistic achievements. We design strategic-but-compromised initiatives that walk the line between aspirational administrative ambitions, best disciplinary practices, and constrained time and resources; assuage the performance anxieties of students and instructors; and confront the boundaries of our own possibility as we labor to meet high personal, professional, programmatic, and pedagogical goals. All of these moves require us as WPAs to navigate tensions between excellence and *adequacy* (far more, perhaps, than between excellence and *failure*). Astute readers will note the parallel placement of *adequacy* and *failure* in the previous sentence, and that link is intentional. While these tensions have long been a significant source of emotional, affective, and invisible labor that some WPAs experience (Cedillo 2021; Costello and Babb 2020; Horner 2007; Micciche 2002; Osorio et al. 2022a, 2022b; Strickland 2011), they intensified dramatically as the COVID-19 pandemic first leveraged urgent demands for high performance amid chaotic circumstances and constrained conditions, and subsequently left a legacy of lingering aftereffects—including, for us, the realization that perhaps we need to imagine our own and instructors' labor differently.

https://doi.org/10.7330/9781646428052.c008

In contexts where anything other than excellence feels like failure, adequacy is a fraught metric and certainly does not seem to be something that we or others should aspire toward. And yet, the impossibility of much of what is asked of WPAs and of first-year composition instructors highlights adequacy as an important benchmark. In this chapter, we define *adequacy* as structurally determined sufficiencies articulated within particular writing program and institutional settings. In this definition, adequacy can be understood as a state of being sufficient for the purpose concerned, a stance that explicitly resists treating anything that is not *excellent* as de facto failure. This definition of adequacy helps us interrogate how WPAs navigate the adequacy-excellence tensions that regularly erupt in the contact zones that comprise WPA work. In this chapter, we focus on one contact zone especially laden with excellence-adequacy tensions: the writing pedagogy seminar or training practicum required of graduate student instructors (GSIs) in many writing programs.

In any format, the GSI training course must balance conflicting goals. On the one hand, it must introduce future practitioners to research-based best practices and model what it means to teach writing in adherence to the highest standards of program, university, and field expectations (Dobrin 2005; Estrem and Reid 2012; Mapes and Miller-Cochran 2019; Restaino 2012). On the other hand, it must support instructors in adequately navigating the terrain of learning to teach, rather than inviting them to hold aloft pedagogical ideals that no one could be expected to meet in their first term with a new class. Such adequacy is human: WPAs and GSIs alike are engaging with others in imperfect ways in a process of learning and growth around writing. In our efforts to support GSIs, we find ourselves responding to performance anxieties; moderating our institutions, colleagues, and GSIs' high expectations; and fielding frustrations directed at WPAs regarding the impossibility of the task GSIs often feel themselves inadequately prepared for. All of this, in the face of GSIs' anxieties about not serving their students well, requires us to underscore and encourage early-career instructors to accept that sometimes, adequacy must be enough (Reed 2020; Saur and Palmeri 2017). And yet, even as we walk that line with GSIs, we also must confront our own lofty goals and field expectations around preparing teachers, creating pedagogical communities, and maximizing preparation—all in the face of compromised institutional conditions and constrained programmatic resources and realities.

These constraints intensified during the pandemic, as each of us, along with instructors in our programs, experienced radically altered conditions of personal, pedagogical, and professional possibility. In other words, the impossibilities of our jobs became even more impossible as we sought to teach current, inclusive, and accessible courses on the teaching of current, inclusive, and accessible courses within highly fraught affective environments. As WPAs, we are regular recipients of GSIs' and colleagues' frustrations about what it means to teach writing well or effectively, as well as feedback that suggests we as WPAs have failed if GSIs do not feel prepared to design and teach a course or if students are not receiving a high-quality educational experience in their composition course. Important here is the explicit recognition that GSIs are not a monolithic group and are complexly positioned against and within institutional and pedagogical structures and language ideologies that regularly enact violence against BIPOC, disabled, queer, and multiply minoritized instructors and students. We feel the weight and urgency of dismantling structures and resisting practices that inflict harm, and to even hint at adequacy, or structurally determined sufficiencies, can feel as if we are evading accountability for the work we need to be doing.

This complex swirl of affect, positionality, and institutional violence offers some insight into why composition pedagogy training feels so high stakes, given its very real consequences for the students and instructors who share space together, as well as the expectations conveyed by Rhetoric and Composition as a field, given its perennial arguments for disciplinary legitimacy and complex relationships within English departments or as stand-alone departments (see, e.g., Kynard 2022). In much the same way first-year writing (FYW) instructors can fall victim to a self-defeating and theoretically flawed mentality that posits we must teach students everything they need to know about writing because who knows what type of writing instruction they'll receive in the future, WPAs can feel as if we must teach new instructors everything they need to know about pedagogy. After all, who knows what type of pedagogical training these instructors will receive in the future?—or we may know all too well that they will receive none at all. The adequacy-excellence tensions we experience in our everyday milieu were heightened amid the pandemic's mandated shift to new pedagogical modes and practices, concomitant transformations of institutional environments, and urgent demands to center antiracist commitments.

We interrogate these tensions by turning to our WPA experiences at three different institutions through a set of reflective narratives. These accounts point to common themes of navigating our own challenges in relation to the emotional and differentially embodied experiences confronted by new GSIs during the pandemic moment. Writing together allows us to engage across these different sites to assess perceptions of and responses to (in)adequacy, taking an especial focus on our experiences teaching pandemic-era pedagogy seminars, encountering structural limits, eliciting mixed responses, and confronting our own senses that we had not met a high bar at a crucial time. Extending from personal reflection to an intersectional reframing of these confrontations, we hope to work toward a way to aim for adequacy.

Adequacy-Excellence Tensions in Composition Pedagogy Training

Across Rhetoric and Composition, a core conviction resonates: This space for "preparing teachers-to-be who will teach undergraduate students" holds "great potential for impact" (Johnson 2016, 95). Sid Dobrin (2005) describes this training as "the largest, most effective purveyor of cultural capital in composition studies" (21) and as a singular opportunity for introducing new practitioners to the field of Rhetoric and Composition. Similarly, Shelley Reid (2017) presents the course to new GSIs as an immersive learning in pedagogy so "personal, dynamic, and multifaceted" that it differs "significantly from how you learn in your other courses" (129). From this idealistic angle, GSI training is an exceptional opportunity to shape the experiences of first-year writing teachers in ways that also shape the lives of first-year writing students.

This idealism, however, can be hard to square with the basic sufficiency of *adequacy* as we are approaching it here. From a more realistic angle, of course, our experiences with writing teacher education courses reveal a constant tension between the elevated bar of *best practice* and the more accessible bar of *actual practice*. Often positioned early in coursework requirements and sometimes taken concurrently with teaching composition for the first time, pedagogy seminars play host to a range of social and academic goals that exceed formal learning objectives. These can range from introducing the expectations of graduate studies, to extending cohort connections into the fuller dimensions of mutually supportive teaching communities, to assuaging impostor syndromes and outsider complexes. GSIs navigating new-to-them courses struggle with their own idealistic expectations amid what Jessica Restaino (2012), in her study of new GSIs, describes as "more of a day-to-day keeping afloat than it is a carefully constructed, planned course" (1), rife with "endless laboring" (50) and thus eased by conscious embrace of a balance between excellence and failure. Expectations of emerging from the course with a *done* syllabus, a *final* teaching philosophy, or a sense of *total* preparedness for the classroom must be dialed back, corrected by reminders that as a single discrete learning experience, the course can initiate but not finalize teaching praxis.

The pressure put on the composition practicum is also influenced by composition's continued efforts to assert disciplinary expertise and legitimacy within universities and departments. Numerous intertwined forces press WPAs to experience the pedagogy practicum as high stakes and with significant risks for achieving anything other than excellence: loss of disciplinary legitimacy; proof of the (in)significance of composition expertise; loss of faith in the value of writing as a field of study; disbelief in pedagogical quality and effectiveness; and the risk of not meeting deep commitments to social justice and equity, given the pernicious and persistent harms of white language ideologies and white language supremacy. Our goal in writing and thinking together is to take seriously what it might mean to approach the composition pedagogy seminar through our articulation of adequacy. What if our goal in teaching the seminar was to achieve a state of being sufficient for the purpose concerned? What shifts for us in imagining answers to that question?

To be real for a minute, it has been very hard to imagine these answers. Even as we acknowledged to one another that we each appreciated so many things about aiming for a generative adequacy, one that recognizes the humanity and everydayness of learning to teach through both curricular encounters and interpersonal engagement with graduate instructors, we noted at the same time our own adequacy-excellency conflicts within those same interactions. As writing studies continually expands and diversifies, it reverberates with tensions between, on one hand, innumerable FYW-relevant urgencies that *could* and *should* be addressed in GSI training and, on the other, the constrained curricular economies of that training itself, making acquiescence to *adequate* necessary. Every year we receive programmatic and pedagogical feedback telling us all the things we did not do or failed to do in our GSI training, messages that are amplified within composition scholarship that increasingly names and points to new and important projects. Take for instance, Parva Panahi's call for "A Multilingual Orientation to Preparing Teaching Assistants to Teach Argumentation in First-Year Writing" (2021), in which she writes that "the growing multilingual (and multicultural) nature of FYW environments makes it *critical* that prospective FYW teachers, especially those working with MLWs, receive *adequate* programmatic support that will help them acquire new knowledge, adapt and transform it to their multilingual classroom contexts, and develop effective pedagogies accordingly" (117; emphasis added). We point to Panahi not to single her out but to note how this quote precisely resonates with myriad other calls within composition studies and our own programs. The words we emphasized in Panahi's quote highlight both the ethical urgency for pedagogical excellence—*"high-quality instruction* based on *up-to-date developments* in relevant disciplines, from *experienced instructors"* (2021, 117; emphasis added)—as well as the acknowledgment that any graduate educator can only address, and any graduate cohort only absorb, so many mandates fully and/or ethically. Even when we concede the functional and material limitations of a single learning experience, achieving "adequate" coverage is likely to leave WPAs with "lingering feelings of inadequacy" (Saidy and Sura 2020, 1) regarding curricular design and delivery.

Another source where WPAs confront adequacy comes through polarized reactions to the materials and topics of the pedagogy course. Different degrees of receptivity to composition theory and pedagogy among GSI cohorts is common. One reason for these differences has to do with disciplinary differences among those who fund their graduate work by teaching composition. Studies of requisite pedagogy courses have long reported on the challenges of navigating "bi-modal" pedagogical responses that separate students with "great enthusiasm for the program" from those who perceive it to be "a waste of their time" (Johnson 2016, 89; see also Grouling 2015; Hesse 1993; Johnson 2021; Reid 2017). There are many degrees of this "bi-modality," and many factors beyond disciplinary allegiance shape orientations toward teacher education: individual dispositions, interests, and embodied experiences; structural forces such as shifting academic programs and job markets; worsening contingent labor trends; and increasing burdens of labor, trauma, and mental and physical health struggles especially borne by minoritized and multiply minoritized GSIs across specialties (Driscoll et al. 2020; Fedukovich and Morse 2017; Osorio et al. 2022a, 2022b; Saur and Palmeri 2017).

In our work developing and teaching these pedagogy seminars, even as we acknowledge the many forces that shape reactions to new disciplinary content and teaching obligations, we also want to listen to Reid's caution against falling prey to "the illusion that once their TAs finish one course, they magically know all they need to know about teaching" (2017, 138) and to prioritize "meaningful training that is responsive to GSIs' needs for well-being and boundary setting" (Schwaller 2022, 113). Consequently, we have also had to recognize that tough encounters *in and with* pedagogy courses are likely to evoke felt reactions that augment numerous forms of labor that "disproportionately falls on the shoulders of WPAs" (Adams Wooten et al. 2020, xiv). As proliferating studies of emotional, affective, and invisible labor poignantly attest (Cedillo 2021;

Costello and Babb 2020; Horner 2007; Micciche 2002; Osorio et al. 2022a, 2022b; Strickland 2011;), WPAs even in "normal" conditions can weather many affective tempests simultaneously, putting our resiliency to the test. It is no surprise that the storms around the pedagogy course have felt uniquely unsettling in our experience: Our conviction in its "great potential for impact" (Johnson 2016, 95) is inflected by our high hopes for programmatic success, our commitments to research-based best practice, and our investment in the experiences of both FYW students and instructors, among other feelings. In other words, as we aspire to at once *model* and *teach* reflective, effective pedagogical practice, we hope for excellence, even as well-recognized structural constraints might in fact endorse a different orientation: adequacy. That is, while adequacy is not "abundance or excellence" in the traditional sense, it may nevertheless represent its own success in that adequacy satisfies what is "absolutely necessary." Such an orientation might prompt more interrogation of the tendency to equate *adequacy* with failure as well as the emotional labor that equation incurs. We think our current moment calls us to recollect, reflect, and reach for a more generative affective relationship to adequacy as an achievement of structurally determined sufficiencies amid the tensions we have describe here. We support that notion next, by turning to our personal pandemic pedagogy course experiences.

Struggling with Adequacy: Our Experiences

Distanced from normal communities and networks during the pandemic, like many WPAs across the United States, we who write this chapter were also fortunate to discover new ones. Indeed, our coming together for this project was facilitated by none other than a Facebook messenger thread that came to life as we first somehow found each other—drawn, perhaps, by affinities among social media posts—then found ourselves routinely processing through the entanglement of personal, programmatic, and professional challenges in which each of us were immured. Alongside the conflicts and crises of administering our respective writing programs through the shifting uncertainties of the pandemic, some of us were also in processes of joining new universities, moving families cross-country, coping with newly diagnosed disabilities, supporting children through acute trauma, and more. Our concept for this chapter emerged from a set of exchanges around writing teacher education that unfolded as we each wrestled with painful gaps between the pedagogy course experiences we hoped to deliver and the experiences our instructors encountered. In what follows, we offer specific vignettes that highlight how various gaps between ideals and reality manifested: first, as sources of grief, guilt, and disappointment; next, through shared reflection and mutual support, as sites of recognition for the structural realities that shaped our conditions of possibilities; and, finally, as resources for reflecting on adequacy-excellence tensions. We conclude by following some threads through these experiences, focusing on what we see as necessary but not readily recognized means of support that should be part of WPA work.

CRYSTAL

Few experiences have challenged me to confront my relationship with adequacy as much as stepping into the pedagogy course as a first-time WPA at a new university, amid a chaotic convergence of pandemic and programmatic transformation. In early 2020, weeks before viral outbreak, I accepted a position as the first faculty writing and rhetoric specialist at Fordham University, a private liberal arts college with two New York City campuses, hired per department tradition as one of two directors who each administered *both* the Writing Program and Writing Center on one campus. If the two-program obligation was daunting, then it was offset by the two-director model, which also promised co-teaching of a two-semester writing studies practicum: GSIs, all doctoral students in literary studies, complete the first half in their second year and the second in their third as they begin teaching composition. The attraction of co-teaching was another draw of the job.

Yet by the time of my first practicum meeting in early 2021, that expectation was in the past along with many others. My family's initial mobilization for a cross-country move had stalled quickly as uncertain university policies, state restrictions, and housing markets ultimately delayed our relocation by a year. If acculturating in a new university is always a steep challenge, then acculturating remotely amid a socially dislocating global pandemic is simply precipitous. I spent my first semester frantically learning programs, policies, and people—days of unbroken Zoom meetings blurring into late nights of "real work" as unprecedented crises called for institutional knowledge I lacked. My partner's job never went online, so I was the sole parent home straining to support three children with moving grief, lockdown loneliness, and remote school agony. To top it all, my department proceeded with plans for an external review of the Writing Program, naming me point person on preparing a self-study, coordinating meetings, and hosting an online site visit. Just before spring semester began, several critical events occurred: my co-director stepped down and those service roles were added to mine, and the external review arrived.

Thus did I greet my first cohort: from half the country away, as a solo WPA and writing center administrator (WCA) on two campuses, back at the bottom of the acculturation hill on a second (much larger) campus; and facing a raft of mandates for comprehensive programmatic overhaul.

If I felt crushed by circumstances, then so did my students. As New York City dwellers in COVID's terrifying onset, their lives had been thrown off course by sickness, uncertainty, and death at its most acute. Some were enduring lockdown in tiny apartments, deprived of the public access that offsets confined city living; others had decamped from expensive isolation to far-flung homes. They had lost loved ones, welcomed babies in isolation, dealt with the havoc that befell international students, and more. All were facing disorder around the comprehensive exams they were expected to take that same semester. As I would soon realize, the timing of that requirement stacks an affective deck against the practicum, as students under pressure to tunnel into literary subspecialties can chafe at the expectation for new disciplinary engagement. Mine felt that friction acutely, not least because my version of that engagement departed from what local lore conditioned them to expect. Over the semester, the problem of misaligned expectations seemed to compound, pulling me into constant confrontation with gaps between my goals for the course and my capacity as I contended with newness, remote work, care work, and an unexpectedly expanded administrative role.

It was distinctively difficult that the worst gaps opened around actions I most hoped would be helpful. Invited by colleagues to take a hand in the graduate curriculum my first semester, for instance, I had suggested shifting this half of the practicum from an uncredited pass/fail to a credit-bearing seminar. My anticipation of a welcome change proved wrong: A graded course signaled a higher-stakes commitment, and students found this overwhelming. My course design likewise caused consternation. The previous tradition had required new GSIs to use a lockstep syllabus with rigid daily materials, and external reviewers had advised significant revision. Yet my expectation that more flexibility would be welcome also missed the mood of the moment. My anxious cohort didn't want to be the first to engage in the disciplinary learning that would resource them to develop syllabi—they just wanted the syllabi, as well as assignments, readings, and lesson plans. New to my role, I lacked access to a wealth of resources, and I struggled to defend best practices endorsed by the review without undermining the traditions of the past. Wanting to respond compassionately to discontents, I embraced radical flexibility by easing requirements, excusing absences, and more. Here again, my efforts misfired: The negative feedback I received after the semester was of a course at once too demanding and too unstructured. My aspirations for excellence, circumstances that left me fighting even for adequacy, and my labor to mediate it all with empathy had produced nothing so much as chaos.

Delivered to my department chair, who was then compelled to (very kindly) address it with me, this feedback initially left me in a quagmire of shame. Here would stand the record of my first graduate course at my new university, and worse—of the cohort that needed my success perhaps more than any ever would. In a theme my coauthors will echo, though, it was our thread that repaired me to perspective. I could appreciate the *uncommon-ness* of *my experience*, but the *common-ness* of *our experience* was what recalibrated my pedagogical reflection away from a rigid framework of ideologically instilled excellencies and toward a more reasonable heuristic of structurally determined sufficiencies generous, importantly, to the emotional distortions of an impossible moment. (It doesn't hurt, either, that that first cohort has done just fine.)

SARA

Since coming to Miami—a large, Midwestern, public university—in fall 2018 as an associate professor and WPA, I have navigated a tumultuous set of circumstances in my personal and professional lives. In fact, the upheaval began a few days before my scheduled campus visit in 2017, when I fell while walking across campus at my former institution and suffered a traumatic, disabling injury to my dominant arm. Since then, I have endured multiple medical crises; my father's death; a global pandemic; the impact of the pandemic on my children's education, social lives, and mental health; and more. While the initial transition to emergency remote instruction and the subsequent year of teaching and administering online were difficult, the 2021–2022 academic year was one of the most challenging I have ever experienced. Early in the summer of 2021, someone I care about experienced a serious trauma that stirred up lingering issues from my personal history and left me with a sense of guilt that I had failed a person I love. Later that summer, I would fall twice, sustaining a severe ankle sprain in the second fall that required nine months of physical therapy. In addition to the physical injuries I sustained in these falls, they further triggered the complex post-traumatic stress disorder (C-PTSD) I developed in the wake of the 2017 fall.

Thus, when I began teaching the two-week, pre-semester, composition theory/pedagogy seminar for new GSIs in August 2021, I was using a walker, my foot was in a walking boot, and I was in tremendous physical and emotional pain. If that were not enough, it was also my first time in a classroom since

March 2020, as Miami's classes had been online since the beginning of the pandemic. I was, in a word, traumatized. I had always conceptualized myself as a caring teacher and WPA whose work was of critical importance, since the training I provide is almost the only pedagogical education GSIs—who teach almost all sections of Miami's first-year writing course—are guaranteed to receive at my institution. When GSIs have failed to live up to my university's Statement of Good Teaching Practice, I have been blamed by administrators and colleagues for their failings; in turn, I internalized this blame, along with our field's impossible standards, and redoubled my efforts to live up to a heroic ideal of a teacher-administrator who is—like Mary Poppins—practically perfect in every way. I was able to maintain that illusion until disability, the pandemic, and the events of the summer 2021 started to make visible what I had tried so long to keep hidden: the physical and mental cost of being a heroic WPA. My arm became more painful and developed additional issues that spread to my shoulders and neck, my C-PTSD symptoms intensified, and I developed an array of physical maladies that were mild but annoyingly persistent, including a thyroid disorder.

I began to realize my body and mind were doing whatever they could to force me to pay attention to their simple but important message: I could no longer strive to be the "perfect" WPA I so desperately wanted to be, as this was impossible for me to sustain, physically and mentally. This realization did not prompt me to consider leaving the academy, because I love being a professor; instead, I started to consider how I could develop a healthier relationship with work. The problem wasn't rooted in academia itself. I would have brought to any job the mentality that I must justify my worth by being perfect, because that belief is rooted in my family of origin. That belief system is most likely why I chose academia in the first place; because it's an environment in which we are often expected to justify our worth through achievements and accomplishments, it felt normal and familiar to me—quite literally like home. These realizations, along with adjusting to life as a disabled person and the tumult of the pandemic, led me to ask a question that previously would have been unthinkable: What if I don't have to justify my worth as a person, scholar-teacher, and WPA by being perfect? What if I simply focused on being sufficient for my purpose as a WPA—in other words, being good enough (Kleinfeld 2020)?

My epiphany that "good enough" is indeed good enough came at a difficult moment, however. As I tentatively began striving for adequacy during the fall 2021 semester, I was confronted with the reality that some of the new GSIs were dealing with their own traumas, a fact that shaped the emotional labor

I was performing but at a time when I was least equipped to give it. I found myself out of my depth in knowing how best to support them in and out of the classroom—a fact that sometimes frustrated them and me. At first I responded by trying even harder to be the perfect WPA, connecting these new GSIs to campus resources and undergoing further training—such as Mental Health First Aid—to learn how to more quickly recognize when they needed professional help. However, as I learned again and again that year, WPAs cannot be all things to everyone, and I was encountering the impossibility of the ideal often imposed on WPAs, as we describe earlier. Looking back, I can see now that I never could have met everyone's needs, especially given all that was unfolding around us and in my own life. However, at the time, being an adequate rather than exceptional WPA felt like failure.

At the same time that I was feeling this pressure to be all things to all people in the new cohort, I also experienced significant resistance to the project of teaching composition and new reactions to what previously had been generally accepted norms in the program. One way I responded to this resistance was by explicitly talking about the importance of self-care, protecting one's health and boundaries—lessons that I was myself painfully learning—only to have a GSI lash out at me frustratedly in class, accusing me of being ableist, antistudent, and unavailable. It was difficult for me to not take these comments personally. The accusation that I was ableist felt like an attack on my identity and experiences as a disabled person. Further, these comments felt like a reaction to my own attempts to set boundaries by not responding to emails at night, by limiting (though not eliminating) my acceptance of late work, and by sharing some of the mentorship load with the two graduate WPAs who assisted me in running the composition program. In other words, pressures to be everything to everyone kept coming, even as I tried to orient differently toward my job and model what I hoped instructors might do for themselves.

These types of remarks and behaviors struck at my deepest fears, guilt, and insecurities as a WPA struggling to reject perfectionism and accept adequacy while coping with C-PTSD. According to the Cleveland Clinic's website as of April 2023, some of the symptoms that distinguish C-PTSD from PTSD include "a negative sense of self involving persistent feelings of guilt, shame, failure, and worthlessness" and "excessive reactivity to negative emotional stimuli," and it is clear to me now how much of my response to the challenges of the 2021–2022 academic year was impacted by C-PTSD. If I did not keep my mind occupied, I ruminated on all of my perceived failings in the parts of the job that troubled me most. I started to recognize this trauma response at the end of fall 2021. In a group chat with Crystal and Stephanie, I found myself ranting and crying as I processed a small set of negative comments and critiques that emerged in the student evaluations from the practicum: Didn't they know what I had sacrificed for them? How much physical and emotional pain I had endured to be in a classroom that semester? How often I prioritized their needs above my own? Never mind the numerous emails and student evaluation comments that praised me for my caring, compassion, and concern; lauded my availability; and acknowledged my strengths as a teacher. Thanks to C-PTSD, I focused on the few negative responses, to the exclusion of everything else.

While Stephanie and Crystal responded to me with kindness and compassion, their gentle questions and encouragement helped me realize that I needed help, because my trauma response—which I assumed was disconnected from my job—was impacting my work more than I realized. Further, I was still acclimating to the realities of life as a disabled mother inside and outside the academy, which reinforced my fears that I was not "good enough." As Marjorie Aunos et al. (2022) argue, idealized discourses of motherhood make it impossible for disabled mothers to be "good mothers," as we can never meet their standards of perfection. In the process, "Mothers with disabilities are bombarded with messages about what it means to be a good mother and or a good mother with a disability. The negotiation of one's identity, particularly in face of multiple and colliding discourses on ideal mothering and ableism, can be confusing" (2022, 7). Being a mother and an academic further contributed to this conflict and confusion, given bias against mothers and systemic gendered inequities in the academy (see Bender et al. 2022; Cucciarre et al. 2011; Minello et al. 2020; Misra et al. 2011; Nielsen 2016; Osorio 2021; Williams 2005; and Zimmer 2020, among many others). I had already failed to meet the academic ideal when I became a mother while still a graduate student; now, I was not only a mother but a disabled mother. My disability meant that against the idealized norms of the academy and motherhood, I was doubly inadequate. Unsurprisingly, I internalized those biases, blamed myself for failing to reach the impossible standards of our field and my institution, and ignored my own trauma.

I'm not doing that anymore. Working with a new therapist specializing in trauma has helped not only in addressing C-PTSD but also in maintaining boundaries and developing a healthier relationship with work, motherhood, and disability. Writing and speaking about disability in both personal and professional contexts have been important in negotiating my still-evolving identity as a disabled person, and I'm learning how to take better care of myself, physically and mentally. I don't have it all figured out; I never will. But that understanding is sufficient for my purpose. That is good enough.

STEPHANIE

I stepped on the University of Washington's (UW's) campus in July 2021 as the university was making preparations to return to campus for the first time since shifting to remote operations in March 2020. I rattled around my empty building and tried to absorb the program's environment and culture while taking on leadership of a large first-year writing program at an R1 university predominantly staffed by graduate students and temporary instructors. Over the previous five years, the program had undergone intense antiracist and institutional transformation (see Rai 2023; Thu et al. 2022), and anxiety infused every part of my job. Some anxieties were shaped by my lack of institutional history and limited relationships on campus, which meant that I rarely felt as if I understood whether or not the things I was doing were in line with or consistent with past practice, while others were shaped by the enormity and the stakes of the job I was doing and amplified further by my own and instructors' fears around teaching in-person during a pandemic.

That quarter, I taught one section of the composition theory course using a syllabus collaboratively developed by previous WPAs and co-teachers. At the same time, as a deaf WPA brand-new to the institution, I was also figuring out my own access needs as an administrator and a teacher in a masked environment. Intensely anxious about—and it feels hard to admit this even in retrospect—establishing credibility and earning respect in my brand-new context, I decided to request an accommodation to teach remotely given the mask mandate on campus. My thinking was that I had at least some modest familiarity (even if not a sense of competence) with navigating teaching using Zoom interfaces, and leaning on whatever familiarity I could find would help as I adjusted to Everything Else is Completely New Which Means I Do Not Know What I Need Much Less Want. At the same time, I wanted to bring a strong commitment to accessibility to my WPA work, and I hoped that by being transparent about my own access needs and making accessibility a cornerstone not just of effective pedagogy but also of navigating the transformed learning environment we faced in fall 2021, instructors would feel similarly empowered to center their own access needs and prioritize self-care and community-building. And yet (this is the topic of a whole other essay), I found myself awake at night worrying about my own inadequacies around what I could and could not maintain, in terms of past program practices and resources.

I did understand—and had numerous colleagues reinforce to me—that I couldn't be everything in every direction to everyone. And in no way did I expect instructors in my program to be everything in every direction to all of the needs their students were revealing to them. And yet, at every turn I felt acutely every single one of my imperfections and shortcomings. So reading the final course evaluations for that first quarter's pedagogy seminar was not unlike getting kicked in the stomach. It was apparent that the course I'd taught had not met everyone's needs, and this course feedback resonated with programmatic feedback coming in through multiple channels. Even as I know, in my heart of hearts, that we all need to set reasonable and realistic goals for ourselves, and that it can be important to enact boundaries around what it is we can and cannot do, something about being confronted with the immediacy of students' and instructors' frustrations and critiques always hits me hard.

Because I've been teaching for more than twenty years, I've gotten a lot of student evaluation comments, and over the years I've developed various skills around soliciting and responding to that evaluation feedback. One of those skills involves connecting with others to get fresh perspective and to process feedback. I reached out to a few trusted colleagues who reassured me that the feedback from my pedagogy course was consistent with patterns of feedback the course routinely got because of the different constituencies it served, constituencies that have different and sometimes even conflicting needs. But I still felt I needed to work harder, to be better, to do more. It didn't matter—or so my brain told me—that I was brand-new at this institution; it didn't matter that I was figuring out all-new-to-me access configurations; it didn't matter that online teaching still felt difficult and awkward (I'm not a natural classroom teacher, and teaching online only exacerbated my feelings of not being good-enough).

In my second year, some of the patterns in the course evaluation and programmatic feedback reemerged. This return brought back familiar anxieties and insecurities from my first year but with an added sense of shame. All of those challenges that might have applied in my first year aren't still the same: I'm more adjusted to this new context; I have a fantastic access structure in place with sign language interpreters I love working with; I understand the program goals and commitments so much better. Consequently, the feedback should—I hoped, desperately—show that I am improving and doing better. But the feedback in my second year wasn't significantly better, so I zeroed in on the obvious target: The problem must be me.

Making matters more fraught, just as in Sara's case, the course critiques pressed on some of my deepest insecurities: I have never felt like an amazing teacher, and I've never gotten the kind of affirmation in student feedback that I've so often celebrated in other teachers' work. Several people, including Sara and Crystal, helped me process this feedback, and they were much kinder toward me than I was to myself, but I didn't want to feel as if I were using adequacy as an excuse for not doing a good enough job at some of the most important work I was supposed to be doing as WPA. Some of the challenges around the feedback were shaped by my newness at the institution: I didn't have a good way of contextualizing for myself what it might mean to do "good enough" at this brand-new job in this brand-new place. But I think a stronger source of my struggle with the feedback was that I had no sense that it was OK for me to be "adequate" in the very same ways that I was encouraging instructors to think of their own first quarter of teaching in our program. Where was I getting these messages from? Why did I think this? Here, I can point to some of the responses I got to questions I was asking about my work on campus. For example, at several points when I would try to articulate a boundary around what I would be doing as WPA, responses from others around me seemed aimed more at helping me figure out how to do everything, rather than to cross things off or to have boundaries (e.g., Am I allowed to say I'm just not going to do XYZ part of the job that was handed to me? What are the possibilities for helping make the enormity of my job more sustainable?). I can also point to the ways that I was still subscribing to the notion of the individual WPA acting heroically and alone, even as I was in a deeply collaborative environment with other department program directors and a fellow WPA just across the hall (hi, Megan Callow!) who enthusiastically embraced opportunities for bringing our programs together and mutually supporting one another. Shifting my frame away from the individual striving for adequacy and toward adequacy as a structural and systemic sufficiency, as perhaps a means of sustainability and of persistence in the face of the enormity of the work, is helpful (my WPA predecessor Candice Rai has written powerfully about what it means to persist in what she calls climate-changing work [2023]).

Writing this essay now, in my third year at UW, I can see clearly that I needed (ok, *still need*) to build some new frames for thinking about what adequacy and structural sufficiency look like, even as I endeavor to create a humane and supportive environment that mitigates as much institutional and programmatic harm as possible. I want to put some pressure on the link between my uptake of instructors' feedback and my own insecurities, not just because critically attending to our insecurities helps us to identify revisions and opportunities for learning but also because for me, my fears tend to get magnified and loom even larger the more they bounce around in my brain. I've learned—after years of making mistakes and screwing up—how important it is to get perspective outside of myself. This is a form of structural sufficiency. It's not a way of excusing our failures or evading accountability: Not all of us are masterful classroom pedagogues, and I *am* bringing a lot of skills and strengths to my WPA work.

While instructor mentoring, including teacher-training and the composition pedagogy seminar, are absolutely some of the biggest parts of my WPA responsibilities, they are decidedly not the entirety of my job. Critiques of WPA work have long pointed out the problems of expecting WPAs to be able to do everything (see, e.g., Adams Wooten et al. 2020; Charlton et al. 2011; George 1999), and Amy Vidali's pointed analysis of these narratives notes how many WPAs report WPA work to be disabling (2015). Recognizing the effects of administrative stress on WPA bodies (including my own, as I've sought out therapy and various forms of healthcare and support in the last two years), I recognize the importance of staying with adequacy, of recognizing structurally determined sufficiencies as a central goal of what I can do with the pedagogy practicum and instructors' sense of overwhelm in their first quarter of teaching. I do not have real answers. It's still, as Candice Rai put it in an email to me, "f-ing hard," to receive all of this feedback and to use it to revise and set personal and professional priorities. But remembering that it's structural and not individual may be one necessary shift I can make toward adequacy.

Conclusion

The COVID-19 pandemic has organized new inflection points around adequacy and excellence, particularly for WPAs. As writing-teacher educators, we experienced numerous forms of inadequacy that were intensified through our experiences with the composition practicum and the COVID-19 pandemic, as detailed in this chapter. We felt torn among the many and endlessly proliferating crises befalling our universities, programs, instructors, students, families, friends, and selves. We also had to confront a truth we found deeply discomforting: Brand-new GSIs were being thrown into a pedagogical reality that was more complex than any of us—as experienced writing teachers—had ever endured and that we ourselves found incredibly fraught and challenging. And we were the ones who had to do the throwing! We also, along with WPAs across the United States, dealt with the intense emotionality of our students' reactions and our own re-reactions amid a dearth of usual resources from pedagogical support communities.

In our narratives, we each trace tensions between the lived realities of WPAs and those of graduate students learning to teach in our programs. As WPAs, we navigated multiple responsibilities toward distinct institutional stakeholders (undergraduate and graduate students, graduate instructors, departmental and university administrators), as well as the responsibilities we had to our loved ones and our own needs as people. WPAs, along with graduate program directors, are among those in a department who have the closest proximity to (graduate) students' experiences. So much of the inhumanity that graduate students experience in English departments and writing programs emerges from systemic and long-standing institutional environments of late capitalism and neoliberalism. By the time institutions were returning to in-person instruction (in the midst of fear, uncertainty, confusion, and concern about masking and vaccines), these systemic inequities and forms of inhumanity kept piling up and, yes, sometimes felt insurmountable when we considered what we as individual WPAs could do. The intractability of meeting each of our stakeholders' sometimes competing needs—combined with the front-row seats we as WPAs had to the harsh realities facing many graduate instructors—meant that it felt impossible for us to accept "adequate" or "good enough" WPA work as emotionally or ethically valid in the face of significant pain, hurt, and trauma.

Further, the pandemic exacerbated another tension we have encountered in WPA work. The more that we try to humanize ourselves and our work, offer meaningful support to graduate instructors, and create safe-er spaces for them to learn and grow as teachers, the more humanity may then be expected of us. This is a predominantly positive phenomenon, of course, but it can generate adequacy tensions of its own. For example, WPAs committed to anti-racist and accessible pedagogies might receive particular blowback when an instructor feels harmed or experiences microaggressions in the program. Sara's story illustrates this tension: When she suggested GSIs consider adopting attendance policies in the future, she received harsh public criticism from a GSI—something that her nondisabled colleagues who had no particular commitments to accessibility or anti-ableist pedagogies did not experience. Too, Stephanie felt acutely the pressure of modeling what it looks like to navigate complex accessibility challenges given that she herself has needs she had to ask instructors and students in her courses to meet.

Writing about her WPA work during the pandemic, Kim Hensley Owens (2023) contends that "WPA roles are notoriously misunderstood, notoriously outsized, notoriously boundary-less (whether by design, demand, or [over]devotion), and notoriously Sisyphean" (74). That has been our experience as well. While there are many systemic issues that contribute to these difficulties, rather than feeling the pressure to be all things in every direction we want to focus here on how we as WPAs can strive for adequacy, rather than excellence. We believe we can practice adequacy by resisting perfectionism and building collaborative, sustainable, and accessible models of WPA work informed by the disability justice work of queer and people of color, an approach Leah Lakshmi Piepzna-Samarasinha (2018) refers to as care work, practices developed and cultivated within communities of multiply marginalized disabled people. She writes that through care work, "we are attempting to dream ways to access care deeply, in a way where we are in control, joyful, building community, loved, giving, and receiving, that doesn't burn anyone out or abuse or underpay anyone in the process" (33). Following Vidali (2015), who has argued that it needs to be OK for WPAs to be disabled and experience disability, without necessarily suggesting that WPA work should be disabling, we contend that our research and professional organizations should encourage this type of reciprocal care.

While we are three cishet white women with varying relationships to disability, we have nevertheless found care work to be a powerful model, and our group chat (which could more accurately be called a support group) is one way we practice care work with each other. We are not collaborators in the day-to-day work of running our writing programs, but we practice mutual support and caretaking as we process challenges and learn new ways to reframe our goals away from perfection and toward adequacy. As WPAs and mothers, we are so often called on to take care of others, but we do not often receive that type of care directed toward us, especially within our institutional contexts. Each of us has had to find multiple sources of care in our personal lives (thank you to loved ones, friends outside of work, therapists, healthcare professionals, exercise accountabuddies, and more), but we are also recognizing that we need forms of reciprocal care in our professional lives. We see this as a way for WPAs to recast "adequacy" away from failure and toward a new orientation to the goals we set for ourselves amid impossible conditions and expectations.

References

Adams Wooten, Courtney, Jacob Babb, Kristi Murray Costello, and Kate Navickas, eds. 2020. *The Things We Carry: Strategies for Recognizing and Negotiating Emotional Labor in Writing Program Administration*. Logan: Utah State University Press.
Aunos, Marjorie, Margaret Spencer, Laura Pacheco, and Evelina Pituch. 2022. "This Changes Everything: A Critical Reflection on the Impact of Internalized Ableist

Constructs on Becoming a Disabled Mother." *Disability and Society*. https://doi.org/10.1080/09687599.2022.2137392.

Bender, Sarah, Kristina S. Brown, Deanna L. Hensley Kasitz, and Olga Vega. 2022. "Academic Women and Their Children: Parenting During COVID-19 and the Impact on Scholarly Productivity." *Family Relations* 71(1; February): 46–67. https://doi.org/10.1111/fare.12632.

Charlton, Colin, Jonikka Charlton, Tarez Samra Graban, Kathleen J. Ryan, and Amy Ferdinandt Stolley, eds. 2011. *GenAdmin: Theorizing WPA Identities in the Twenty-First Century*. Anderson, SC: Parlor Press.

Cleveland Clinic. 2023. "CPTSD (Complex PTSD)." Last modified April 5. https://my.clevelandclinic.org/health/diseases/24881-cptsd-complex-ptsd.

Cedillo, Christina V., ed. 2021. "Invisible Labor in the Academy" issue. *Journal of Multimodal Rhetorics* 4 (2): 1–100. http://journalofmultimodalrhetorics.com/issue-4-2.

Costello, Kristi Murray, and Jacob Babb. 2020. "Emotional Labor, Writing Studies, and Writing Program Administration." In *The Things We Carry: Strategies for Recognizing and Negotiating Emotional Labor in Writing Program Administration*, edited by Courtney Adams Wooten, Jacob Babb, Kristi Murray Costello, and Kate Navickas, 3–16. Logan: Utah State University Press.

Cucciarre, Christine Peters, Deborah E. Morris, Lee Nickoson, Kim Hensley Owens, and Mary P. Sheridan. 2011. "Mothers' Ways of Making It—or Making Do?: Making (Over) Academic Lives in Rhetoric and Composition with Children." *Composition Studies* 39(1; Spring): 41–61.

Dobrin, Sidney I, ed. 2005. *Don't Call It That: The Composition Practicum*. Urbana, IL: National Council of Teachers of English.

Driscoll, Dana Lynn, S. Rebecca Leigh, Nadia Francine Zamin. 2020. "Self-Care as Professionalization: A Case for Ethical Doctoral Education in Composition Studies." *College Composition and Communication* 71, no. 3 (February),: 453–480.

Estrem, Heidi, and E. Shelley Reid. 2012. "What New Writing Teachers Talk About When They Talk About Teaching." *Pedagogy: Critical Approaches to Teaching Literature, Language, Composition, and Culture* 12, no. 3 (Fall): 449–480.

Fedukovich, Casie J., and Tracy Ann Morse. 2017. "Failures to Accommodate: GTA Preparation as a Site for a Transformative Culture of Access." *WPA: Writing Program Administration* 40, no. 3 (Summer): 39–60.

George, Diana, ed. 1999. *Kitchen Cooks, Plate Twirlers, and Troubadours: Writing Program Administrators Tell Their Stories*. Portsmouth, NH: Heinemann.

Grouling, Jennifer. 2015. "Resistance and Identity Formation: The Journey of the Graduate Student-Teacher." *Composition Forum* 32 (Fall) https://compositionforum.com/issue/32/resistance.php.

Hesse, Doug. 1993. "Teachers as Students, Reflecting Resistance." *College Composition and Communication* 44, no. 2 (December): 224–231.

Horner, Bruce. 2007. "Redefining Work and Value for Writing Program Administration." *JAC* 27 (1/2): 163–184. http://www.jstor.org/stable/20866772.

Johnson, Jennifer K. 2016. "TA Training in an Independent Writing Program: Revisiting the Old Comp/Lit Split in a New Venue." In *A Minefield of Dreams: Triumphs and Travails of Independent Writing Programs*, edited by Justin Everett and Cristina Hanganu-Bresch, 87–110. Fort Collins, CO: WAC Clearinghouse.

Johnson, Jennifer K. 2021. "Disciplinarity, Enculturation, and Teaching Identities: How Composition and Literature TAs Respond to TA Training." In *Standing at the Threshold: Working Through Liminality in the Composition and Rhetoric TAship*, edited by William J. Macauley, 60–85. Logan: Utah State University Press.

Kleinfeld, Elizabeth. 2020. "From Great to Good Enough: Recalibrating Expectations as WPA." In *The Things We Carry: Strategies for Recognizing and Negotiating Emotional Labor in Writing Program Administration*, edited by Courtney Adams Wooten, Jacob Babb, Kristi Murray Costello, and Kate Navickas, 237–250. Logan: Utah State University Press.

Kynard, Carmen. 2022. "Fakers and Takers: Disrespect, Crisis, and Inherited Whiteness in Rhetoric-Composition Studies." *Composition Studies* 50, no. 3 (Fall): 131–136. https://compositionstudiesjournal.files.wordpress.com/2023/03/kynard.pdf.

Mapes, Aimee, and Susan Miller-Cochran. 2019. "Framing Graduate Teaching Assistant Preparation Around Threshold Concepts of Writing Studies." In *(Re)Considering What We Know: Learning Thresholds in Writing, Composition, Rhetoric, and Literacy*, edited by Linda Adler-Kassner and Elizabeth Wardle, 208–226. Logan: Utah State University Press.

Micciche, Laura R. 2002. "More than a Feeling: Disappointment and WPA Work." *College English* 64, no. 4 (March): 432–458. https://doi.org/10.2307/3250746.

Minello, Alessandra, Sara Martucci, and Lidia K. C. Manzo. 2020. "The Pandemic and Academic Mothers: Present Hardship and Future Perspectives." *European Societies* 23 (1): 1–13. https://doi.org/10.1080/14616696.2020.1809690.

Misra, Joya, Jennifer Hicks Lundquist, Elissa Holmes, and Stephanie Agiomavritis. 2011. "The Ivory Ceiling of Service Work." *Academe* 97, no. 1 (January–February): 22–26. https://www.aaup.org/article/ivory-ceiling-service-work?wbc_pur.

Nielsen, Mathias Wullum. 2016. "Gender in Equality and Research Performance: Moving Beyond Individual-Meritocratic Explanations of Academic Advancement." *Studies in Higher Education* 41 (11): 2044–2060. https://doi.org/10.1080/03075079.2015.1007945.

Osorio, Ruth. 2021. "Constellating with our Foremothers: Stories of Mothers Making Space in Rhetoric and Composition." *constellations: a cultural rhetorics publishing space*, no. 4 (August 18). https://constell8cr.com/articles/mothers-making-space-rhet-comp/.

Osorio, Ruth, Vyshali Manivannan, and Jessie Male, eds. 2022a. "Special Issue on Carework and Writing During COVID: Part I." *Journal of Multimodal Rhetorics* 6 (2). http://journalofmultimodalrhetorics.com/6-2-issue-intro.

Osorio, Ruth, Vyshali Manivannan, and Jessie Male, eds. 2022b. "Special Issue on Carework and Writing During COVID: Part II." *Journal of Multimodal Rhetorics* 7 (1). http://journalofmultimodalrhetorics.com/7-1-issue.

Owens, Kim Hensley. 2023. "When Too Much Really Is Too Much: On WPAing Through the COVID Years." *WPA: Writing Program Administration* 47, no. 1 (Fall): 68–75.

Panahi, Parva. 2021. "A Multilingual Orientation to Preparing Teaching Assistants to Teach Argumentation in First-Year Writing." In *Argumentative Writing in a Second Language: Perspectives on Research and Pedagogy*, edited by Alan R. Hirvela and Diane Belcher, 115–135. Ann Arbor: University of Michigan Press.

Piepzna-Samarasinha, Leah Lakshmi. 2018. *Care Work: Dreaming Disability Justice*. Vancouver: Arsenal Pulp Press.

Rai, Candice. 2023. "Institutional Climate Changing." In *Rhetorical Climatology*. By a reading group: Chris Ingraham, John Ackerman, Jennifer Lin LeMesurier, Bridie McGreavy, Candice Rai, and Nathan Stormer, 99–119. East Lansing: Michigan State University Press.

Reed, Meridith. 2020. "Enacting Bricolage: Theorizing the Teaching Practices of Graduate Writing Instructors." *WPA: Writing Program Administration* 44, no. 1 (Fall): 107–128.

Reid, E. Shelley. 2017. "On Learning to Teach: Letter to a New TA." *WPA: Writing Program Administration* 40, no. 2 (Spring): 129–145.

Restaino, Jessica. 2012. *First Semester: Graduate Students, Teaching Writing, and the Challenge of Middle Ground*. Carbondale: Southern Illinois University Press.

Saidy, Christina, and Thomas Sura. 2020. "When Everything Changes over Night: What We Learned from Teaching the Practicum in the Era of Covid-19." *Teaching/Writing: The Journal of Writing Teacher Education* 9, no. 1 (Summer): 1–5.

Saur, Elizabeth, and Jason Palmeri. 2017. "Letter to a New TA: Affect Edition." *WPA: Writing Program Administration* 40, no. 2 (Spring): 146–153.

Schwaller, Emily Jo. "Rethinking Graduate Student Instructors' Resistance as Acts of Well-Being." *Composition Studies* 50, no. 2 (Summer): 112–131.

Strickland, Donna. 2011. *The Managerial Unconscious in the History of Composition Studies*. Carbondale: Southern Illinois University Press.

Thu, Sumyat, Katie Malcolm, Candice Rai, and Anis Bawarshi. "Translingualism and Anti-Racist Writing Praxis." In *Writing Across Difference: Theory and Intervention*, edited by James Rushing Daniel, Kate Malcolm, and Candice Rai, 195–217. Logan: Utah State University Press.

Vidali, Amy. 2015. "Disabling Writing Program Administration." *WPA: Writing Program Administration* 38, no. 2 (Spring): 32–55.

Williams, Joan C. 2005. "The Glass Ceiling and the Maternal Wall in Academia." *New Directions for Higher Education* 2005, no. 130 (Summer): 91–105. https://doi.org/10.1002/he.181.

Zimmer, Katarina. 2020. "Gender Gap in Research Output Widens During Pandemic." *Scientist*. Last modified June 25. https://www.the-scientist.com/gender-gap-in-research-output-widens-during-pandemic-67665.

9
Laboring Through the Lifecycle

Toward a Disciplinary Approach to Faculty Evaluation

LAURIE A. PINKERT AND LAUREN MARSHALL BOWEN

In recent years, higher education has experienced significant and publicly debated shifts in the landscape of accountability. Some of these pressures to change the standards of evaluation and productivity are built on a generalized suspicion of the academy, raised by critiques of academic institutions in general, and of tenure in particular (Worthen 2021). By legislating curricula, hiring, and promotion activities, and by increasing the decision-making power of appointed boards, politicians have become increasingly involved in the standards by which faculty are evaluated (American Association of University Professors 2023). Further pressures from corporations that have moved into the landscape of higher education challenge the primacy of universities and colleges (Miller and Selden 2014) and the centrality of faculty governance and expertise.

Not all changes, however, have been motivated by an interest in curtailing or restricting faculty behaviors. Some have been motivated by a desire to radically revise evaluation to support more meaningful and equitable processes. Amid the many challenges that the COVID-19 pandemic presented, the global disruption of labor forced a moment of reckoning, as colleges and universities had to account for the pandemic in all of its facets, including faculty evaluation, tenure, and promotion. In some cases, the emergency measures prompted more enduring change (McMurtrie 2023). At Lauren's institution, for instance, a task force recommended that departments shift teaching evaluation from numerical student scores toward more developmental practices (Joint Task Force of Faculty Council and Provost 2022). And yet, the opportunity that the pandemic presented to think more expansively about faculty evaluation has been generally lost, and temporary solutions, such as pausing the tenure clock, seemed to recommit to evaluation as defined by the "uninterrupted and predictable march toward a singular objective" (Gannon 2021).

Questions about how to define and evaluate productivity aren't new to the discipline of Rhetoric, Composition, and Writing Studies (RCWS) and its ongoing struggle for legitimacy and recognition. The field has regularly wrestled with defining "success" and has attempted to shape the ways in which adequacy is measured. One thread has focused on considerations of what counts as legitimate intellectual labor, as historically RCWS scholars and practitioners have needed to justify applications of their disciplinary expertise for institutions that routinely fail to recognize its value. Scholars have argued for the inclusion of perspectives, epistemologies, and research methods that have not been privileged by academia or the field (Perryman-Clark and Craig 2019; Powell 2002); early advocates for digital and multimodal scholarship have demonstrated the rigor of such work (Ball 2004); and professional organizations have advocated for unrecognized disciplinary labor to be recognized as intellectual activity (Council of Writing Program Administrators 1998). Furthermore, members of the field have urged us all to be sure that activities such as caregiving, often associated with invisible ceilings in the academy (Williams 2005), do not become a barrier to success in RCWS (Ballif et al. 2008; Cucciarre et al. 2011). These calls most often expand our definitions of "what counts."

We too have called for change in the ways we understand our disciplinary labor, challenging the prevalent metaphor of the "career arc," which all too often instantiates an ages-and-stages model of development that slopes upward toward midcareer and downward toward retirement, in favor of a more realistic imagining of the contours common to a RCWS career that acknowledges that expertise is lifelong and "lifewide" (Smith et al. 2020). We offered disciplinary lifecycling as a framework that could better account for the ways that the variously positioned members of our field apply their disciplinary knowledge across space and time (Pinkert and Bowen 2021). But what might lifecycling mean for the evaluation of our labor and definitions of success, adequacy, and failure for faculty in RCWS?

In this chapter, we test the strength of the disciplinary lifecycle metaphor to help us rethink the practical and very nonmetaphorical process of faculty evaluation. We explore the potential of disciplinary lifecycling to provide a generative frame for evaluation in RCWS; acknowledge the positionality of individuals across our field and within our institutions; develop measures of adequacy that center the discipline rather than the institution; and provide a framework that values the continuation of disciplinary development.

In doing so, we envision a more participatory, disciplinary-based model of evaluation, thereby disrupting neoliberal valuing and positioning of faculty expertise, as called for by scholars such as Genesea Carter and Rickie-Ann Legleitner (2021) and Arianna Kezar and colleagues (2019). We further imagine a means of evaluating labor in the discipline that does not rely on reductive, often quantitative measures of "success" that render invisible or irrelevant much disciplinary activity that takes place throughout one's lifecycle. Our aim is to help RCWS stakeholders—from those who develop shared standards to those who conduct annual reviews—use lifecycling to rethink the evaluation in a way that centers the disciplinary labor that occurs throughout the lifecycle.

Tensions in Evaluation: Competing Logics and Contrasting Discourses

Our interest in exploring the relevance of lifecycling to faculty evaluation grew, in part, out of Laurie's experiences on a committee tasked with revising the standards and procedures for annual review for her department, a stand-alone Writing and Rhetoric department within a large public research university. This experience provided the opportunity to examine not only the standards by which faculty were evaluated but also the ways in which evaluation was conceptualized more broadly across the institution. At Laurie's institution, faculty are evaluated based on their respective assignments in teaching, research, service, and other duties. Faculty are only evaluated in the areas in which they have assigned "time" (i.e., assigned responsibilities). Each department is responsible for developing their own standards for annual evaluation. These standards are reviewed regularly and may be revised at any interval with a corresponding faculty vote. Faculty-elected standards must be approved by a faculty-supporting unit that reports to the provost before going into effect. This system maintains administrative oversight but also allows for faculty participation through the required departmental committee and the required vote for approval.

The revision of annual evaluation standards in Laurie's department exposed competing narratives about adequacy: Sometimes, it seemed that individuals within the department were doing too much and, yet, the department as a whole wasn't doing enough. Despite the existing checklist-style annual evaluation standards that could have promoted certainty around evaluative expectations, faculty experienced heightened anxiety, uncertain how to define adequacy on individual or collective scales. The process also exposed the ways that the annual evaluation process drove commitments to things faculty perceived that they "must" do in order to be evaluated highly, whether or not these "musts" were perceived as important to their individual professional development or to collective goals like student success. Furthermore, the process raised questions about whether it should be possible for everyone to be excellent or whether excellence should be reserved for the few. Saving high praise for rare occasions becomes a practical problem when the limited merit pay available will be distributed only to those who meet standards of excellence (not adequacy) on their faculty evaluation.

The acknowledgment of limitations and contradictions in university evaluation systems is not new (Bogt and Scapens 2012; Dobija et al. 2019; Guthrie and Neumann 2007), nor is it isolated to institutions like Laurie's. Similar situations in which faculty evaluation is constrained by unclear goals or competing priorities can emerge from institutions of all shapes, sizes, and missions and has been linked to rising neoliberalism in higher education. In fact, Martin Cave and colleagues described "new managerialism in higher education" as early as 1989, raising the still-unresolved questions about why faculty so often "fee[l] like their evaluations are an externally imposed constraint rather than the means by which they judge themselves" (11). These tensions echo the issues inherent in contrasting discourses (e.g., national governance strategies vs. institutional missions vs. individual goals), which arise especially in public universities, where there is a high need to attract funding amid significant reductions in resources (Manes-Rossi et al. 2022). Such contrasting discourses are further complicated by competing logics (e.g., commercial logics vs. professional and public service logic) behind performance evaluation in universities (Grossi et al. 2020). All in all, the project forced Laurie and her RCWS colleagues to reckon with their lack of a shared framework for evaluation and to consider: What constitutes *adequate* individual and collective labor?

Our discipline has, on occasion, attempted to intervene in constraining institutional evaluation procedures through public statements by its professional organizations. For example, the "CCCC Statement on Working Conditions for Non-Tenure-Track Writing Faculty," while primarily concerned about evaluation processes being equitable and offering protection from arbitrary dismissal of RCWS faculty, acknowledges the value of "rigorous, systematic evaluations" as "essential faculty development tools" (Conference on College

Composition and Communication 2016). In another example, the Council of Writing Program Administrators' (1998) "Evaluating the Intellectual Work of Writing Administration" is an effort to increase recognition of RCWS faculty administrative work as intellectual labor that contributes to disciplinary knowledge and expertise. The statement indicates a fundamental difficulty with quantifiable measures of products as "professional accomplishments," since "activities other than research and teaching... have little exchange value" and are often relegated to "the ill-defined and seldom-rewarded category of 'service' in promotion and tenure evaluations." The very existence of these statements suggests that common practices of faculty evaluation are often reductive and obscure the intellectual work performed by many RCWS faculty, and that RCWS faculty may not experience evaluation that fully accounts for the breadth and impact of their work.

Commonplaces in Evaluation: Accounting for Activities

To better understand the ways that RCWS faculty might experience evaluation, we first examine an often used model of evaluation: an activity-based model. The activity-based model centers the quantification of activities an individual performs, often providing a list of accepted or suggested activities within each category of a faculty member's assigned duties, and then requiring that a faculty member conduct a certain number of activities to meet a certain rating. For example, an activity-based evaluation system might provide a list of activities like the abbreviated version in table 9.1 and instruct faculty to indicate which activities were completed in the review period.

An activity-based system might require that the faculty member complete four activities for an excellent rating, two activities for an above satisfactory rating, and a described baseline for a satisfactory rating. A baseline for teaching might include holding class meetings as scheduled, submitting syllabi on time, holding office hours, responding to student work, and submitting grades in a timely fashion. On the surface, the activity-based system may look transparent: Just do the things on the list, and you get credit; earn enough credits, and you get a high evaluation. But further examination can expose some of the inconsistencies and complexities.

One problem with this approach is that the checklist flattens the variation inherent in these activities. Each activity may require different kinds of resources or different positionalities. For example, if someone needs to teach four different course preparations in order to check that part of the teaching

TABLE 9.1. Abbreviated example of an activity-based evaluation system rubric

Teaching Activities

___ Receives course evaluation ratings above the department average
___ Teaches four or more course preparations in a year
___ Mentors a student in publishing their writing
___ Participates in faculty development seminar related to teaching

Research Activities

___ Publishes an article or book chapter
___ Presents a paper at a conference
___ Receives a research grant
___ Is recognized with a research award

Service Activities

___ Serves on a committee for a disciplinary organization
___ Serves on a university committee
___ Serves in a college committee
___ Serves on a department committee

Administrative Activities

___ Conducts orientations, staff meetings, and/or workshops for program stakeholders
___ Oversees and submits programmatic assessment
___ Chairs programmatic committee(s)

list, but they get a grant that reduces their teaching load, or a class gets cancelled due to low enrollment, they may not have the opportunity to receive credit in that area. Similarly, some committees may offer only elected positions or may limit membership to those of certain ranks or position types, eliminating the opportunity for some faculty to get credit in this area.

Yet another problem is that the listed activities often don't account for the bulk of faculty labor in that category of their assignment. If a faculty member is teaching four classes a semester (eight classes in an academic year), the majority of their teaching time and labor is spent on teaching those four classes—preparing lessons, conducting class, responding to student inquiries, reading student writing, conferencing with students, grading student projects, meeting with students in office hours, and building online course content. These activities take up the greatest proportion of time but likely do not appear anywhere in their checklist. Even if these activities comprise the baseline of teaching expectations, the checklist approach presents a situation in which one cannot be excellent for the quality of their teaching in the classroom. Rather, they can only be excellent for the quantity of additional activities they do beyond their classroom teaching. This problem is exacerbated by the fact that some of the activities listed aren't really activities at all; they are the end results from activities, or the resources needed to do activities. For example, "publication of an article" does not name an activity but a result that comes from several activities, including generating the idea, conducting the research, and spending the time writing, submitting, and revising.

While activity-based systems aren't the only ones in use for faculty evaluation, the examination of the activity-based model highlights how inconsistencies might inhere in evaluation systems. Faculty might lack the resources needed to meet certain standards placed upon them, and/or they might find that the bulk of their labor is not recognized in the systems they experience. Such examination left us wondering about how faculty in RCWS might account for the diversity of their labor and accomplishments, and whether disciplinary lifecycling could offer a framework for doing so.

Disciplinary Lifecycling: New Possibilities for Development and Evaluation

Proposed as an alternative to the linear, rising-and-falling, age-biased model of the "career arc," we developed the lifecycling model from our collection of quantitative and qualitative survey data, in which members of the field described the experiences they associated with their disciplinary expertise (Pinkert and Bowen 2021). The framework has several key features that, if used to frame RCWS faculty evaluation, might help to mitigate the inconsistencies and inadequacies of other approaches. In this section, we outline three strategic shifts in faculty evaluation based on lifecycling's primary features: centering the discipline as a standard for disciplinary labor, acknowledging environments and varied spaces of action, and reimagining the timelines involved in intellectual labor.

SHIFT 1: CENTER THE DISCIPLINE AS A STANDARD FOR DISCIPLINARY LABOR

Disciplinary lifecycling centers the development, production, and reproduction of disciplinary knowledge: "The disciplinary lifecycling model . . . recenters career development on relationships to the discipline rather than employing institutions" (Pinkert and Bowen 2021, 38). This reorientation to the discipline provides two important possibilities for evaluation in RCWS. First, it provides an opportunity to reconceptualize and reposition the work of research, teaching, service, and administration in equitable ways. Such a move might counter the wide gap that Ernest Boyer (1997) and others have identified in truly assigning equal merit to the categories of assignment. Such a move could center, for example, the role that teaching plays in the discovery, application, and circulation of disciplinary knowledge. This could offer the necessary space for faculty members to more fully consider how disciplinary best practices can be demonstrated through one's teaching and to counter the evaluative structures that can sometimes dissuade faculty from productive activities like implementing *new* teaching practices. For example, a focus on quantity metrics such as the number of students who rate a teacher highly on their course evaluation or the number of students who pass/fail a given course can dissuade teachers from the work of disciplinarily relevant teaching in favor of metrics that don't always capture quality.

This approach can also create the possibility of differentiating the ways that disciplinary knowledge can be refined even within a single category of assignment. For example, faculty might serve on an institutional parking and transportation committee that reviews policies and needs on their campus. This might seem far afield from the faculty member's expertise in RCWS, but in fact, it presents an opportunity to engage the faculty member's disciplinary expertise in the ways that they conduct the work of the committee. For example, they might employ best practices for public participation that draw from our field's knowledge of power dynamics and development of critical rhetorical approaches. In other words, they have the opportunity to apply their disciplinary expertise to the coordination of the committee. On the other hand, a member of the department may serve on the university's general education committee, which oversees the development and review of general education courses, including composition. In this role, they may provide crucial insight into the ways that students in composition courses benefit from certain class sizes that allow for routine and detailed faculty feedback, and they may draw from and share professional statements and research studies to demonstrate the best practices within the discipline that can inform this work. They might circulate their knowledge of disciplinary documents to inform the committee's work. This differentiation not only offers a means of acknowledging the contribution of service work to discovery, application, and circulation, but it also creates opportunities for faculty to consider and select roles and projects with individual and/or collective development in mind.

For many, this shift away from the institutional focus of faculty evaluation will be significant, but we see it as a possibility for raising the visibility of disciplinary knowledge in RCWS both as a contribution to and metric for research endeavors and as a way to bring value to the work we do across our categories of assignment, in teaching, service, and administration as well. Taken further, differentiating work based on disciplinary knowledge may create a means of resisting what we, and many of our colleagues, have experienced as a gradual increase of faculty responsibilities—not always distributed equitably (Allen et al. 2023)—that may overextend and thereby exploit faculty roles, particularly as universities continue to make extensive cuts to hiring and staff in anticipation of enrollment shortages. Rather than saying yes to everything because it needs to get done, differentiation of labor may allow the individual to consider the activity for its implications for disciplinary development before they opt into or out of specific opportunities. In addition, this approach may allow institutional units to focus their attention on the activities that best refine their collective expertise.

SHIFT 2: ACKNOWLEDGE ENVIRONMENTS AND VARIED SPACES OF ACTION

Lifecycling makes possible nuanced acknowledgment of faculty activities' contributions to disciplinary development, and it does so by recognizing the variability of context: that is, the ways that the same environment can operate as a disciplinary space of action for some but not others and that the same actions, when prompted from different environments, can have different consequences:

> We differentiate environments—the places in which our activities occur—from spaces of action—those particular environments in which individuals experience agentive possibilities for disciplinary development... Environments certainly provide a background for disciplinary activity that is necessary to acknowledge but an environment shared by two individuals does not necessarily indicate equal access to a space of action... which are created by organizational contexts, position responsibilities, reporting structures, and so forth. (Pinkert and Bowen 2021, 31)

This acknowledgment of environments as potential, but not guaranteed, spaces of action that enable different kinds of disciplinary development can be used to reframe and explore the inconsistencies faculty may have experienced in access to the resources needed to meet certain standards or accomplish certain goals.

A disciplinary lifecycle approach would allow for and, perhaps, require the discussion of context in an attempt to reflect on and recognize that spaces of action offer access to particular activities. For example, this might provide context for the disparate experiences of faculty who teach similar courses but for whom teaching plays very different roles in their disciplinary development. Many qualified teacher-researchers may be discouraged from applying for pedagogically focused research grants or may not be eligible for teaching the kinds of courses that would most acutely apply their disciplinary expertise. This constraint may have little to do with one's expertise or credentials, and more to do with the distinctions many institutions draw between the role of "teaching" faculty (e.g., non-tenure-track lecturers) and "research" faculty (e.g., tenure-stream professors). While both faculty roles may operate in the same environment—the university classroom—this context may not provide the same "space of action" for both roles. Both might receive positive evaluations for innovative course design or positive student evaluations, but one might be privileged in support for teacher-research while another might be limited in or not recognized for the same kind of activity. For instance, research-active faculty often have travel funding (however modest) to support conference attendance. Seen as a necessity for sharing research findings, conferences often create avenues for learning about practices that can inform teaching and would be otherwise inaccessible to those who do not have travel allowances.

While we would not simply want to endlessly expand the list of valid activities for teacher evaluation to include things like research as a necessity and, thereby, contribute to the silent but steady bloat of faculty labor, by acknowledging that contexts are experienced variably we propose a way to narrate and more fully describe the disciplinary environments that allow faculty to implement new content or pedagogies, which may incentivize access to disciplinary spaces of action commonly restricted to research and scholarship. Further, it might allow faculty within the same institution to have productive conversations about the ways that activities like conference attendance might enable teaching faculty to bring disciplinary best practices into their pedagogy, supporting justifications for funding to support disciplinary development regardless of domain (teaching, research, service, administration). As a discipline, it might help us rethink the ways we can provide more equitable transformative access (Banks 2006) to activities like conferences without requiring travel resources out of reach to so many of the laborers in our field.

SHIFT 3: REIMAGINE THE TIMELINES INVOLVED IN DISCIPLINARY KNOWLEDGE DEVELOPMENT

The third shift necessitated by a lifecycling framework is a reorientation toward time that situates one's activities within the ongoing process of expertise development by the individual and knowledge development by the discipline. A lifecycling approach cannot ignore timing as it affects both the possibilities for and contexts of disciplinary development: "Over time and across contexts . . . disciplinary knowledge is conceived and regenerated through a range of activities and practices that make up the ongoing process that we call lifecycling" (Pinkert and Bowen 2021, 29).

Such a time-aware approach acknowledges that disciplinary expertise isn't developed once and for all but is refined in continual renegotiation with changing aspects of one's own knowledge, the field's scholarship, one's applications of knowledge, and/or the absences of conceptual and practical experiences related to one's areas of expertise. It also acknowledges that the process of expertise development contains different experiences. When one aims to develop expertise in a new area, more interaction and engagement with varying sources of knowledge may be needed for the sake of learning, whereas when one aims to test the transferability of their knowledge, they may need opportunities to apply that knowledge within various contexts.

This approach recognizes that although the listing of annual activities can momentarily stabilize the ongoing process of disciplinary development, reflection on and articulation of the roles and purposes of the activities can better inform a trajectory that is cognizant of the discipline that exists beyond the institution. This approach pushes back against the typical notion of activities as counted once and counted only when "done"—a notion that runs counter to our disciplinary knowledge and that likely motivates some of the sense of overwork that members of our field experience.

We recognize that annual evaluations are bound by a specific timeframe and are typically not cumulative. We believe, however, that it is not only possible but productive to approach the singular "snapshot" of annual review from a lifecycle view. Such an approach suggests that even if bound by timeframes, the annual review can be more than a quantitative accounting of activities or products within a calendar or academic year; it also can invite participants to reflect on and articulate the roles that their activities are playing within their lifecycle.

Evaluating Labor Across the Lifecycle: Practical Moves

We expect, of course, that transitioning to this model would necessarily involve not-inconsequential startup costs in terms of faculty labor, as we imagine that, for the vast majority of RCWS faculty, the modes of evaluation we describe here represent a significant departure from the status quo. While it is not possible to prescribe a one-size-fits-all set of criteria for faculty evaluation, here we offer a heuristic that we hope illuminates the possibilities of a disciplinary lifecycle model for faculty evaluation, and perhaps provides a starting point that might expedite some of the groundwork necessary to establishing a new approach to evaluation.

When we think about developing standards for evaluation with disciplinary knowledge development in mind, we imagine that initial conversations about how the evaluation can center disciplinary development would be grounded in questions such as, *What does disciplinary development look like for faculty within our unit?* And, *how do faculty within our unit engage with disciplinary knowledge in each of the categories of assignment?* To acknowledge and examine the environments in which disciplinary knowledge development takes place and the contexts that create transformative access (Banks 2006), faculty might discuss the environments in which disciplinary labor takes place across the categories of assignment, and the infrastructures that encourage or constrain disciplinary development within those environments. And, finally, to recognize the varied roles that activities play in the ongoing process of disciplinary development, faculty involved in setting or revising evaluation standards might consider the following questions: *How might a faculty member within our context discover, apply, or circulate disciplinary knowledge for themselves? For others? What processes of development do we want to center and encourage for faculty within our unit?* These questions can promote the development of disciplinary-oriented evaluation frameworks and challenge the institution-centric approach to most faculty evaluation standards.

What if, for example, instead of asking faculty members to perform a certain number of completed activities in each category of assignment (as in the activity-based system we examined previously), we ask them to narrate the following in each of their assignment categories: one activity that is contributing to their development of new disciplinary knowledge, one activity that is contributing to their application of disciplinary knowledge, and one activity that is enabling them to share disciplinary knowledge with others? This could reorient faculty toward the discipline, toward the varied contexts, and toward the roles that each activity is playing in the micro-cycles of their larger lifecycle. We might imagine a lifecycle-based evaluation form could look something like table 9.2.

Such reorientation toward cyclical development can be a mechanism for narrating activities across typical categories of assignment. For example:

TABLE 9.2. Sample lifecycle-based evaluation system rubric

For each category in which you have assigned duties, identify and describe an activity through which you discovered, applied, or circulated disciplinary knowledge. If you do not have assigned duties in an area, leave that section blank.

Name the activity.	Indicate the role this activity plays in your disciplinary development.	Describe the ways you discovered, applied, or circulated disciplinary knowledge.	Note any relevant resources or infrastructures that enabled this development.	Highlight, if relevant, the ways you hope to continue to develop your expertise in this area.
Teaching				
___ Discovery				
___ Application				
___ Circulation				
Research				
___ Discovery				
___ Application				
___ Circulation				
Service				
___ Discovery				
___ Application				
___ Circulation				
Program administration				
___ Discovery				
___ Application				
___ Circulation				

- For teaching, one can be learning about a new pedagogy (discovery), deploying best practices (application), and sharing vetted or approved course materials with a new faculty member in the department (circulation).
- For research, one can be collecting data on a new study (discovery), employing a new method or process (application), and publishing an article about the results of a completed research project (circulation).

- For service, one can join a committee to learn about local context of the institution (discovery), draw from disciplinary expertise to guide a committee's actions or approach (application), and introduce findings or literature in the field to other committee members to inform committee activity (circulation).
- For program administration, one can attend a conference or workshop to learn about new administrative perspectives or approaches (discovery), implement research-based findings into program design or revision (application), and present program self-assessment results at an institutional forum or conference (circulation).

By offering a heuristic that features discovery, application, and circulation as ways that we might individually and collectively develop disciplinary knowledge, we don't mean to suggest that these are the only experiences along the lifecycle. Instead, we hope to suggest a way to revise evaluation to validate the labor that goes into the process of disciplinary development. Such a move can resist notions of adequacy that center only on the products of disciplinary activities rather than the value of the activities themselves.

Possibilities for Evaluating Individual and Collective Labor Through the Lifecycle

We see disciplinary lifecycling as not just a metaphor for reimagining the RCWS career but also a generative way to resituate disciplinary development as a key facet of and potential framework for faculty evaluation. Such an approach would necessitate important conversations about the ways that faculty want to describe their disciplinary knowledge and to account for the development of that expertise across their labor categories and across their lifecycles. Ideally, the collaborative creation of new evaluative standards through a lifecycling framework would push faculty toward shared understanding of their individual and collective goals and possible ways to reach those goals together. For those laboring in RCWS, disciplinary development could become a standard for adequacy, thereby reinforcing the necessity of ongoing disciplinary development for those who teach, research, serve, and coordinate programs within the discipline. If faculty collectively set their standards for what adequate annual disciplinary development might look like, this can preempt notions of stagnation or laziness that sometimes accompany stereotypes of the college professor. It can also give us opportunities to plan for and reflect on our development, taking responsibility for and an active role in our evaluative processes.

While we are hopeful that disciplinary lifecycling might encourage a generally positive shift in perspectives of RCWS faculty evaluation and what constitutes "adequate" faculty labor, we recognize that the practical value of our proposal is limited by the varying access RCWS faculty members may have to influence evaluation processes and criteria at their own institutions. We recognize that different configurations of faculty roles and responsibilities, differences in institutional governance structures, and current approaches to faculty evaluation will constrain how much agency and support departments and faculty evaluation committees might have to self-determine a significant perspective change in faculty evaluation.

Furthermore, the shift in orientation from institution to discipline inevitably bumps up against a common challenge for RCWS faculty in multidisciplinary departments: how to be evaluated, and *valued*, by non-RCWS colleagues. RCWS faculty members positioned in English departments, for instance, might wonder about what it would mean to be evaluated in terms of disciplinary development if department-level faculty evaluators (i.e., review committees and chairs) include non-RCWS faculty. While we argue that the challenge of cross-disciplinary evaluation is already widely experienced, we are cautiously optimistic that this shift might precipitate important, edifying discussions about what constitutes disciplinary development and expertise for RCWS faculty, as it stands apart from other English Studies disciplines. Further, implementation of this perspective into documented criteria and procedures would codify those disciplinary distinctions in ways that could better serve the assessment of RCWS faculty in their home departments.

As we encourage faculty evaluation to orient toward RCWS disciplinary knowledge, it is not our intent to call for a retreat into disciplinary isolationism, thereby "silo-ing" faculty from colleagues and practices in other disciplines. RCWS faculty have historically developed, applied, and circulated their expertise from and among other disciplines. Therefore, we see enormous adaptive potential for RCWS expertise across the full range of teaching, research, service, and administrative activities that RCWS faculty perform. While we are less certain that the disciplinary lifecycling approach would have similar transformative possibilities for other disciplines (physics comes to mind), we anticipate that RCWS faculty would find enormous potential for the often invisible work they already do to build interdisciplinary connections to be recognized and rewarded in the disciplinary lifecycling vision of faculty development.

Furthermore, this approach, with its disciplinary orientation, offers a way for faculty to acknowledge for themselves so many of the affordances that they want to offer students and so many of the realities that they describe in studies of writers/writing in context. For example, by focusing on the process of discovery/application/circulation of knowledge, faculty might find space to describe not only their successes but also the failures they experienced along the way. Failure, for example, has been theorized within our field as an important part of writing development (Brooke and Carr 2015). If faculty image themselves as ever-developing writers within the field of RCWS, this opens space to narrate and acknowledge all the activities, including failures, that lead to learning.

Such an approach might also help mitigate any tendencies to negate experiences beyond the institution as relevant to one's application of disciplinary expertise, further expanding the boundaries of our intellectual gaze beyond the composing that individuals and collectives do within "schooled" spaces (Mahiri 2005) and/or in their early lives (Bowen and Pinkert 2020). Many of the participants in our interview-based study of retirement in RCWS described the ways that they put off civic and public activities until retirement because these activities were not part of their institutionally recognizable or institutionally sponsored work (Bowen and Pinkert 2020). However, a lifecycle approach might encourage more active, present engagement in a range of activities that hone our disciplinary knowledge across contexts. This could hold generative potential for individual RCWS faculty and also establish meaningful feedback loops for the discipline as well. By integrating the breadth of our field's disciplinary knowledge and practices—which recognize that individuals will and already do compose far beyond a singular institution—we might better develop our own expertise to support curricula, initiatives, and community-based projects that position our collective expertise as central to learning, literacy, and writing across contexts. Lifecycling can remind us of our responsibility to create such opportunities toward literacy development in a yet-to-be-experienced future. And, maybe, just maybe, our attempts to define adequacy for evaluation within our institution might also drive us to discover, apply, and circulate our disciplinary knowledge beyond the institutions in which we labor, toward the needs of the communities in which to live.

References

Allen, Tammy D., Michelle Hughes Miller, Kimberly A. French, Eunsook Kim, and Grisselle Centeno. 2023. "Faculty Time Expenditure Across Research, Teaching, and Service: Do Gender Differences Persist?" *Occupational Health Science*, May 1–14. https://doi.org/10.1007/s41542-023-00156-w.

American Association of University Professors. 2023. "Political Interference in Higher Ed." AAUP. March 2. https://www.aaup.org/issues/political-interference-higher-ed.

Ball, Cheryl E. 2004. "Show, Not Tell: The Value of New Media Scholarship." *Computers and Composition* 21 (4): 403–425. https://doi.org/10.1016/j.compcom.2004.08.001.

Ballif, Michelle, D. Diane Davis, and Roxanne Mountford. 2008. *Women's Ways of Making It in Rhetoric and Composition*. New York: Routledge.

Banks, Adam J. 2006. *Race, Rhetoric, and Technology: Searching for Higher Ground*. Mahwah, NJ: Lawrence Erlbaum.

Bogt, Henk J. ter, and Robert W. Scapens. 2012. "Performance Management in Universities: Effects of the Transition to More Quantitative Measurement Systems." *European Accounting Review* 21 (3): 451–497. https://doi.org/10.1080/09638180.2012.668323.

Bowen, Lauren Marshall, and Laurie A. Pinkert. 2020. "Identities Developed, Identities Denied: Examining the Disciplinary Activities and Disciplinary Positioning of Retirees in Rhetoric, Composition, and Writing Studies." *College Composition and Communication* 72 (2): 251–281. https://doi.org/10.58680/ccc202031037.

Boyer, Ernest L. 1997. *Scholarship Reconsidered: Priorities of the Professoriate*. Princeton, NJ: Jossey-Bass.

Brooke, Collin, and Allison Carr. 2015. "Failure Can Be an Important Part of Writing Development." In *Naming What We Know*, edited by Linda Adler-Kassner and Elizabeth Wardle, 62–63, Logan: Utah State University Press.

Carter, Genesea, and Rickie-Ann Legleitner. 2021. "Prioritizing Ourselves and Our Values: Intersectionality, Positionality, and Dismantling the Neoliberal University System." *Academic Labor: Research and Artistry* 5 (1): 2–20. https://digitalcommons.humboldt.edu/alra/vol5/iss1/1.

Cave, Martin, Maurice Kogan, and Stephen Hanney. 1989. "Performance Measurement in Higher Education." *Public Money and Management* 9 (1): 11–16. https://doi.org/10.1080/09540968909387519.

Conference on College Composition and Communication. 2016. "CCCC Statement on Working Conditions for Non-Tenure-Track Writing Faculty." *Conference on College Composition and Communication* (blog). April 2016. https://cccc.ncte.org/cccc/resources/positions/working-conditions-ntt/.

Council of Writing Program Administrators. 1998. "Evaluating the Intellectual Work of Writing Administration." Rev. 2019. https://wpacouncil.org/aws/CWPA/pt/sd/news_article/242849/_PARENT/layout_details/false.

Cucciarre, Christine Peters, Deborah E. Morris, Lee Nickoson, Kim Hensley Owens, and Mary P. Sheridan. 2011. "Mothers' Ways of Making It—or Making Do?: Making (Over) Academic Lives in Rhetoric and Composition with Children." *Composition Studies* 39 (1): 41–61.

Dobija, Dorota, Anna Maria Górska, Giuseppe Grossi, and Wojciech Strzelczyk. 2019. "Rational and Symbolic Uses of Performance Measurement: Experiences from Polish Universities." *Accounting, Auditing and Accountability Journal* 32 (3): 750–781. https://doi.org/10.1108/AAAJ-08-2017-3106.

Gannon, Kevin. 2021. "Advice | Faculty Evaluation After the Pandemic." *Chronicle of Higher Education*, June 9. https://www.chronicle.com/article/faculty-evaluation-after-the-pandemic.

Grossi, Giuseppe, Dorota Dobija, and Wojciech Strzelczyk. 2020. "The Impact of Competing Institutional Pressures and Logics on the Use of Performance Measurement in Hybrid Universities." *Public Performance and Management Review* 43 (4): 818–844. https://doi.org/10.1080/15309576.2019.1684328.

Guthrie, James, and Ruth Neumann. 2007. "Economic and Non-Financial Performance Indicators in Universities." *Public Management Review* 9 (2): 231–252. https://doi.org/10.1080/14719030701340390.

Joint Task Force of Faculty Council and Provost. November 2022. "Holistic Evaluation of Teaching." University of Massachusetts Boston. https://www.umb.edu/faculty-staff/faculty-council/minutes-and-reports/minutes/.

Kezar, Adrianna, Tom DePaola, and Daniel T. Scott. 2019. *The Gig Academy: Mapping Labor in the Neoliberal University*. Baltimore: Johns Hopkins University Press.

Mahiri, Jabari. 2005. *What They Don't Learn in School: Literacy in the Lives of Urban Youth (New Literacies and Digital Epistemologies)*. New York: Peter Lang.

Manes-Rossi, Francesca, Riccardo Mussari, and Denita Cepiku. 2022. "Introduction to the Special Issue: 'Performance Measurement Systems in Universities: Threats or Opportunities for Governance?'" *Journal of Management and Governance* 26 (2): 327–335. https://doi.org/10.1007/s10997-022-09638-5.

McMurtrie, Beth. 2023. "Could Reflection Be a Key to Better Teaching?" *Chronicle of Higher Education*. August 31. https://www.chronicle.com/newsletter/teaching/2023-08-31.

Miller, J. Elizabeth, and Peter Selden. 2014. "Changing Practices in Faculty Evaluation." American Association of University Professors. https://www.aaup.org/article/changing-practices-faculty-evaluation.

Perryman-Clark, Staci M., and Collin Lamont Craig. 2019. *Black Perspectives in Writing Program Administration: From the Margins to the Center*. Urbana, IL: National Council of Teachers of English.

Pinkert, Laurie A., and Lauren Marshall Bowen. 2021. "Disciplinary Lifecycling: A Generative Framework for Career Trajectories in Rhetoric, Composition, and Writing Studies." *Composition Studies* 49 (1): 16–41.

Powell, Malea. 2002. "Rhetorics of Survivance: How American Indians Use Writing." *College Composition and Communication* 53 (3): 396–434. https://doi.org/10.2307/1512132.

Smith, Anna, Autumn J. West, and Sarah J. McCarthey. 2020. "Literacies Across Sponsorscapes: Mobilising Notions of Literacy Sponsorship." *Literacy* 54 (2): 22–30. https://doi.org/10.1111/lit.12199.

Williams, Joan C. 2005. "The Glass Ceiling and the Maternal Wall in Academia." *New Directions for Higher Education*, no. 130 (Summer): 91–105. https://doi.org/10.1002/he.181.

Worthen, Molly. 2021. "Opinion | The Fight over Tenure Is Not Really About Tenure." *New York Times*, September 20, sec. Opinion. https://www.nytimes.com/2021/09/20/opinion/tenure-college-university.html.

10
This Is Fine

Reflecting on (Missed) Opportunities and Adequate Moments of Departmental Collaboration, Labor, and Care

BRIGITTE MUSSACK

We are all *spent*: emotionally, mentally, physically. As a writing program administrator (WPA), as nontenured faculty, as a woman laboring in academia, much of my professional identity involves unseen and uncompensated labor (Näring et al. 2006). I am often tasked with caring for my undergraduate and graduate students in a way that helps to protect them from exploitative labor practices upon which the university is founded (e.g., Fox 1999; Giroux 2001; Gore 1993). While Writing Studies defines its own disciplinary identity as collaborative and student centered (Elbow 1973; Gore 1993) it cannot deny the neoliberal, capitalist framework of the university, which imagines care and well-being in terms of productive output. As faculty in a technical communication program, I situate my understanding of labor and social justice work within the field of technical communication. Specifically, I grapple with scholarship in technical communication that calls for the collaborative building of coalitions, a move that is met with direct opposition to the structure of a corporate university (Walton et al. 2019). Catherine Chaput (2008) articulates the connections between capitalist culture and the global university and emphasizes the constraints that grow out of collapsing economic and cultural structures. How can we work to build coalitions for social justice within such a corporate structure while recognizing and honoring the inherent labor involved in such work?

In "What Does a Good Teacher Do Now," graduate instructors analyze their own tentative positionalities and how they might create communities of care within an institution that has failed to live up to its promises of well-being (Day et al. 2021). But how do we create these communities of care in this moment when we are already "drowning in the labor of hope" (Hubrig 2023)? Herein lies dissonance: At a moment when we have the least to give, we need that collective labor the most. While Richard Young and colleagues (1970) position dissonance as fruitful sites for inquiry, I invite us to rest in the dissonant spaces without attempts at resolution.

This piece presents critique and reflection of specific moments of (missed) attempts to value collective departmental labor and well-being. I describe dissonant situations and offer that inhabiting these dissonances *without resolving them* is important as we work toward departmental change. Specifically, I analyze two key moments:

- An open-source textbook: I reflect on a grant-funded project to create an open-source text centered on access and social justice. Through this project I attempted to build coalitions as social justice work and ran into the very real problem of uncompensated labor involved in this "ask."
- Professional development: I analyze attempts to use professional development spaces that already exist as opportunities to engage in rest, reflection, and community care and share artifacts from these meetings.

In this chapter, I operationalize *adequate* by emphasizing the dissonances that emerged in each moment. Under the framework of capitalism, dissonance *is* adequate when embarking on departmental DEI work. Further, neither dissonance nor adequacy should be understood as a means to an end or even as "good enough." Dissonance can be reimagined as *the goal* when confronting departmental labor and DEI efforts. Adequate outcomes, marked by dissonance, are the very outcomes that shift culture and impart change under this capitalist structure of the corporate university. My own adequate attempts aim to address "the need to restructure workplace policies so that equity efforts are central to everyone's professional responsibilities, which means they need to be both expected and supported" (Kahn and Lynch-Biniek 2022, 321). Of course, this is a huge goal, and none of these attempts met that goal. They did, and continue to, push the conversation toward the goal of care work and collaboration, of organization around departmental care, as a central goal in departmental training and curriculum development. Further, I hope that these efforts, even in exposing various dissonances implicit in DEI attempts, can foster a way of "thinking about [departmental] *solidarity* grounded in trust, mutual care, and mutual responsibility as the antidote to hegemonic unity-in-fear" (322).

As the Barbie movie claims, just recognizing the contradictions can allow us to do the work: The inherent dissonance *is* where we work and live. In a corporate university, existing and operating within the framework of late-stage capitalism, adequacy *is* the earmark of significant change. Further, adequacy highlights commonplace gatekeeping structures—which are often ignored or invisible—antithetical to DEI work within the university. These dissonances grow from the realities that DEI work is, so often, incompatible with universities when these institutions exist within a capitalist, neoliberal framework.

Dissonance and Love

When teaching research writing, I rely on the text by Richard Young and colleagues (1970) that frames research as inquiry and that emphasizes how inquiry grows out of a dissonance. Young et al. describe when a researcher encounters something that bumps up against their worldview or previous experiences, it creates discomfort: Research is an impulse to resolve the discomfort. This framework is useful for students developing research questions. However, the text does not discuss unresolved dissonances, or the recognition of two opposing "facts" in itself. When it comes to implementing DEI initiatives, the dissonance rises between the goal of promoting equity and the fact of increasing labor. As Seth Kahn and Amy Lynch-Biniek (2022) point out, "The COVID-19 pandemic has both amplified labor equity problems and created new ones" (323)

My own attempts at departmental care expose these labor problems and this inherent, unresolvable dissonance. Along with labor, I focus on values. The shared values of collaboration, reflection, and community appear throughout our scholarly work and curriculum. However, it is difficult to *enact* these values within the framework of academia. In my own context, I support an undergraduate program in Technical Writing and Communication (TWC). As such, I position my own work within the field of TWC and in foundational texts on social justice and technical communication. When Angela Haas and Michelle Eble (2018), in their touchstone text, claim that "technical communication does important work in the world—and we have the position, agency, and obligation to identify and intervene in discourses that authorize injustice" (17), how does that mandate echo into our departmental labor? How is it true, and how can it be acting as the very roadblock to taking those important and terrifying first steps?

Under a capitalist framework, dissonance *is* adequate; dissonance is often the best we can hope for given how capitalism and, by extension, the university, work against access, diversity, and care. Not only is dissonance an expected result of our own DEI initiative; it is adequate in demonstrating limitations and inherent spaces of conflict or discomfort. Dissonance is also adequate when framing departmental DEI efforts as love. We still exist in spaces under capitalism, *and* we can shift departmental culture toward love and care. Finally, dissonance is adequate when part of our work must also shift away from wanting clear deliverables or from usefulness as a metric. Under capitalism, dissonance is adequate because it allows us to grapple with labor and care even as we push against the structures that would measure our worth by our output.

Love allows us to operationalize dissonance as adequate because love highlights the hope in dissonance and in DEI labor. Adequacy, love, and dissonance are concepts that can inform each other and frame projects in a response to the horrors of capitalist calls to continual production and improvement while *actually* working toward change. Adequate is *not "quiet quitting"*; it is not doing just enough or a way to disconnect with our own labor. Rather, adequate is recognizing, embracing, and sitting with the dissonances without the need to emerge from that dissonance with a "better version" or a "more perfect project." It is the rejection of improvement without recognizing and honoring how our labor is at odds with the capitalist machine that relies on that labor. Adequacy is a way to resist capitalist imperatives; I do this work by recognizing and reflecting on the connections between adequacy, dissonance, and love. Love is the thing that moves dissonance into the realm of care and compassion. Love remakes dissonance as *the thing*. Love gets into this framing of dissonance by emphasizing connection without resolution. Love frames dissonance as an end rather than a problem by focusing on connection and on the labor of that connection.

I understand and operationalize *love* as care and community engagement that not only resists framing dissonance as negative or as a problem to be solved but that actively leans into dissonance as a measure of *adequate* community building. I understand bell hooks's work (2018) on love, specifically, as an anticapitalist framework that does not rely on production success metrics and that recognizes both dissonance and adequacy as *necessary* features of forming coalitions for social justice work.

Social Justice and Love in the field of Technical Communication

While love may seem like a strange framework to bring into departmental administrative tasks, "indeed, all the great movements for social justice in our society have strongly emphasized a love ethic" (hooks 2018, xix). I frame the work of creating an open-source textbook, of planning and executing professional development sessions, and of reshaping departmental meetings as spaces for community building through a lens of love. Love, care work, and social justice texts help move past viewing dissonance as a beginning and toward inhabiting unresolved dissonance as a goal. These frameworks, taken together, push against a narrative of continual improvement. Further, they challenge the notion that our goals should be to labor toward impossible ends under impossible conditions. Love, care work, and social justice push against the capitalist university that can only imagine dissonance as something to be resolved toward one end or another, often in favor of the dominant culture. Moving past dissonance that is understood only as useful IF it is resolved, we can frame dissonance—and adequate achievements that highlight dissonance—as a useful space to hold multiple truths and work in solidarity. Love highlights administrative tasks as social justice work, and highlights how seemingly innocuous work can either uphold problematic institutional values or lend themselves to care. This type of social justice work relies on adequacy as a benchmark, rather than capitalist metrics of "success."

Although the field of technical communication is invested in social justice, research in technical communication articulates a "gap" between scholarly work and engaging that work at the departmental level (Agboka and Dorpenyo 2022). Natasha Jones (2019) describes an "obligation for positive change," and Godwin and Agboka and Isidore Dorpenyo (2022) press the urgent need for action and change. Jones (2019) further says that teachers need to "examine the design and dissemination of communication critically with a focus on understanding how oppressive conditions can be rearticulated and reinforced" (346). My own attempts model a way to do this work—not perfectly but adequately—at the level of an academic department. Further, I hope that the dissonances I describe belie the ways that departments struggle. Building social justice coalitions is always a struggle, and any attempt without inherent dissonance or "failings" should be held suspect.

Acknowledging shared dissonance, along with shared values, can be understood as an act of love. As hooks (2018) claims, "Far too many people in our culture do not know what love is. And this not knowing feels like a terrible secret, a lack that we have to cover up" (11). The adequate nature of the attempts—the dissonance between what worked and what did not—reveals this lack. Adequate, here, rests in dissonance. I believe that just as interpersonally many of us do not know what love is, we do not really know what it means to love each other in a professional context, and that not knowing can feel shameful. Bringing to the surface where we *don't know* is necessary to engage in departmental culture shifts toward care. The institutions of the nuclear family, as hooks demonstrates, have left us unprepared to love, and the institutions of capitalism and academic institutions have left us unable to really care. Love is possible, but we need to recognize, through adequate projects, where the "cracks" are in our departmental relationships.

When certain (impossible) success metrics are not met, such projects as those described in this chapter might be viewed through a capitalist, production-focused lens as failures. If we instead rest in and celebrate the dissonances that surface through these projects, *adequate* becomes a way to understand how projects are embedded within an entire institutional structure that often works against its own DEI goals, particularly given that these goals require labor.

The Open-Source Textbook: A Collaboration Opportunity

My first adequate attempt involves the creation of an open-source technical communication textbook and the labor necessary for collaboration.

Open-source textbooks have been touted as a way to enact social justice (e.g., Griffiths et al. 2022; Richter and McPherson 2012). Collaborative authorship, similarly, can shift frameworks and promote inclusion of diverse departmental voices. In 2019, I received a grant through the university libraries for access to create an open-source textbook for a university-wide technical communication course. The previous textbook was difficult to access because of price and format, and its content did not align with the values of the department and the course. My grant application promised a collaborative, accessible text that would frame technical communication through social justice. While this grant awarded support of librarians and publication through the library system, it came with only $1,000, which was not enough to compensate contributors for the incredible time commitment and labor involved in composing a textbook.

In their introduction to *Key Theoretical Frameworks*, Haas and Eble (2018) emphasize that "injustice is not just a problem in technical communication but also one that we can solve with technical communication" (8). Likewise, this open text addresses social justice through its use, its creation, and its content. It is a dual-purpose document: It works to frame technical communication as social justice work for student readers, *and* it positions social justice work in technical communication departments by emphasizing collaborative creation and inclusive content. Understanding this dual purpose, it is necessary to grapple with the labor involved in its creation and to frame an imbalance of labor *as* related to departmental justice and DEI work.

Creating this text provided an opportunity for inclusion and equity; it also placed disproportionate labor expectations onto already marginalized faculty. As a non-tenure-track faculty member, myself, I am cognizant of how labor is distributed and compensated in academic departments. As such, I work hard not to add more labor to contingent faculty and graduate instructors. However, there is always labor involved in change. Throughout this open-source project, I struggled not to find interested colleagues but to find colleagues who were able to contribute their labor without compensation, on top of all their other responsibilities. The lack of official contributors felt like a "fail"; repositioning this problem as a dissonance provides opportunity to grapple with how curricular changes require significant labor from our instructors. Social justice work is *necessary*; it also requires labor. We cannot do this work without examining how such labor is distributed. While it is important to frame open education resource (OERs) as engaged with social justice, it is necessary to engage with the labor that is required in their creation and maintenance. They have, in the works cited here, been engaged as artifacts that work toward social justice without adequate engagement in how or whether the creation of these artifacts aligns with social justice work. Importantly, the labor involved in the creation of open-source texts is not often accounted for; labor concerns are social justice concerns (Kahn and Lynch-Biniek 2022), and, as such, there is a tension between DEI efforts for students and whether these efforts support DEI for faculty and staff.

My own project failed, in its inception, to recognize labor as part of social justice, because I was so focused on a utopian framing of collaboration. Research in OERs across disciplines suggests that open texts are a way to work toward social justice in higher education by providing access to students. This research typically focuses on cost. While OERs work to remove cost barriers for students, there is labor involved in creating such resources, and this labor is often uncompensated. The grant that funded the creation of my own open-source text, for example, did not cover the labor required to write a textbook. Ultimately, I authored most of the text, with various collaborators contributing sections and feedback. I learned ways to allow for contributions without committing too much time, but the text was not as *genuinely* collaborative as my goal.

As I reflect on this experience, and push against the academic training that moves me to label it a "failed" attempt, I am struck by several things:

- Labor is not evenly distributed across academic departments, and while as a field we claim to be invested in DEI, labor distribution and lack of recognition of different types of academic labor, or even hesitancy to view certain types of academic work as labor, are things that academic departments should continue to address.
- Collaboration can look like many things, and a project can still be a "successful" collaboration even if the labor is not evenly distributed across all contributors. In this case, I did the bulk of the labor, but this book is still an adequate example of a collaborative text.
- Research on open texts and DEI focus more on how these texts contribute to DEI for students and less on how their creation does or does not align with DEI goals and values.

The points I have outlined center around how we understand labor, broadly, and how our theory meets departmental practice. What does our departmental praxis look like when it comes to valuing labor? Further, how do we understand, embody, and practice the notion that rest is productive, that knowledge generation comes in forms other than publishing peer-reviewed articles, and that adequate gets the job done? As was my experience with the creation of this textbook, "The tendency to leave the bulk of the work to the faculty who are the most vulnerable" is the default in many academic contexts (Kahn and Lynch-Biniek 2002, 321).

Creating this open text was an attempt to do what Kahn and Lynch-Biniek (2002) suggest: to shift from activism to organizing. While the open text included organizing at a program level, it pushed to center DEI without necessarily framing this work as activism. The content of the text itself centered DEI, and the creation of an open text also framed departmental curricular development as inherently invested in DEI by providing a platform to honor instructor voices and by creating a shared, collaborative text that relied on building coalitions and explicitly articulating departmental values. Interestingly, this project highlighted not only shared values but also where members of our department do not align. Honoring diversity means pushing against consensus and instead valuing dissonance. While falling far short of my collaborative authorship goals, the text is an adequate artifact.

The lack of contributors to the finished product reveals the shortcomings of encouraging and sponsoring collaborative departmental efforts without understanding how labor plays into these efforts. Reflecting on both this process and finished product, I resist framing it as a failed attempt at collaboration and instead frame it as adequate, sitting in the dissonances highlighted through open-source creation. We should not add more labor to the lowest-compensated department members. It is also the case that "intersectional work should include contingent faculty" (Khan and Lynch-Biniek 2002, 328). While the labor fell on contingent faculty and graduate instructors, these voices were also highlighted in the text. This labor shapes how we teach this course, which impacts not only department culture but also students across the university.

As I continue to revise and develop this text, I wonder: *Is this project successful? Is it adequate? How can we live in the dissonances that encourage growth and that celebrate labor without the imperative of improvement or perfection?*

When taking stock of how this project turned out, relative to its initial goals, I am left with the unresolvable dissonances that (1) creating accessible texts AND collaborating to create these texts rest on labor, and this labor is often un- or undercompensated; and (2) collaborating to create accessible texts is important DEI work for students and for departmental DEI efforts as they work to create coalitions around shared values and articulate goals toward departmental social justice efforts. Highlighting this dissonance, and recognizing the dissonance as adequate, shifts us away from the capitalist framework that works *against* collaborative labor while also voicing the struggles involved in collaborative labor.

Professional Development: A Reflection Opportunity

Developing the open-source text, and the various realities around instructor labor made apparent through that process, led me to consider how reflection and rest might become a central component to department culture without relying on more labor from already overworked department members. One such existing space: required professional development that instructors were already contracted to complete. As a program head, I help organize and lead fall orientation and spring symposium. All our advanced writing instructors are required to attend. I have long wrestled with how to make these required events as useful as possible without adding more work. Of course, that goal is impossible to reach: Can professional development be both useful AND require no extra labor from instructors? How can I tap into work that they are already doing? Or, how might I reframe some of these professional development sessions as spaces of reflection and rest?

Fall orientation and spring symposium work as bookends at the beginning and end of the academic year that foster community and provide space for discussion and reflection. Orientation includes sessions that directly discuss labor, DEI, social justice, and how instructors can work to create personal and professional boundaries around their own labor with their students and with the demands of the department. In this context, boundaries mean that instructors have clear delineations between work and rest, that they do not have to be "on" all the time, and that they feel supported by the department in their right to say "no" and to prioritize their own well-being. For example, instructors can create clear expectations around responding to student emails and do not need to share phone numbers or be "on-call" outside of working hours. The onboarding orientation emphasizes boundary making and enforcing as one way to care for our students, as one way to promote labor justice. Of course, it is not perfect and places that work on the instructor. However, departmental leadership works to create a culture of support, and we remind instructors that we are here to help them enforce their boundaries, to help them manage students when they need help, and to generally support them as valued members of our community.

bell hooks (2018) tells us that "bringing love into the work environment can create the necessary transformation that can make any job we do, no matter how menial, a place where workers can express the best of themselves. When we work with love, we renew the spirit; that renewal is an act of self-love, it nurtures our growth" (65). This need for love echoes what Gérard Näring and colleagues (2016) found to be true about burnout in teachers, that lack of community and lack of alignment between how one feels and how one acts lead to burnout in the workplace. Love is rooted in community (hooks 2018), and social justice must be grounded in both love and in building coalitions (hooks 2018; Walton et al. 2019). Teacher training, textbooks, and professional development often fall under menial tasks, or are viewed as less important than scholarship and research, but these tasks are the cornerstones of our departmental culture and directly impact how we connect with students and with our own work. It has felt, for me, almost silly to frame these tasks as care work, or as acts of departmental love. This dissonance, between how I have been enculturated as part of the academy and what I believe to be true, highlights the need for change. Framing my own work in these areas as adequate and celebrating adequacy allows me to practice my own self-love and to then bring love into my work.

Some adequate attempts we've made to frame the fall orientation as care, to value our instructors as individuals, and to weave DEI throughout the two-day trainings include

- sessions that focus on how instructors can set and respect boundaries, and reminders of how program directors can support or facilitate that;
- sessions that work to set goals, collaboratively with instructors, related to DEI in our department;
- sessions that highlight support available to instructors through the library, writing center, and technology center;
- less tangible efforts that include emphasizing instructors as valued individuals by framing sessions as reflective workshops that invite collaboration and ask instructors to help us name, trouble, and address shared challenges and goals;
- not asking attendees to prepare anything ahead of time;
- making space for workshopping syllabi and assignments;
- framing both days in terms of what the university and college set as standards or guidelines, then moving into how our department functions within that structure, sitting with any dissonance or troubling spaces together and setting goals or brainstorming how policies and institutional guidelines / do not shape our teaching practices.

This symposium is the other end of this "onboarding" professional development. As an attempt to again emphasize community building, care, and support—to build a coalition based in care—we frame the spring symposium as a day of collective reflection and rest. For this day, the Director of Undergraduate Studies (DUS) and I ask instructors to choose topics for workshops and to collaboratively lead workshops or presentations. My approach to shifting the spring symposium toward collaboration and reflection follows bell hooks's assertion that "there can be no justice without love" and that "there can be no love without justice" (hooks 2018). While care work is not necessarily the same as what she describes and defines as *love*, part of this restorative departmental practice must concern valuing individuals as individuals, as human beings, in a structure or system that fails to do so (Day et al. 2021).

Just like with the open text, herein lies the dissonance: The more collaborative something becomes, the more labor is required of participants. It is *easier* to attend a professional development session and to passively listen to presenters. It requires more work to collaborate to plan and present a session or participate in a workshop. It is also more useful and more engaging, and collaboration works toward building the necessary coalitions that engage the voices, ideas, values of department members. How can care happen without labor? How can the dissonance between rest and labor be understood *as love?* My own answers to these questions look like operationalizing love through community building within the spaces where some form of (corporate) community already exists. These answers are adequate; my attempts are not enough to overcome the very real labor placed on myself and on instructors, nor are they enough to overcome the barriers to enacting social justice work in my own department. However, the adequacy of these attempts does not mean that my answers were wrong. Rather, they mean that these questions can call us into a space of dissonance, and when that dissonance is framed as loving, it can be restorative.

Some adequate attempts we have made to shift the spring symposium away from "training" and towards "reflection and collective rest" include:

- inviting instructors to participate by suggesting session topics or leading workshops;
- emphasizing reflection and shared goals, using the space to openly discuss both what went well and what "failed" or what didn't work out the way we wanted;
- creating space for sharing struggles and sharing in frustrations *without* necessarily framing these conversations as opportunities to find solutions;
- drawing from the text "What Does a Good Teacher Do Now?" and introducing care work as a framework for building our departmental culture;
- reiterating support available to instructors and building community through sharing experiences;
- emphasizing reflection and discussing boundaries, labor, and rhetoric of "self-care."

These professional developments "fall short" of my own goals in that they are still mandatory training, and they require time and labor. They require time, which is always a finite resource, during the beginning and end of the academic year, times that are generally already filled with labor and stress. Would it be more supportive to just give instructors that time so that they can focus on preparing their courses or completing grading? Perhaps, but I hope that these sessions are useful spaces that provide some respite or even community-based comfort: We are all stressed; let's feel stressed together; and let's share some strategies that have been helpful or vent frustrations that we can likely all relate to. So, even while they take time and require labor, they also provide space for community building and collective engagement. Just like with the open-source text creation, collaborative work is always *work*. If we stopped offering professional development, instructors might miss out on this collaborative work and on the chance to engage with each other.

These professional development sessions are adequate spaces for community building and for collective instruction. They highlight the dissonance of how professional development is framed as both necessary and as, often, a waste of time. Leaning into that dissonance allows for critique of the corporate university and for reframing of such professional sessions. What if this work were just as important as our scholarly labor? What if we leaned into the discomfort and messiness of the mundane parts of our jobs? What if, instead of capitalist wastes of time, teacher training sessions were spaces to push at the boundaries of the most exhausting aspects of our jobs and to gain strength in solidarity?

Ultimately, as a Writing Studies department that values its members, "we want to live in a culture where love can flourish" (hooks 2018, xxix). To engage in social justice work, we need to develop an ethic and culture of love and to make the members of our department feel valued. Care work too rests on a foundation of love, and of finding opportunities to practice love. I have to push against how I define or imagine "usefulness" in the context of professional development: What does usefulness "look like" if the goal is dissonance, and if dissonance is a measure of adequacy? How do we understand usefulness if we are pushing against a problematic notion of progress?

Conclusions

Rest is productive and important for care. However, rest is difficult to measure in a culture that values achievements, accomplishments, and measurable goals. Dissonance is a valuable, productive space to occupy. Dissonance is also difficult to measure in a culture that views it as a means to an end. But how can we resolve dissonances that are unresolvable under the current structures in which we exist and work? How can we achieve unachievable goals? So much of academia is focused on moving toward some goal, with "toward" being the operative word. How can we honor where we are, right now—dissonances and missteps and failures and all? How can we rest with the lovely messes that we make of these projects? Recognizing the rest and labor are dissonant and rely on each other is an adequate move in anticapitalist work. Valuing dissonance as an adequate outcome in these attempts, not as something that we need to resolve or improve upon, is a way to push back on capitalist imperatives. Put differently: dissonance *is* adequate, and adequate *is* enough.

Each of these adequate attempts bridge theory to practice, engaging mundane texts and tasks as artifacts and as spaces for care work. I have also, in each attempt, fallen far short of my goals. As Khan and Lynch-Biniek (2022) emphasize, "Academics need to pay more attention to how we care or are cared for, and recognize that as worthy work and *real shit*, particularly up against white supremacist, neoliberal hegemonic regimes that work so hard to make sure we don't care for each other" (325). Do my adequate attempts count as "real shit"? Do my students and colleagues feel cared for in these professional development sessions, in teaching group meetings, and through the creation and maintenance of a collaborative text? Assigned student readings and professional development can be coded as "service and organizing," which can "affect the very make-up of faculty and student communities" and impact "the futures of institutions" (326). These tasks are important, and in making spaces for care and love through these important tasks, we can engage with social justice. Adopting a love ethic, as hooks reminds us, does not require us to move mountains. Rather, it requires us to sometimes be okay with dissonances that arise out of our efforts.

Even as I draft this chapter, I wrestle with feelings of inadequacy tied to both institutional expectations and the simple truth that there is not enough time in the day (or enough money in the budget) to do things the way that I *want* to do them. Some of the work of shifting toward an adequate mindset—of finding value in what we *have done* as much as what we *would like to have done*—depends on an adapting mindset, a cultural shift. Folks who teach technical communication are familiar with the fact that "technical communication scholarship, practice, conferences, and pedagogies have rich histories of adapting with cultural, technological, and scientific changes" (Haas and Eble 2018, 5). It stands to reason that Writing Studies departments can likewise adapt to reflect value shifts away from excellence rooted in bad labor practices and problematic hierarchies. These adequate attempts are adaptive and add to the pile of growing efforts toward redefining usefulness and toward valuing care.

Sample Artifacts
- Open text on technical communication and social justice (https://pressbooks.umn.edu/techwriting/)
- "Teaching and Self Care: Questions for Discussion" (https://docs.google.com/document/d/1QyQzihHne-Qs85uePsOQKA4bNDz0PvrB/edit?tab=t.0)

References

Agboka, Godwin Y., and Isidore K. Dorpenyo. 2022. "Curricular Efforts in Technical Communication After the Social Justice Turn." *Journal of Business and Technical Communication* 36 (1): 38–70.

Chaput, Catherine. 2008. *Inside the Teaching Machine: Rhetoric and the Globalization of the U.S. Public Research University*. Tuscaloosa: University of Alabama Press.

Day, Jathan, Sarah Hughes, Crystal Zanders, Kathryn Van Zanen, and Andrew Moos. 2021. "What Does a Good Teacher Do Now? Crafting Communities of Care." *Pedagogy: Critical Approaches to Teaching Literature, Language, Composition, and Culture* 21 (3): 389–402.

Elbow, Peter. 1973. *Writing Without Teachers*. New York: Oxford University Press.

Fox, Tom. 1999. *Defending Access: A Critique of Standards in Higher Education*. Portsmouth, NH: Heinemann.

Giroux, Henry. 2001. *Theory and Resistance in Education*. Westport, CT: Bergin and Garvey.

Gore, Jennifer. 1993. *The Struggle for Pedagogies: Critical and Feminist Discourses as Regimes of Truth*. New York: Routledge.

Griffiths, Rebecca, Jessica Mislevy, and Shuai Wang. 2022. "Encouraging Impacts of an Open Education Resource Degree Initiative on College Students' Progress to Degree." *International Journal of Higher Education Research* 84 (5): 1089–1106.

Haas, Angela M., and Michelle F. Eble. 2018. *Key Theoretical Frameworks: Teaching Technical Communication in the Twenty-First Century*. Logan: Utah State University Press.

hooks, bell. 2018. *All About Love*. New York: William Morrow.

Hubrig, Ada. 2023. "Hope Is a Fickle Thing." Paper presented at Conference on College Composition and Communication, Chicago, February.

Jones, Natasha. 2019. "The Technical Communicator as Advocate: Integrating a Social Justice Approach in Technical Communication." *Journal of Technical Writing and Communication* 46 (3): 342–361.

Kahn, Seth, and Lynch-Biniek, Amy. 2022. "From Activism to Organizing, from Caring to Care Work." *Labor Studies Journal* 47 (3): 320–344.

Näring, Gérard, Briet, Mariette, and Brouwers, Andre. 2006. "Beyond Demand Control: Emotional Labour and Symptoms of Burnout in Teachers." *Work and Stress* 20 (4): 303–315.

Richter, Thomas, and McPherson, Maggie. 2012. "Open Educational Resources: Education for the World?" *Distance Education* 33 (2): 201–219. https://doi.org/10.1080/01587919.2012.692068.

Walton, Rebecca, Moore, Kristen, and Jones, Natasha. 2019. *Technical Communication After the Social Justice Turn: Building Coalitions for Action*. New York: Routledge.

Young, Richard E., Becker, Alton L., and Pike, Kenneth L. 1970. *Rhetoric, Discovery, and Change*. New York: Harcourt, Brace, and World.

INTERLUDE 3

We Will Never Be Enough (Because Academia Will Always Demand More)

A Letter from a Fledgling "Crip Doula"

ADA HUBRIG

Dear one—kind human,

I'm responding, with as much care and gentleness as I know how, to "the ask."

What I call "the ask" is somewhat nebulous, a rhetorical shapeshifter. I've become familiar with many of its iterations. Sometimes these asks come from someone I've known for years, sometimes an acquaintance, sometimes a friend-of-a-friend, sometimes a stranger. The *real* ask often follows some version of "Ada, can I ask you a personal question?"

Maybe your own version of "the ask" is rooted in something personal and specific, even if you choose to ask it through a more vague and generalized framing. Maybe your "the ask" is about autistic experiences, being "mentally ill," inhabiting a chronically ill body, dealing with pain.[1] Maybe your ask is about gender and transness and disability. Whatever your version of the ask, I try to respond to your ask with gentleness and patience, understanding that the ask often leaves so much unsaid and, if you're asking, you may be learning to navigate these things too.

---

1. I won't betray any personal details, here, and I am intentionally withholding anything personally identifiable of those kind humans who have made "the ask."

But most often, "the ask" is tied to questions about how to navigate what it is to be a Mad, disabled academic, how to handle spillages of the personal into the professional.

I don't mind your ask; in fact, I am quietly honored to be trusted to provide such care, and I treat your trust with reverence. I am honored they have trusted me with such vulnerable, complicated feelings, and see my role as being a "crip doula," a concept I borrow from late disability activist Stacey Milbern, who writes about how disabled people welcome others into disabled identity and disabled existence, or changing disabled experiences. Milbern writes, "The transition itself, of becoming disabled or moving along the ability spectrum, is frequently invisibilized, to the point that these changes do not even have a name" (qtd. in Piepzna-Samarasinha 2018, 240). In these conversations, we talk through and give name to some of these invisibilized experiences, and I am often asked for some form of guidance.

I will do my best, kind human. But the simple truth is I don't know what I'm doing either.

I don't feel I have much guidance to offer; I'm not someone who has it *figured out*, nor do I have a solid grasp on what "it" is that requires our figuring. I am a silly little queer who doesn't know what I'm doing but am trying desperately to figure it out because I don't want my own actions—or inactions—to cause harm.

So I do what I *can* do: Sometimes all there is to do, all I can do, is listen. Being present with you, trying to prioritize *care* and *community*, even within institutional superstructures and value systems antithetical to my perhaps naive and childlike hopes that we might exist differently.

I do my best to sit with you, here, to be present with you. I'm doing my best to get it right because I want to show up for you, for us, in these pages. As I've drafted and redrafted these words, I've had several conversations with early-career disabled, Mad, and queer/trans scholars, with "the ask," and I have returned to these words—to this letter—after each one, to reshuffle the words and try to get it right. While I gesture at the broad themes of conversations with others about their asks, I won't offer details beyond this, because they are not mine to share.

But I do turn to a central theme of these asks that I suspect may be lurking in your ask: a shared fear/anxiety/reluctance that they'll be seen as incompetent or inadequate because of these bodyminds we are—and these anxieties are understandably elevated for multiply marginalized colleagues who are already disproportionately scrutinized.

Put another way, kind human: At the center of most of these asks is an anxiety that whatever disabled or divergent way of being asked about makes you *not enough*, makes you a bad teacher or scholar or person. At the center of so, so many of people's own iterations of "the ask" are feelings of inadequacy, of feeling like we are not enough, that institutional demands outpace our capacities. And this is the part of "the ask" and its follow up conversations that often breaks my heart, because I see in these feelings reflected back at me my own struggles to be enough.

An often-used codeword for these feelings of inadequacy is "unprofessional." The one making the ask often reports a fear of judgment, of retaliation, of being denied a job or other opportunity, of being seen as unable to perform their job because they are disabled, and many share doing *extra work*, that they do unpaid labor of all kinds to be seen as able, as worthy, as professional. Some report fearing to ask for what they need to survive or too worried to take a rest or to ask for help because of the stigma around disability, Madness, and other forms of marginalization—especially multiply marginalized disabled colleagues.

I am happy to be present, to listen, but I don't have some sage advice to fix it. I wish I had it figured out, but I don't. I experience these same pressures. I still catch myself subconsciously hiding my stims, worried that if I bounce my leg or fidget with my hands too much, I will be seen as incompetent, infantile, inadequate. I have been told that even my most innocuous and harmless behaviors are "unprofessional."

The word escapes the mouths of even well-meaning mentors and colleagues I've long considered friends. They might say something they think is reassuring, like telling me I'm "smart" *for an autistic person*, or that I "work so hard" *for someone with disabilities*. Or that they'd "never have guessed" *I'm mentally ill*. Somewhere along the way, I internalized a message that if I work hard enough—coming in early and staying late to make up for the days I'm too sick to work; if I hide and mask my disabilities well enough; I might be accepted as properly "professional," just as the colleagues who've made "the ask" explain to me about being seen as "professional" too.

These comments are extensions of the stories academia likes to tell about marginalized bodies, the way they narrativize our experiences to suit institutional agendas (Hubrig 2023). Creating language around what is "professional" that excludes disabled and other marginalized bodyminds allows institutions to blame me for their ableism and bigotry. I am made to feel inadequate, not as a marker of my actual performance or an evaluation of my work but because *I* am not the kind of "professional" that fits institutional norms.

"Professional" is a lexical chameleon, a bit of corporate lingo used to brand what suits institutional agendas and demarcate what doesn't. Calls to be "professional" are thinly veiled demands, as Christina V. Cedillo

(2018) has noted about the intersections of race, gender, and disability, that we "leave our identities at the door." My disabled and otherwise marginalized friends and colleagues share—in their conversations following "the ask"—a pressure to overwork, to do *even more labor* because we're not seen as "professional," a mantel conferred by default to some of our other colleagues by overlapping markers of privileges.

To heck with this sense of professionalism always on the periphery, a cursed moon about to crash into your world. It's high time professionalism be dismantled, especially when it is at odds with care and community. You, dear one, are adequate. You do not owe your institution "above and beyond," validating their barriers of "professionalism" that ask us to contort our bodyminds to fit in their ableist, privileged frameworks of being.

The problem is not you; it is not us. The problem is the "professional" standards of the glorified hedge funds that market themselves as public goods and call themselves a university while conveniently (to the bottom line, at least) ignoring institutional harms in favor of professionalization. Down with professionalism, embrace all the ways we are already adequate—accepting that there is no bar at which we will be "good enough" to our institutions, because under institutional logics "there is always room for improvement"—a greed for further return on institutional investments but not for the rest vital to our well-being.

Whatever it is at the center of your "the ask" does not make you a "bad academic," or a "bad teacher," or a "bad person." It may make you, make us, "unprofessional" but only so far as "professional" is a word levied selectively, almost always to chastise marginalized colleagues because our very habitus doesn't match institutional biases. It's deployed to gaslight marginalized colleagues who are challenging and calling out the white supremacist, ableist, sanist, cisheteropatriarchal systems and values of university spaces and the many abuses and harms of these systems.

As I try to understand, myself, what such dismantling of professionalism would mean, I share this with you as I try to develop what Yanira Rodriguez et al. (2021) call "an ethos of refusal," which they theorize as *more than* exercising the right to refuse additional labor but a refusal to be complicit in "re-inscribing as norm capitalist labor practices that privilege productive performance above quality of life." Rodriguez et al., in their introduction and three-part performance addressing invisibilized labor in academia, describe how the labor expectations further the white supremacist, capitalist logics that target BIPOC people and offer "an ethos of refusal" as antithetical to the "coerc[ive] compliance" of the white, oppressive normativities of our institutions. As Sherri Craig states in her section of Act II of the performance:

I refuse to be on the menu as our institution cannibalizes its young and its vulnerable . . . none of this will help my career. None of this will help me make tenure. None of this will be seen by, or could ever be seen by the university. You were consumed by the institution when you were young, and made room for us to be chewed but now swallowed by the system you are now complicit in. I refuse. You will see me as inedible.—Sherri Craig (qtd. in Rodriguez et al.)

As a person who inhabits a *white* marginalized body, I learn alongside and in community with my BIPOC colleagues in forming an ethos of refusal. I don't know, yet, what becoming inedible means for me. To be vulnerable and honest with you, kind human, as someone living with complex post-traumatic stress disorder (C-PTSD) and working to unpack how traumas inform shape my psyche because *I desperately do not want to harm others*, my instinct is to lean into people-pleasing behaviors, to marinade myself and get the spices to make myself as edible and easily digestible as possible.

But I'm learning, from Craig and other BIPOC, disabled, LGTBQ, and otherwise marginalized colleagues, that my willingness to be cannibalized, to have so willingly put myself on the menu, doesn't just harm me *but makes me complicit in harming others*. And that, that I cannot abide.

When pressed for advice beyond my presence—what I humbly offer those that make "the ask" of me as a crip doula, is that despite what messaging we've heard about ourselves, that we're enough. Our presence *as ourselves*, dear one, can invite others in. And our refusal to be edible—our refusal to hide our stims or overwork ourselves, our insistence on choosing care and community—is the work itself. I'm learning to show up—on my campus, in my collegiate relationships, in my writing, in *this document*—as my whole self, and to find ways to be present with others who are trying to do so as well. I—we—are enough. We're adequate. And I hope you'll show up with me as your whole self, in our adequacy.

References

Cedillo, C. V. 2018. "What Does It Mean to Move? Race, Disability, and Critical Embodiment Pedagogy." *Composition Forum* 39. https://www.compositionforum.com/issue/39/to-move.php.

Hubrig, A. 2023. "Beyond (Favor) Access: Constellating Communities Through Collective Access." *College Composition and Communication* 75 (1): 117–136.

Piepzna-Samarasinha, L. L. 2018. *Care Work: Dreaming Disability Justice*. Vancouver, BC: Arsenal Pulp Press.

Rodriguez, Yanira, Sophia Sunshine Vilceus, and Laquana Cooke, et al. 2021. "Foolery, Refusal, and Possibility: On Labor Relationalities at Predominately White Institutions." *Journal of Multimodal Rhetorics* 4 (2). https://journalofmultimodalrhetorics.com/4-2-issue-rodriguez-et-al.

Afterword

Maturing and Organizing Toward/with/for Adequacy

SETH KAHN AND TONY SCOTT

Adequate is challenging to respond to, er, adequately. As a starting place, we recognize that our habitual ways of responding to scholarly work reflect our age (professionally) and career status—we finished our PhDs the same year (2002) and benefitted from getting credentialed—and eventually tenured/promoted—based on standards (norms/expectations), many of which the chapters in this book are resisting. We also need to say something the contributors haven't already said (otherwise what's the point of an afterword?) but without misappropriating the work that's here. We decided, therefore, to pose ourselves among the audiences for the book—faculty in leadership positions who need to support our siblings fighting to make healthy expectations into something usable. The two of us see some things differently, and rather than trying to find agreements, we offer our differences as ways people might react to what's here, in hopes that it helps others set your own expectations for what might happen when you use the book. We also hope that our dialogue can serve as a primer for sorting and synthesizing the issues and ideas you've encountered in these chapters. As such, after quick introductions, the rest of the piece moves conversationally. Imagine we ran into each other at the publisher's booth at CCCC and realized we'd both read the book, started talking about our reactions to it, and decided to keep that conversation happening over lunch (except we wrote it down).

Who are we and where are we coming from?

SETH: I grew up in a comfortably middle-class Jewish neighborhood in Atlanta, and I don't recall a single conversation about class identity or consciousness, or anything about workplace rights or organizing, until I was in college. Nobody I knew (maybe one high school friend) was *antiunion*, exactly. We just never talked about it, because we were all safe and secure. The fact that I'm a white cishet man reinforced that sense of security, of course, and still does.

My labor "epiphany" happened during my PhD program, around 2000. Since then, and especially since 2007 or so, I've seen myself first as a labor organizer and activist, second as somebody who does research about how to *organize* academic workers to "build and use collective power" (Taylor 2016). I've focused mostly on contingent faculty equality, and how tenured/tenure-track (TT) faculty can organize with contingent faculty without colonizing them—and more broadly, about how cadres within a larger movement keep from undercutting each other. In 2018/2019, thanks to Lamiyah Bahrainwala and Dana Cloud, I was on two conference panels that posited academic contingency alongside racialized/gendered/ableist precarity as *intersectional*, and I began to see how hegemonic power uses the complexities of those intersections to pit marginalized people's interests against each other. Recently I've been working on a project that's focused on how faculty in US higher education build solidarity among ourselves, with other campus workers, and across the larger labor movement, and arguing that the central problem of collectivizing faculty is *academic exceptionalism*. We (especially tenured folks) have deep faith in our powers of analysis and discernment; we spend most of our time working without direct supervision; we articulate our mission in lofty terms; and as a result, we don't easily form networks of trust, mutual support, and mutual responsibility. We're too smart and too busy doing important things to get distracted by such proletarian concerns, to put it flippantly.

TONY: My interest in labor and higher education is most deeply rooted in my lived experiences with precarity and work. By the time I graduated from high school and enrolled in a university as a first-generation college student, I had moved fourteen times, living in rented houses, apartments, and a mobile home that was parked in three different places before it was repossessed. As I moved through higher education in my teens and twenties, I financed my education with the help of Pell Grants and through working short-term jobs: landscaper, dishwasher, waiter, tree farm worker, temp, and so on. When I earned an MA in English Literature, I got a job as an adjunct at an urban community college. I taught writing courses in the mornings and loaded and unloaded trucks at a UPS distribution hub in the evenings. During that period, I became aware that I was a contingent worker teaching courses in which most of the students were also contingent workers going off to afternoon and evening jobs after their classes. I also began to compare my work as an adjunct with my work as a package handler. On the adjunct job, I was contracted by the course with no benefits and no guarantees of teaching past any given term. I taught at satellite campuses, rarely encountering any other teachers, and I had minimal contact with the writing program administrator. I used texts and assignments that were mandatory for the courses, but no one was in a position to know much about what I was really doing. Both jobs were alienating and exploitative but more so the adjunct instructor position. At UPS, I was a member of the Teamsters. I could not be fired without cause and formal arbitration, and I had a benefits package that included family health and dental insurance and sick pay. Also, while the work at UPS was physically demanding and sometimes dangerous, I worked in teams alongside my coworkers, and the proximity and intensity of the work created a sense of camaraderie. In contrast, my work as an adjunct was "as needed," and it was performed without support. Any sense of accountability to others in my teaching work was necessarily self-generated because there was no professional development, no basis for mutual accountability with co-workers, and no sense of common purpose and belonging.

 When I went back to graduate school and moved, over years, into tenured positions and writing program administration, it was with an awareness of how precarity and alienation shapes the conditions and embodied experience of our work, even among those of us who have tenure. This collection interests me, in part, because the various ways that adequacy is imagined in the chapters evoke new questions about the emotional elements of our work ecologies.

What are our "gut reactions" to this collection?

> SETH: I read everything about academic work as an organizer, that is, as a contribution to or a deflection from building solidarity, so I cheered a lot. I especially want to applaud chapters that demonstrate the value

of building informal networks of mutual support (Lee, Wan, and Lopez Amezquita; Colombini, Kerschbaum, and Webb-Sunderhaus; Loe, Kumari, and Johnson; Cedillo, Manivannan, Hubrig, and Olivas; Wingard and Joplin; Silber, Fernandes, Jamdol, Nelson, Tan, and Tian; Hubrig) alongside more formal ones (Pinkert and Bowen; Wood; Mussack), since homegrown support networks are a key element of effective organizing (see Dixon et al. 2004). Sure, I have quibbles with a claim here and there, but the basic argument of the book rings clear to me: Doing enough should be enough.

TONY: I also read them within the context of decades of scholarship that has focused on composition "work" and aspects of its deep relationship with precarity (e.g., Bousquet et al. 2004; Daniel 2022; Hassell and Phillips 2022; Horner 2016; Kahn and Lynch-Biniek 2022; LaFrance 2019; Schell 1998; Strickland 2011; Welsh and Scott 2016, etc.). "Adequacy" is, as far as I know, new to the ongoing conversation about the terms of academic labor in our field. In my reading, the collection contributes to earlier ways of framing academic work through its focus on the emotional consequences of taken-for-granted conditions. Among my own quibbles is that it doesn't engage with that work. Elements of the deep sense of dissatisfaction that pervades the chapters surfaced decades ago, for instance, in James Sledd's speech at the closing of the 1987 Conference on College Composition and Communication, which brought into the open simmering disagreements among the attendees about whether the emerging field should be focused primarily on research, professionalization, and establishing disciplinary legitimacy within institutions or on addressing the disaffection created by the terms of labor for the largely non-tenure-line faculty who teach writing (see McDonald and Schell 2011; Sledd and Freed 1996).

The labor conversation in Rhetoric, Composition, and Writing Studies (RCWS) has been conducted in vocabularies drawn from the labor and social justice movements, Women's and Gender Studies, and writing program administration. Its focus, however, has typically been more on the effects of contingency on non-tenure-line academic workers and the effects of race and gender on professional life. This collection brings further attention to the emotional alienation and material precarities that can extend across levels of professional "advancement." That said, if someone at a conference in some multiverse in which publisher booths still existed asked me about this collection, I would say that the questions it raises about adequacy contribute to, and potentially extend, that ongoing, vital conversation about terms of work, professionalization, organizing and administration in our field. So, like you Seth, I have quibbles and questions about claims and elisions in some chapters. That said, I also join you in being interested in the possibilities described by, for instance, Lee, Wan, and Lopez Amezquita; Colombini, Kerschbaum, and Webb-Sunderhaus; Loe, Kumari, and Johnson; and Wood. It is heartening to read about instances in which people are working together and acting intentionally to address the alienation, anxiety, and feelings of insecurity that so many of us feel in our work.

SETH: Tony, that history is woven in the subtext of the whole book—the willingness, maybe compulsion, to overperform is clearly a result of the tension Sledd articulates. Sometimes it *feels* resolved, for better or worse (hint: worse), in favor of a prevailing discourse of professionalizing/legitimizing instead of organizing for better working conditions. Sure, sometimes that's posed as a necessary but not sufficient condition for improving the labor situation, but often it's not. One ripple effect of that focus is faculty who are tenured but not fully promoted worrying that they're "not doing enough," even though they're relatively safe, while pre-tenure TT faculty are increasingly alarmed by the prospect of losing positions they worry they can never reattain in this market, and non-tenure-track (NTT) faculty who hoped to move into tenure lines increasingly despair at the prospects. In short, ironically, as we've gotten clearer about the grounds for disciplinary legitimacy, the institutions that house us have gotten less hospitable. I don't want to make a causal argument, but they've both happened.

Along with all that, faculty (less for adjunct and graduate student instructors, for sure) are used to seeing ourselves as *self-managed* because we work with so little direct supervision. That makes it easy to underthink labor problems: how we get evaluated, compensated, renewed/tenured/promoted—or not. . . . And it's too easy, even when we think about that layer of the workplace, not to think about it in collective terms. At face value, "adequate" should answer all of that—do your job adequately, and you can keep doing it.

TONY: I completely agree with what you say about "underthinking" labor problems, Seth. One way to bring work and labor more to the fore in RCWS is to recognize that *how* we do what we do shapes *what* we do, and a way to complicate academic exceptionalism is to turn the "backstage light" on to illuminate the conditions and work ecologies that led to the production of that work, so readers are encouraged to reflect on how material conditions shape what is represented and how it is represented. Some of the chapters in this collection move in that direction. The collection also has me thinking about adequacy and performance. The lived reality and pervasive fear of precarity have long been recognized as an essential disciplining mechanism in capitalism. Recent work (e.g., Lorey et al. 2015; Taylor 2023) examines how the intentional production of insecurity has now become an explicitly recognized and legitimated aspect of political economy in neoliberal capitalism. The ever-present fear of falling is a taken-for-granted source of public discipline and a pervasive condition of academic work. Among the reasons that tenure has steadily diminished over the past three decades is that the level of job security it provides diminishes the threat of impending precarity. Within an economy that is driven more by a fear of falling than a promise of stability, overperforming is construed as just enough—or maybe not. This is hardly unique to those who are tenured, pre-tenure, or in untenable positions in higher education. What may be somewhat unique is that some faculty in tenured or tenurable positions still feel that we can unilaterally change the terms of our labor, and this could indicate that we still feel an unusual amount of agency in our workplaces.

SETH: Those of us in unions certainly can't unilaterally change the terms of our labor—it's literally illegal—but some people can. Your ending point is one consequence of that—it makes some people feel like they have agency and that they often come by that agency in ways that harm other people (see, e.g., Richard Hall, *The Alienated Academic* [2018]). But collectively we can change our conditions. For understandable reasons, there's a tone of defense/protectiveness in a lot of the book, especially among faculty who are marginalized in multiple ways, and, honestly, I think the ideas provide more grounds for genuine optimism and organizing potential than many of the authors articulate. I realize my optimism starts from privilege; it's easier to take the long view when it's not my livelihood at risk. (I also get how much I sound like a manager saying, "It's not a challenge; it's an opportunity!"). But organizing at scale benefits from involving people who aren't directly at risk, who can use our positions of relative safety and our resources to connect and amplify a lot of work that otherwise happens in isolation.

TONY: I agree, Seth. I happened to be reading Vanessa Machado de Oliveira's *Hospicing Modernity: Facing Humanity's Wrongs and the Implications for Social Activism* (2021) when I first read this manuscript. Machado de Oliveira points to the entanglement of factors that auger the collapse of modernity: climate change, forced migration, mass extinction, loss of faith in liberal democracy, crumbling infrastructures, growing political violence, and so forth. She argues that among the reasons that modernity is unraveling and unequal to the immense social, political, and ecological challenges that humans now face is that it has kept humans in a state of immaturity, which she associates with valorizing individual achievement, self-sufficiency, and the pursuit of "progress" without adequate regard to histories or consequences. For Machado de Oliveira, becoming mature means looking with courage at the dire realities of the Anthropocene and embracing "a political practice of healing, of radical tenderness that can help us to step up, to grow up, and to show up differently. This involves unlearning our learned ways of thinking and imagining; of sensing and feeling; of relating to one another, the earth and the cosmos; of facing life, fear, pain, loss and death" (xxi). I see in most chapters of this collection an emergent, "mature" sensibility that we need to work toward better, less emotionally damaging, more mutually accountable and satisfying working lives and conditions.

The relationship between precarity and adequacy in higher education is worth exploring, especially when adequacy is seen as a means toward creating the conditions that enable people to work cooperatively toward something that is "mature" in terms of how we see our current situation, and also creatively in terms of how we can imagine and create a better future. A part of being mature might mean more fully accounting for the qualitative, material conditions of academic labor in theories and research, for instance, scholarship in antiracism, pedagogy and administration, where work remains largely invisible. Adequacy might contribute to conversations about "showing up differently" for those we feel accountable to in a troubled historical moment. Mature explorations of "adequacy" in RCWS might be linked to other emergent movements and ideas about how to live with resiliency, mindfulness, and hope in this moment—for example, eco-socialism, the slowness movement, Indigenous epistemologies and futurism, and rewilding and degrowth movements—through thinking, imagining, and acting with intention.

What do we see happening in the chapters that they don't already say for themselves? And what else can we say because of what we've learned from these chapters?

SETH: I'm going to take a long turn here. Circulating through the book is the question of determining how much and what quality of what kinds of work should be enough to be safe in our jobs, as well as physically and psychologically safe, situated against the generalized threat of precarity that you describe, Tony, and that I generally see as Gramscian hegemony. I understand why the editors parse work and labor for the purposes of articulating the positions in the chapters, but workers don't get to set their own standards unilaterally. Michael Burawoy's *Manufacturing Consent* offers a potentially double-edged way of thinking about deciding how much work is enough, which is helpful, and how management uses ambiguities around that to garner worker compliance, which is dangerous for workers. He calls the concept "making out": As a simple example, assembly-line workers who were paid a piece rate had some latitude about how fast they worked, but because they were on production lines, that latitude was limited. So they had some autonomy to decide for themselves how hard to work for what pay, and also they had to come to terms with other workers about speed so that they didn't erase other people's autonomy to make those same decisions.

The danger, for Burawoy, is that such narrow autonomy serves management's compliance-gaining interests better than the workers' interests because it directs their individual and collective decision-making to a singular problem, thus deflecting their attention from other issues (like organizing to get better pay in the first place so they didn't need to bust their [ahems] to make survival wages). I'm not arguing that we should get paid piece rate (per-section pay for adjunct faculty is a strong argument for why we shouldn't) or that we should see our curricula/programs as assembly lines. But there's something to be said, and lots of people in this book are saying it, for needing to understand how decisions about productivity land on each other. There's also something to be said for thinking about the spaces our managers leave for us to make decisions because we'll get consumed enough by those that we don't organize around issues management doesn't want us to notice.

Without putting it this way, part of what all the multiauthored chapters in the book do is to show how such decisions can get made, supported, and reinforced in small groups. I encourage readers to think about how we build that recognition, mutual support, and mutual accountability beyond these initial informal networks. Research on organizing (Dixon et al. 2024; Lind 2015; McAlevey 2020; Reich and Bearman 2018) makes clear that these kinds of homegrown/DIY networks are crucial to successful solidarity-building. And I hope it's clear that I'm not criticizing folks for focusing on the value of taking care of each other and themselves; I don't want to put people who are already squeezed on the hook for even more work (same as I've argued that contingent faculty shouldn't have to solve the crisis of contingency), but I do want to put people who are leading solidarity-building efforts on the hook to encourage these networks/systems, support them as fully as you can, and try to build from them without threatening or undercutting or appropriating them. Sue Doe et al. (2016) describe such work as "culture change" (214) and describe it in nearly identical terms to Astra Taylor's (2016) description of "organizing": long, slow, sidewalk-level trust building and commitment-making, along with systems for making people answerable for breaking that trust. And your reading of Machado de Oliviera is part of this too; none of it happens with the kind of maturation she's calling for.

For example, if one aspect of organizing around adequacy is figuring out how much work is enough, then another needs to be figuring out how to demand more from peers (and managers) who currently aren't doing enough. Shot through your earlier comments here and your book *Composition in the Age of Austerity* (Welch and Scott 2016) is the point that the workforce is constantly threatened with DOOM if we don't all overperform, and yet we all know (and several contributors to this book point out) that in any department there are people who chronically *under*perform. They need to meet a standard of adequacy too. We need, as I was saying earlier, to establish that with management too—if the goal is to do more than make ourselves feel cared for by peers, then all this good work needs to turn into something sustainable. Olivia Wood's chapter points out that sometimes we need yes/no answers to direct questions, as much as our rhetoric training wants us to resist certainty and binaries. I want people to be happy with their work because they're good at it and care about it. I don't want that to substitute for material support, what Michael Stein (1989) calls "emotional" or "psychological wages," a concept lots of us RCWS learned via Eileen Schell (1998). Satisfying work and tenable working conditions shouldn't compete, but all too often they're deployed rhetorically as a wedge.

This logic holds in non-collective-bargaining environments too. Joe Berry (2005) is (in)famous for arguing, if you don't have a union, just act like you do! That's great advice, unless you have no idea how unions work. Anyway, I think this principle is portable: If we're going to act like we've consented to a constituting set of policies, then we have to live under its terms. One aspect of corporatism we don't talk much about in academic labor discourse is the ability of corporate leadership to deflect responsibility away from anyone when they break the rules. Faculty can guard against that and call it out when we see it, even without a legally enforceable contract—a contract makes it easier, but the provost (or whoever signed off on the faculty manual) is on the hook for living with it too. That's what the signature *means*.

Pulling apart the ways technocratic meritocracy works against workers is hard, especially for people in a profession that's been literally built on the foundations of technocratic rationality and meritocracy. So I'm not rosy eyed about this, but I think we can cut through that knot. As an example, if you follow the arguments about educational technologies designed to supplant faculty, you'll generally find that supporters toggle between two rationales: efficacy (this works better, so it's worthwhile even if it costs more) and cost (it costs less, so even if it doesn't work as well, we can't afford to keep paying people). One of the responses to this, lifting again from Olivia Wood, is just to call out the stasis shifting every single time it happens. Another, extending Brigitte Mussack's argument, is to say that management's duplicitous position shows that the technologies are neither cheaper nor better (i.e., they're *right both times*, and somehow that makes them all wrong!), but we know that well-trained and supported people can do outstanding work. How we organize around that is local and particular, just like always, but the groundwork for it is right there.

TONY: Seth, I like that you bring attention to how accountability to others becomes an issue when we make decisions about adequacy. In my reading of these chapters, I kept thinking about the vexing, perhaps irresolvable frictions between what is individually adequate for self-care, and our accountability to students, co-workers, institutions, and the profession. Joshua and Timothy offer a useful initial working definition of adequacy in the introductory chapter:

> In building this collection, we imagined adequate as a deliberate choice to value our needs and desires as workers against the material and structural realities of our present. On the one hand, we know that there's always more to do, and we value what we need to do; on the other hand, we are equipped with decreasing resources (financial, temporal, emotional, physical) to do them. Adequacy in this context, then, emerges as a form of [personal] agency—a goal for thriving by empowering ourselves to focus on the work we choose to do and to let other things go. (page 6)

The introduction is written in a spirit of solidarity and with regard to the material realities of work in academia, but it frames decisions about adequacy in personal terms. A number of the ensuing chapters argue that the affordances and consequences of agencies are personal and ecological. Personal agencies are negotiated among a variety of other agencies within our work ecologies. This is also true of desire and valuation:

To what extent can we distinguish our individual needs, desires, entitlements, and agencies from the professional and institutional actants, privileges, constraints, and conditionings of our work ecologies? Those of us who have advanced degrees and do teaching and administrative work in tenurable or otherwise stable positions inescapably *constitute* institutions, even as we work to create the critical and personal distance in order to reimagine and change them. What work can we eschew for our personal well-being without rippling consequences for others?

Some of the chapters in the collection answer this question through modeling ways to navigate self-care and survival, while also being accountable to colleagues, communities and students. As you point out Seth, the multiauthored chapters demonstrate how decisions can "get made, supported, and reinforced in groups." Olivia Wood's chapter is among those that advocate for the pursuit of adequacy within a broader and more institutionally engaged scope. Rather than using adequacy just to refer to a threshold of work that we determine based on our needs and situations, Wood makes the case that adequacy should refer to a broader, collective struggle for adequacy: "[We] might understand 'adequacy' as being just 'good enough' to keep our jobs, along the lines of 'quiet quitting' or 'acting your wage,' but I want to invert the concept into a positive call for action: What pay and working conditions do we want to consider genuinely adequate for our needs, and not just 'better than other jobs'? And what are we willing to do to achieve these adequate working conditions?" (page 68). Also aiming for change with a broader scope, Eunjeong Lee, Amy J. Wan, and Sara P. Lopez Amezquita emphasize our underrealized relationality and cast adequacy as part of an effort to create greater solidarity through community engagement, and "[building] humanizing spaces in the sometimes violent institution" (page 34). With emphasis on emotional damage and well-being, Crystal Broch Colombini, Stephanie L. Kerschbaum, and Sara Webb-Sunderhaus describe an institutionally situated approach that seeks to, for instance, challenge the use of "the pursuit of excellence" as a threshold metric for performance and replace it with "structurally determined sufficiencies articulated within particular writing program and institutional settings" (page 160). This with the goal of rejecting standards that cast "anything that is not excellent as de facto failure" (page 160). What these chapters show is that questions about adequacy can be a part of efforts to galvanize people toward common purposes, mature relations, and more healthy conditions within a profession that too often feels hypercompetitive, factional, emotionally battering, and unsupportive.

References

Berry, Joe. 2005. *Reclaiming the Ivory Tower: Organizing Adjuncts to Change Higher Education*. New York: Monthly Review Press.

Bousquet, Marc, Tony Scott, and Leo Parascondola. 2004. *Tenured Bosses and Disposable Teachers: Writing Instruction in the Managed University*. Carbondale: Southern Illinois University Press.

Burawoy, Michael. 1982. *Manufacturing Consent: Changes in the Labor Process Under Monopoly Capitalism*. Chicago: University of Chicago Press.

Daniel, James Rushing. 2022. *Toward an Anti-Capitalist Composition*. Logan: Utah State University Press.

Dixon, Marc, Vincent J. Roscigno, and Randy Hodson. 2004. "Unions, Solidarity, and Striking." *Social Forces* 83 (1): 3–33.

Doe, Sue, Maria Maisto, and Janelle Adsit. 2016. "What Works and What Counts: Valuing the Affective in Non-Tenure-Track Advocacy." In *Contingency, Exploitation, and Solidarity: Labor and Action in English Composition*, edited by Seth Kahn, William B. Lalicker, and Amy Lynch-Biniek, 213–234. Fort Collins, CO: WAC Clearinghouse. https://doi.org/10.37514/PER-B.2017.0858.2.14.

Hall, Richard. 2018. *The Alienated Academic: The Struggle for Autonomy Inside the University*. New York: Palgrave/McMillan.

Hassell, Holly, and Cassandra Phillips. 2022. *Materiality and Writing Studies: Aligning Labor, Scholarship, and Teaching*. La Vergne: National Council of Teachers of English.

Horner, Bruce. 2016. *Rewriting Composition: Terms of Exchange*. Carbondale: Southern Illinois University Press.

Kahn, Seth, and Amy Lynch-Biniek. 2022. "From Activism to Organizing, from Caring to Care Work." *Labor Studies Journal* 47 (3): 320–344.

LaFrance, Michelle. 2019. *Institutional Ethnography: A Theory of Practice for Writing Studies Researchers*. Logan: Utah State University Press.

Lorey, Isabell, Derieg, Aileen, and Judith Butler. 2015. *State of Insecurity: Government of the Precarious*. London: Verso.

Lind, Staunton. 2015. *Solidarity Unionism: Rebuilding the Labor Movement from Below*. 2nd ed. Chicago: PM Press.

Machado de Oliveira, Vanessa. 2021. *Hospicing Modernity: Facing Humanity's Wrongs and the Implications for Social Activism*. Berkeley, CA: North Atlantic.

McAlevey, Jane. 2020. *A Collective Bargain: Unions, Organizing, and the Fight for Democracy*. New York: Harper-Collins.

McDonald, James C., and Eileen E. Schell. 2011. "The Spirit and Influence of the Wyoming Resolution: Looking Back to Look Forward." *College English* 73 (4): 360–378.

Reich, Adam, and Peter Bearman. 2018. *Working for Respect: Community and Conflict at Walmart*. New York: Columbia University Press.

Schell, Eileen E. 1998. *Gypsy Academics and Mother-Teachers: Gender, Contingent Labor, and Writing Instruction*. Portsmouth: NH: Boynton-Cook.

Sledd, James, and Richard D. Freed. 1996. *Eloquent Dissent: The Writings of James Sledd*. Boynton/Cook.

Stein, Michael. 1989. "Gratitude and Attitude: A Note on Emotional Welfare." *Social Psychology Quarterly* 52 (3): 242–248. https://doi.org/10.2307/2786719.

Strickland, Donna. 2011. *The Managerial Unconscious in the History of Composition Studies*. Carbondale: Southern Illinois University Press.

Taylor, Astra. 2016. "Against Activism." *Baffler* 30 (March): Np. https://thebaffler.com/salvos/against-activism.

Taylor, Astra. 2023. *The Age of Insecurity: Coming Together as Things Fall Apart*. Toronto: Anansi.

Welch, Nancy, and Tony Scott. 2016. *Composition in the Age of Austerity*. Logan: Utah State University Press.

Index

activism, 206; Black feminist, 18–19; disability, 216; labor, 26, 67, 222; student, 10, 68
adequate, adequacy, 5–6; as agency, 20; as coalition-building, 95–96; as response to institutional constraints, 128–130, 152–153, 160, 163; as response to labor conditions, 11–16; as solidarity, 40, 93–94, 227; as success, 127, 165; as utopian potential, 17–18, 68–69, 200
administration, university administration, 8, 69, 72, 78, 82; administrative burden, 8; evaluation of, 16, 184–186, 193–195; as social justice work, 16, 176, 203; WPA coalitions, 103–105, 231; writing program administration (WPA), 4–5, 8–9, 91–94, 159, 203
affect, 10, 13, 18–20, 21, 34, 92, 125, 130, 152n3, 159, 161, 164–165, 167
Ahmed, Sara, 11, 18, 48, 142, 152
Americans with Disabilities Act (ADA), 82, 108
anti-racism, 23, 57, 94, 98, 161, 227
anxiety, 14, 98, 110, 130, 147, 172, 184, 216; anxiety attacks, 117
assessment, 18, 115; of curriculum, 82; of faculty, 195; programmatic assessment, 186; self-assessment, 194

Atlanta, Georgia, 222
austerity, 5, 104, 108
autonomy, 228

Bahrainwala, Lamiyah, 222
Barnard College, 66–67
Barrino, Fantasia, 19
Berlant, Lauren, 13, 19
best practice, 5, 101–102, 160, 162, 165, 167, 188, 190, 193
Black July (pogrom), 113
Black Power (movement), 68
Boquet, Elizabeth, 126, 135
Brown University, 67
Browne, Robert M., 70–71
budgets, 108, 212; budget crises, 7; budget cuts, 78
burnout, 95, 128, 133, 208

California, 47, 239; State University, 67, 239; University of, 66–67
capital: cultural, 12, 91, 162; as system, 54
capitalism, 23, 107, 130, 131n1, 176, 200, 201, 204, 226
care work, 51, 60, 177, 203

236 : INDEX

City College of New York, 71–72, 245
class, 53, 78, 93, 123, 222; consciousness, 67, 74; middle-class whiteness, 42-49, 55, 78; ruling, 70; struggle, 67, 71, 73–79; working-, 67–68, 78, 117, 125
Cloud, Dana, 222
collaboration: collaborative labor, 209; collaborative writing, 123, 204–207; across difference, 50, 59–60, 177, 204–207; as mutual support, 34–37, 40–41, 43, 177, 194, 199
College Composition and Communication (CCC), 14
colonialism, 24, 33–35, 42, 45–46, 116, 125, 128
Columbia University, 66
community, 20, 105, 115–116; as accountability, 95, 97–100; community building, 33–45, 101, 105, 209–211, 223; disability communities, 115, 216–219; disciplinary, 48, 59–61
compensation, 9, 84–85, 205
composition: classes, 8, 161, 188; directors of, 105; as a discipline, 15, 73; instructors of, 160; pedagogies, 161, 163, 175; practicum, 172–178; processes, 113; teaching of, 162, 164, 166; theory, 164, 172; university programs in, 78; the work of, 16, 72, 224
Conference on College Composition and Communication (CCCC), 73, 91, 184, 221, 224; statement on working conditions for non-tenure-track faculty, 184–185
consent, rhetorical, 67
contingent workers, 223, 228; contingent faculty and labor organizing, 66–67, 69, 78, 222; contingent labor, 164; proliferation of, 108, 164; teaching as contingent faculty, 135; training and supervising contingent faculty, 205, 207
Corbett, Edward P.J., 67–70, 73–74
Council of Writing Program Administrators (CWPA), 16, 92; statement on intellectual work of writing program administrators, 16, 91, 185
Crowley, Sharon, 125
COVID-19 pandemic, 103, 133, 145–146; effects on labor conditions, 7, 107–108, 151, 159, 172, 181–182, 201; effects on teaching, 161–162, 165–168, 175–176; isolation as a result of, 133, 146, 167
culture, 113, 203, 211–212; of academia, 17, 42; of capitalism, 199; culture shifts, 93, 96, 101, 200, 204, 229; departmental culture, 202, 207–208; of higher education, 7, 54; institutional culture, 35, 38, 40, 172; of neoliberalism, 35, 43, 45; of Niceness, 49, 52; of overwork, 67, 117, 119, 124; of writing, 96

decolonial pedagogy, 126
DEI, 43, 102, 200–209
democracy, 58, 72, 226
departmental culture, 202, 204, 208, 210
disability, 56, 76, 169, 118, 217–218; activism, 216; communities, 49, 115; disabled bodyminds, 61, 116; disabled faculty, 108–109, 112; disabled parents, 171; disabled POC, 110–111, 113, 161; disabled students, 14, 101; disabled teachers, 169; and internalized ableism, 117; justice, 17; solidarity, 61, 216; stigma, 55, 218
dissonance, 201–212; dissonant spaces, 200; in thinking, 98; theories of, 26
diversity, 40, 11, 202, 206; and inclusion, 102; diversity, equity, and inclusion, 35, 102; language diversity, 72; of labor, 187

economics, 92, 142, 199, 135; economic crises, 5; economic disparity, 118; economic dominance, 77; economic production, 93; economic solvency, 7; political economy, 26, 226
embodiment, 19, 53, 92, 113, 161, 164, 223
employment, 7, 12, 14, 18, 56, 112; non-academic employment, 85, 108
English as a second language students, 123, 134
Ervio, Cynthia, 19
expectations, 13, 35, 53, 55–57, 84, 92–93, 97–98, 115, 123, 125–128, 131, 138, 160–162, 167, 177, 184, 186, 205, 208, 212, 218, 221

faculty, 4, 13, 51, 135, 166, 182, 222–229; administrators, 104; BIPOC faculty, 11, 37; BIPOC junior faculty, 37; of color, 56; contingent, 26, 66, 207; development, 4; directors, 124; disabled faculty, 108, 111; evaluations of, 25–26, 181–196; governance, 181; graduate faculty, 205; junior faculty, 34; marginalized faculty, 54, 56, 205; meetings, 156; mentors, 138, 141; minoritized faculty, 56–67; mobility, 139; multiply marginalized faculty, 25; Native faculty, 111; pre-tenured faculty, 41, 92; organizing, 50, 66–67, 69, 78; responsibilities, 82, 92; tenured, 41, 91; tenure track, 139, 190; senior faculty, 144; non-tenure track, 190, 199, 205; white faculty, 111; women of color faculty, 24; working conditions of, 24, 51
failure, 6, 21, 33, 38, 138, 151–153, 159–160, 162, 170, 177, 182, 196, 231; institutional, 83; as pedagogy, 123–125, 129; queer, 25, 128, 131, 142-143; state, 17
fear, 83, 176, 226, 227; of being seen as incompetent or unprofessional, 216; of enforcing

oppressive structures, 20, 134; of retaliation from the university, 69; of judgment, 217; of the tenure clock, 39
Federal Pell Grants, 81, 223
feminist theory, 73–76, 86, 140, 152; Black feminist thought, 10, 17–20, 93; feminist mentorship, 140
first generation, 36, 81, 102, 123, 139, 222
First-year writing, 15, 67, 99, 100, 163–164; instructors, 160–161; students, 82, 127, 162
Fordham University, 66–70, 166, 238
Freire, Paulo, 126
funding, 97, 127, 184, 190; grant funding, 94, 96

García-Peña, Lorgia, 35–37
gay. *See* Joshua and Timothy
gender, 102, 215, 218, 224; gendered inequalities, 171; gendered norms, 53–54; gendered precarity, 222; gendered whiteness, 53, 57
genderqueer, 117
generosity, 23–24
Goldberg, Whoopi, 18
graduate students, 39, 91, 100, 115, 138–139, 171, 176, 199; as instructors, 66, 91, 160, 172, 176, 225; as workers, 67, 79, 95
Gurner, Tim, 107

Halberstam, J., 128, 131, 142
higher education, 4, 6, 53; culture of higher education, 7, 15, 85, 112; DEI in, 102; economics of, 66; emotion in, 57; leaders of, 8; history of, 125; institution of, 135; labor organizing in, 66, 77, 222; marginalized in, 33; neoliberalism in, 54, 103, 184; Niceness in, 58; precarity in, 227; shifting landscapes of, 181; social justice in, 205
Houston, Texas, 151, 241, 245
Huffington, Arianna, 107

identity, 50, 78, 85–87, 109, 170, 171; class identity, 78, 222; disabled identity, 216; identity politics, 20; linguistic identity, 100; professional identity, 199
inequality, inequalities, 123, 128
Indiana University–Purdue University Indianapolis, 125
individualism, 6, 9, 13, 17, 34–35, 41, 54–55, 72
instructors, 100; composition instructors, 73, 160, 172–173; graduate instructors, 66, 161, 172, 200, 205, 207, 225; new instructors, 159, 208–209; support for, 160, 161, 165, 174–176, 208–210; temporary, 172
intersectionality; intersectional dilemmas, 125; intersectional frameworks, 22, 162;

intersectional positions, 128; intersectional precarity, 222
isolation, 125, 133, 167, 226

Jewish rhetorics, 49–50, 58–59
job market, 42, 81–87, 93, 112, 130, 139–140, 145, 148–152
Judaism, 49, 58–61

Kahn, Seth, and Amy Pason, 9, 108; Kahn and Amy Lynch-Biniek, 50–51, 108, 200–201, 205–206, 224
kindness, 38, 109, 142, 171; coalitional kindness, 25, 50, 58–61
Kynard, Carmen, 10–11, 33, 37, 93, 96–97, 101, 103, 161

labor, 9, 93–94, 182–183, 185, 192, 199–202, 205–208, 210; conditions of, 5–6, 107–108, 151, 227; exploitation of, 7; evaluation of, 185, 189–190, 194–195; labor organizing, 67–68, 222, 224; labor of teaching and mentoring, 159, 164–165. *See also* work
lecturers, 66, 72, 109
LGBTQIA+, 219
life experiences, 36
linguistic identity, 100
linguistic justice, 96–97, 101, 126
Lorde, Audre, 19, 113
Love, Bettina, 34, 36–37
Love, Black feminist love-politics, 19–20; DEI and, 202; as rhetorical, 202–204, 208–211; as ethic, 212
Lynch-Biniek, Amy, and Seth Kahn, 50–51, 108, 200–201, 205–206, 224

marginalized, marginalization, 37, 217; bodies, 217; bodyminds, 217; communities, 49, 103; faculty, 205; in the university, 33, 52, 86; multiply marginalized scholars, 54, 56, 114, 118, 177, 216–219, 225–226; people, 109, 222; scholars, 113, 115, 118; white marginalized scholars, 219
Menand, Louis, 7
mental health, 52, 83, 148, 168, 170
mentoring, 86, 123–124, 135–136, 175, 186; graduate mentoring, 140–143, 152–153
Milbern, Stacey, 216
Miller-Cochran, 5, 93; Mapes and Miller-Cochran, 160
mission, 103, 150, 222; institutional mission, 35, 43, 127
Mullivaikkal massacre, 113
multilingualism, 34, 41, 127, 163

Nash, Jennifer C., 18–20
neoliberalism, 7–8, 183–184, 201, 226
New School (university), 66–67
New York City, 66, 166–167, 238, 239, 241
neurodivergence, neurodivergent, 49, 56, 86, 116, 118, 126

O'Leary, Kevin, 107
outsider status, 62

Pason, Amy, 9, 108
patriarchy, patriarchal, 77, 75; white patriarchy, 57
Patterson, GPat, 23
Peitho (academic journal), 141, 144–145
performance, 53, 141, 217–218, 226, 231; adequate, 96; anxieties, 159–160; demands, 159; evaluation, 184, 43; gendered, 54; job, 33–34; performance-based policies, 126
Piepzna-Samarasinha, 49–50, 60–61, 177, 216
Powell, Malea, 87, 141, 152
positionality, 36–37, 49, 93, 116–117, 123–124, 185, 200
privilege, 23
professional development, 200, 203, 207–212; faculty professional development, 184

queer, queerness: queer academics, 86, 116, 151–152; queer failure, 25, 128, 131, 142–143; queer Rhetoric and Composition studies, 181; queer students, 86, 101; queer theory, 18–19
Queens College, 35–39, 41–43, 241, 244
quiet quitting, 13, 21, 68, 107, 202, 231. *See also* work-to-rule

race, 52–53, 56–57, 76, 93, 102, 123, 218, 224
racism, 24, 37, 47–48, 52–53, 57, 114
reflection, 3, 123, 125, 150, 151, 153, 162, 166, 168, 191, 200, 201, 207–210
retirement, 87, 182, 196
Rhetoric and Composition, 1–24, 50, 67–69, 73, 77, 84, 95, 97, 101, 148, 161–162
rural, 39, 117

sexism, 52, 57
shame, 44, 114, 133, 168, 173, 204
Shark Tank (series), 107
Sledd, James, 224–225
Strickland, Donna, 7, 16, 93, 159, 165, 224
structural, structural conditions, 123; structural forces, 164; structural limits, 162, 165; structural operations, 57; structural positions, 67, 78; structural realities, 5–6, 17, 166, 230; structural sufficiency, 174–175; structural transformation, 19
student-centered learning, 126

teaching, 14–15, 72, 193, 195, 200; evaluation of, 185–188, 193, 195; as knowledge production, 39, 190; teacher training, 53–55, 160–163, 175–177, 208–210
technical communication, 199, 200–205, 212
Temple University, 67
Tetlow, Tania, 69–70
Texas (US state), 7, 47, 102, 139, 146, 151, 239, 241, 245
trauma, 52, 103, 151, 164, 165, 176; institutional, 17, 52; personal, 117, 119, 168, 171; trauma-informed work, 104; responses, 170–171
Tufts University, 66

unions, 10, 66–67, 69, 74, 77–78, 223, 226, 229
United Parcel Service (UPS), 223
United States of America, 5, 12–13, 47, 52, 66, 82, 165, 175
University of Houston, 138, 141, 151, 239, 241, 245; Clear Lake campus, 238
University of Illinois (Chicago), 66
University of Michigan, 66
University of Oregon, 67

violence, 73, 75, 103; epistemological, 10; institutional, 161; against marginalized communities, 103, 161; police, 73, 103

wages, 11, 25, 66–68, 124, 150, 228, 231
Welch, Nancy, 7, 73, 78, 130, 229
Wesleyan University, 122
whiteness, 33–34, 49
work, 9–10
work-to-rule, 13, 21
writing, 35, 91, 95; agitational writing, 67; centers, 8, 93, 96, 101–102, 117, 122–136, 167, 209; classes, 68–69; collaborative writing, 37, 41, 108, 125; first-year writing, 15, 67, 99, 162, 169; grant writing, 83; groups, 24; mentors, 124; processes, 45; programs, 4, 91, 172; projects, 112, 114, 116–117, 147; public writing, 72; research writing, 201; scholarship on, 5, 14; standards, 123, 125; student writing, 186; teaching of, 4, 13, 14, 101, 127; technical writing, 201; tutoring of, 128–135; voices, 41; workshop, 133

Zeno of Citium, 68

About the Contributors

Joshua Barsczewski is an assistant professor of English and the Writing Program director at Muhlenberg College. He has published in *Peitho, Composition Studies, WPA: Writing Program Administration,* and *The Journal of the Assembly for Expanded Perspectives on Learning*.

Lauren Marshall Bowen (she/her) is an associate professor of English at the University of Massachusetts Boston, whose upbringing was supported by the labor of her parents: a chemical engineer and a human resources administrator, both of whom worked at a paper mill in rural Maine. During working hours, she teaches courses on writing, literacy, and composition pedagogy; directs a large and vibrant first-year writing program; and collaborates on research projects with smart people who share her scholarly interests, including writing development and disciplinary identity through the lifespan and age inclusivity in higher education (among other things). Publications about these projects have popped up in *College Composition and Communication, College English, Composition Studies, Literacy in Composition Studies, enculturation, Community Literacy Journal,* and a variety of edited collections. During her nonworking time, she reads as much fiction as she can, watches her talented daughter dance, makes her wonderfully supportive partner laugh, and snuggles with her two lazy cats.

Crystal Broch Colombini is an associate professor of English at Fordham University in New York, where she currently directs the Writing Program and the Writing Center at both the Rose Hill and Lincoln Center campuses. Her research focuses mainly on economic rhetoric and writing, with a growing number of WPA-related projects as well, and her work has appeared in a range of journals in the field, including *College English, Rhetoric Society Quarterly,* and *Journal for the History of Rhetoric*. As a midcareer scholar with multiple administrative responsibilities, three kids at home, and a never-ending list of goals and tasks, she feels strongly that adequacy is a concept to embrace and celebrate, and she is honored to contribute to a collection on the topic.

Christina V. Cedillo is an associate professor of writing and rhetoric at the University of Houston–Clear Lake. Christina's research draws from cultural rhetorics and decolonial theory to focus on embodied rhetorics and rhetorics of embodiment at the intersections of race, gender, and disability. Their work has appeared in *College Composition and Communication, Rhetoric Society Quarterly,* the *Journal for the History of Rhetoric, Composition Forum,* and various other journals and edited collections. Christina's current project examines the multimodal rhetorics of twentieth- and twenty-first-century women of color activists. They are the lead editor of the *Journal of Multimodal Rhetorics*.

Sara Doan (she/her) is an assistant professor of experience architecture in the Writing, Rhetoric, and American Cultures Department at Michigan State University. In her teaching and research, she examines how expertise is framed and enacted across different genres, such as instructor feedback on resumes and cover letters, misleading data visualizations about COVID-19, project management, audience co-creation in public service announcements, and the content strategy of Southeastern state health departments. Doan's work on data visualizations, preventive health behaviors, and feedback in technical communication courses has appeared in the *Journal of Business and Technical Communication, IEEE Transactions on Professional Communication,* and *Business and Professional Communication Quarterly*.

Malaika Fernandes (she/her) is a senior theater and economics double-major at Wesleyan University. She is a playwright who uses her plays to deal with her complicated relationships with home, diaspora, and language. As a writer and a tutor at the Writing Workshop, Malaika believes in collaboration and community as ways to escape the terrors of isolating and paralyzing perfectionism. She founded the student group Writing Circle to bring these values to student writing spaces at Wesleyan. Outside of theater and writing, Malaika enjoys dabbling in things she doesn't understand: running, contact improvisation, and piano, to name a few. She dreams of playing the violin terribly.

About the Contributors : 241

Mara Lee Grayson is a writer and teacher-scholar whose research focuses on antiracist writing instruction and rhetorics of racism and antisemitism in education. Her books include *Teaching Racial Literacy: Reflective Practices for Critical Writing*, *Race Talk in the Age of the Trigger Warning: Recognizing and Challenging Classroom Cultures of Silence*, and *Antisemitism and the White Supremacist Imaginary: Conflations and Contradictions in Composition and Rhetoric*. Her poetry has been nominated for fancy awards but hasn't won any of them. Born and raised in Brooklyn by leftist Jews, Mara Lee is, in the coded words of a colleague, "so New York," but she navigates Southern California with the help of an engineer husband and two opinionated cats. She works as an associate professor and faculty coordinator of general education assessment at California State University, Dominguez Hills.

Ada Hubrig (they/them) is an autistic, genderqueer, disabled caretaker of cats. They live in Huntsville, Texas, where they work as an assistant professor and co-director of composition at Sam Houston State University. They've decided to use this little space to wish you and yours all the best and encourage you to be your favorite version of yourself ♥.

Tenzin Jamdol (she/her) is pleasantly surprised to be a part of this project because she originally applied to work at Wesleyan's Writing Workshop with an evil scheme of uncovering the untold secrets of how to be an awesome writer while also having the authority to say she got mentoring experience. Having been continuously welcomed into the space with unwavering warm and open arms despite the weight of her initial selfish intention, Tenzin has grown to be sincerely grateful for learning to accept and work with her deep insecurities and frustrations with writing. She is certain that three years of working with the Writing Center will leave her with lessons and a love of literature that will last for a lifetime and truly wishes for everyone to feel this level of genuine and raw acceptance. She also wants three cats just as badly.

Gavin P. Johnson (he/him) works as an assistant professor and the director of composition at Texas Christian University. He has published widely and been recognized for his research on multimodal pedagogy, digital cultural rhetorics, surveillance studies, anti-oppressive writing assessment, and queer worldmaking grounded in coalitional praxis. He serves as managing editor at *Composition Forum* and is the founding section editor for *Multimodal + Justice + Action*, a pedagogical companion to the *Journal of Multimodal Rhetorics*. Not often enough, he spends time with his two long-haired dachshunds, Archie and Henry, and his long-time partner. He is a proud first-generation college graduate from southeast Louisiana.

Rachelle A. C. Joplin (she/her) earned her PhD in Rhetoric, Composition, and Pedagogy from the University of Houston. Her dissertation focused on the movement of memories within various JRPGs and their fan cultures. Her work has been featured in *Peitho* and *Presumed Incompetent II*. After many ups and downs, she finally found a job that feels like home. She currently resides in Minneapolis, Minnesota, where she is the academic advisor for the School of the Arts at Augsburg University. Her priorities include empowering students to navigate the higher education landscape in healthy ways that feel successful to them, centering herself around holistic work/life balance, and burying herself in many niche fandoms.

Seth Kahn is a professor of English at West Chester University of Pennsylvania, where he teaches courses in writing, rhetoric, propaganda, and research methods. His research focuses on academic labor organizing. Recent publications include "From Activism to Organizing, From Caring to Carework" with Amy Lynch-Biniek (*Labor Studies Journal*, 2022); "What Do We Mean by Academic Labor (in Rhetorical Studies)? A Conversation" with Amy Pason (*Rhetoric and Public Affairs*, 2021); "We Value Teaching Too Much to Keep Devaluing It" (*College English*, 2020); and the collection *Activism and Rhetoric: Theories and Contexts for Political Engagement*, coedited with Jong-Hwa Lee (2019). With Sue Doe, he coedits the book series Precarity and Contingency, published by the WAC Clearinghouse and the Center for the Study of Academic Labor. He also serves as chair of his union's (APSCUF) Statewide Mobilization Committee, treasurer of Tenure for the Common Good, and co-chair of the CWPA Labor Committee.

Stephanie L. Kerschbaum is a professor of English and director of the Program in Writing and Rhetoric at the University of Washington. She is the author of *Toward a New Rhetoric of Difference* (NCTE, 2014) and *Signs of Disability* (NYU, 2022), and coeditor, with Laura T. Eisenman and James M. Jones, of *Negotiating Disability: Disclosure and Higher Education* (Michigan, 2017). She is currently editor of the Studies in Writing and Rhetoric series published through NCTE and spends a lot of time thinking about how to support communities of writers, teachers, and scholars through writing program administration, scholarly editing, and intellectual connection.

Ashanka Kumari (she/her) is a first-generation college graduate, daughter of immigrant parents, and parent of the coolest toddler you've ever met. Her work lives at the intersection of writing, teaching, community, and care, focusing on the hidden curriculum, graduate education, multimodal composition, and feminist and antiracist pedagogies. Her research appears in *Computers and Composition*, *Kairos*, *Composition Studies*, *The Journal of Popular Culture*, and multiple edited collections. She is co-editor of *Mobility Work in Composition: Translation, Migration, Transformation* (Utah State University Press). Currently, she works as Associate Dean of the Graduate School and Associate Professor of Rhetoric and Writing at East Texas A&M University.

Eunjeong Lee (she/her/hers) is a Korean immigrant–generation scholar-educator who is committed to equitable language and literacy education and justice for multilingual students and communities of color. She currently works at University of Houston as assistant professor, teaching courses on sociolinguistics, first-year and advanced composition, and translingualism. Eunjeong strives to pursue different ways of thinking, learning, and teaching language and writing, away from the colonial, monolingual ideology in her work. Her work has appeared in *Written Communication, Composition Forum, World Englishes*, and other journals and edited collections, including *Linguistic Justice on Campus*. When she is not working, Eunjeong likes to go for a walk with her pug or to check in with her communities in Seoul and Busan, South Korea; Queens, New York; and Austin and Houston, Texas.

Kelin Loe is an assistant professor of English and Writing Center director at Texas A&M University–Commerce. Her first collection of poetry, *These Are The Gloria Stories*, was published by Factory Hollow Press in 2014, and she continues to publish poetry widely, including serving for a stint as the founder and coeditor of *SPOKE TOO SOON: A Journal of the Longer*, which emphasized long-form poetics. Her scholarly research, which focuses on the circulations of rhetoric and affect in late capitalist networks of exchange, disability studies, and animal rhetorics, has been published in *Rhetorical Animals: Boundaries of the Human in the Study of Persuasion* (2018).

Sara P. Lopez Amezquita (ella, her, hers) is associate professor of English at Queens College, City University of New York (CUNY). Her qualitative research focuses on the language and literacy practices of self-outed US undocumented young adults. Sara is also interim co-principal investigator with CUNY's, first of its kind, Initiative on Immigration and Education (CUNY-IIE). Sara's works have appeared in *Literacy in Composition Studies* and *Journal of Adolescent & Adult Literacy*, among other journals and edited collections. Sara's most recent publication, titled "Multilingualism Beyond Walls: Undocumented Young Adults Subverting Writing Education," is included in the edited collection, *Writing on the Wall*.

Vyshali Manivannan (she/her/hers) is an assistant professor in the Department of Writing and Cultural Studies and director of the Writing-Enhanced Course program at Pace University–Pleasantville. She is an interdisciplinary creative-critical scholar who has written extensively about the experience of nonapparent chronic pain and fatigue and about the ethnic conflict in Sri Lanka. Her scholarship has appeared in publications such as the *Journal of Multimodal Rhetorics*, *Digital Health*, *Fibreculture Journal*, and *enculturation*, and her creative work has been featured in literary journals like *Fourth Genre*, *The Paris Review*, *Consequence*, and *Black Clock*.

Katie Manthey is an associate professor of English and director of the writing center at Salem College, a small women's college in Winston Salem, North Carolina. Her research and teaching bring together professional writing, cultural rhetorics, dress studies, and fat studies to see how the visible self, with attention to size, is constructed rhetorically. Her work has appeared in *Peitho: The Journal of the Coalition of Women Scholars in the History of Rhetoric & Composition*, *Jezebel*, the *Journal of Multimodal Rhetorics*, and *Computers and Composition Online*.

Brigitte Mussack (she/her) holds a PhD in rhetoric and scientific and technical communication and is a senior lecturer in the Department of Writing Studies at the University of Minnesota, where she teaches courses in technical and professional communication. Her research focuses on metaphor, epideictic rhetoric, voice, community, and writing in online spaces. She is published in such journals as *Prompt*, *Rhetoric Review*, and the *Journal of Communication Pedagogy*. In addition, she created and maintains a collaborative open-source text on technical writing instruction and social justice. Her work emphasizes writing as value laden and rhetorical and lies at the intersection of rhetorical theory, philosophy of language, pedagogy, and writing studies. Her research grows out of her administrative work, her teaching, and her joy in watching the language development in her two young children. Her least favorite genre is the author bio.

Audrey Auerbach Nelson (she/her) is a second-year anthropology major at Wesleyan University. Originally from Bainbridge Island, Washington, Audrey is passionate about creative writing, contact sports, interfaith advocacy, romance novels, and eating dessert. She has worked as a copy editor, a literary magazine editor, a bookseller, and a journalist. Currently, she tutors and mentors at Wesleyan's Writing Workshop, where she loves telling prospective tutors that they don't have to be English majors to apply. Her favorite part of her work at the workshop is that if she does her job well, she can help change the way students view themselves in relation to their writing. Audrey spent all of her freshman year trying to be perfect; now, as a sophomore, she is thoroughly enjoying being "enough."

Timothy Oleksiak (he/they) is a low-femme associate professor of English and the Professional and New Media Writing Program director at University of Massachusetts Boston. His works have appeared in *College English*, *QED: A Journal of LGBTQ Worldmaking*, *College Composition and Communication*, *Peitho*, *Composition Studies*, *Pedagogy*, *Pre/Text*, and in various edited collections. He watches way too much television and loves his given and chosen families. He hopes one day to be on *Fresh Air* with Terry Gross.

Bernice Olivas teaches writing and rhetoric at Salt Lake City Community College. She specializes in first-generation students, antiracist and inclusive pedagogy.

Laurie A. Pinkert (she/her) is an associate professor of writing and rhetoric and director of Writing Across the Curriculum at the University of Central Florida. She comes from a family of plumbers and mechanics; teachers and preachers; business owners, hourly workers, and stay-at-home laborers who go unpaid in traditional ways. The physical labor that supported her intellectual pursuits pushes her to broadly understand "work" within the academy, to teach in collaboration with communities, and to investigate the values that welcome and sustain individuals within their careers/disciplines. She finds as much satisfaction in reroofing a house with her dad as in co-writing articles with colleagues and as much joy discovering thrift-store deals with her mom as in choosing the right words as the right time. Her readily recognized academic labor can be found in venues like *College Composition and Communication* and *Composition Studies* and has been funded by the National Science Foundation.

Tony Scott is an associate professor in the Department of Writing Studies, Rhetoric and Composition at Syracuse University. His scholarly work has focused primarily on labor in higher education, political economy and literacy, writing assessment, and writing program administration. His publications include *Dangerous Writing: Understanding the Political Economy of Composition*, and the coedited collections *Composition in the Age of Austerity* and *Tenured Bosses and Disposable Teachers: Writing Instruction in the Managed University*.

Lauren Silber (she/her) is the assistant director of academic writing and assistant professor of the practice in academic writing at Wesleyan University. She works closely with the writing tutors and mentors at Wesleyan's Writing Workshop and teaches courses in writing studies, US literary and cultural studies, migration studies, race and ethnic studies, and gender and sexuality studies, with interests in affect, emotion, and the felt. After over a decade in writing centers and academia, Lauren feels certain that play, experimentation, and failure are central features of learning. She thoroughly enjoys exploring these concepts with her students and collaborators, and has recently published in *Pedagogy* on how failing led to new ways to teach close reading.

Xiran Tan (they/she) is an English and East Asian studies double major. Coming from Southern China, they swim in the interstices of different languages and political spaces. In addition to working at Wesleyan's Writing Center, they have also been a farmer, a docent at a Buddhist cave temple complex, and a mentor at different education nonprofits. They also do a range of random stuff on campus—playing badminton, writing and translating stories, community organizing, particularly among Chinese international students, building a home and learning space within the institution, attempting at STEM, and sleeping early—but sometimes get frustrated when they can't say they excelled at any one of these. But that's okay. The friends and experiences Xiran had along the journey are the most valuable thing that will always be part of them.

Shaoxuan Tian (she/her) is graduating from Wesleyan (in May 2023). She regards writing as a necessity and learns by stealing vocabulary from all flows of conversations. Writing across multiple languages/disciplines, she is dedicated to creating spaces via words and believes that every voice is adequate to be heard and held. She meditates on the politics of narratives, is obsessed with talking to people about writing while constantly being utterly embarrassed by such processes, and tries her very best to keep her desk(top) clear. In surviving institutional time, Shaoxuan daydreams, rhythms in poems and lame puns, yields to whale videos, leaves herself drifting while taking random walks, and learns to enjoy being both excessive and enough. Please feed her with your favorite dystopian and apocalyptic stories. She also wants to adopt cats (as terribly as Tenzin).

Amy J. Wan (she/her/hers) works as a professor of English at Queens College and the CUNY Graduate Center and has been a writing program administrator at Queens College for most of her career. She was thrilled to recently learn that her first publication in *Radical Teacher* is still assigned and is part of at least one university library module on zine making. The DIY ethic of zines reflects the trajectory of her research, which has all, in some way, been about the impact of literacy on people's material realities, the building of community, and the possibilities for gaining agency. Her current project analyzes how to create spaces for change and resistance within the global US university through a historical and contemporary study of policies addressing access, diversity, race, and language.

Sara Webb-Sunderhaus is an associate professor of English and the former director of composition at Miami University (Ohio). Acquiring a disability in October 2017 and surviving (so far) a global pandemic have led her to finally internalize the importance of striving for adequacy as a method of preserving her physical and mental health. With Kim Donehower, she is the coeditor of *Re-Reading Appalachia: Literacy, Place, and Cultural Resistance* (University Press of Kentucky, 2015). Her work has appeared in various other edited collections, as well as journals such as *College English, Community Literacy Journal, Composition Forum, Journal of Basic Writing,* and *WPA: Writing Program Administration.*

Nafis White (she/they) is a multidisciplinary fine artist who creates her work using objects commonly found in beauty supply stores; natural, industrial, and irrigation components; and the seemingly limitless horizons of our global and political landscapes. Through weaving, hairdressing, sculpture, and installation, White centers the uncanny audacity of self-affirmation and love by means of repetition as a form of change. Through play and continuous exploration, White employs her research on the intricate customs of Victorian hair weaving and mourning traditions and appropriates them using Black hair, beauty products, and African and African American hairstyling techniques, where they were never imagined to take up space and esteem. White's formal training is in sculpture, printmaking, and digital media. She uses concept as anchor and medium as message in her work, moving within conceptual and durational realms. Community engagement, beauty, and the political root deeply in White's work. White's work is in the permanent collection of the RISD Museum and University of New Mexico Art Museum and has been exhibited at The de Young Museum, The RISD Museum, National Queer Arts Festival, The List Gallery at Brown University, New Museum, Goldsmiths University, Autograph ABP, OXO Tower in London, Overture Center for the Arts Madison, and the Rhode Island School of Design, among many others. White holds a BFA and MFA and from the Rhode Island School of Design. She lives and works in Providence, Rhode Island.

Jen Wingard PhD is an associate professor of rhetoric, composition, and pedagogy at the University of Houston. She writes about neoliberalism, Texas, Houston, and how the rhetoric of gender and immigration are used to create scapegoats in political rhetoric and legislation. She is fascinated by Houston and exhausted by Texas. She loves all animals but especially cats.

Olivia Wood (she/her) sells her labor as a writing teacher in exchange for wages at the City College of New York (CUNY). For the time being, to quote and then more loosely adapt the words of Karl Marx in *The German Ideology*, "[she] must remain [a writing teacher] if [she] does not want to lose her means of livelihood; while in communist society, where nobody has one exclusive sphere of activity but each can become accomplished in any branch [they wish], society regulates the general production and thus will make it possible for [her] to do one thing today and another tomorrow," perhaps to teach writing in the morning, literature in the afternoon, history in the evening, and politics after dinner, just as she has a mind, without ever becoming a rhetorician, literary critic, historian, or politician.

www.ingramcontent.com/pod-product-compliance
Lightning Source LLC
Chambersburg PA
CBHW060556080526

44585CB00013B/586